REPUTATIONAL CHALLENGES IN SPORT

D0916377

Issues of reputation management are negotiated in a wide array of contexts, yet arguably one of the most visible of these areas involves how such stories unfold within the sporting arena. Whether involving individual athletes, teams, organizations, leagues, or global entities, the process of navigating issues of image repair and/or restoration and crisis-based communication has never been more byzantine, with a plethora of communicative media outlets functioning in myriad manners.

Reputational Challenges in Sport explores the intersection of reputation, sport, and society. In doing so, the book advances theory and then explores individual, team, and organizational applications from varied methodological perspectives as they relate to reputation and identity management and crisis orientations. The book provides a synthesis of previous works while offering a contemporary advancement of these subjects from a variety of epistemological approaches. It gives voice to a variety of perspectives that offer a robust advancement of issues relating to reputation, sport, and modern society.

Andrew C. Billings is the executive director of the Alabama Program in Sports Communication and Ronald Reagan Chair of Broadcasting in the Department of Journalism & Creative Media at The University of Alabama. He also serves on many editorial boards, including as an associate editor of the journals *Communication & Sport* and *Journal of Global Sport Management*.

W. Timothy Coombs is a full professor in the Department of Communication at Texas A&M University and an honorary professor at Aarhus University in Denmark. He is currently the editor of *Corporate Communications: An International Journal*.

Kenon A. Brown is associate professor in the Department of Advertising and Public Relations at The University of Alabama. He is also the programming director for the Alabama Program in Sports Communication.

REPUTATIONAL CHALLENGES IN SPORT

Theory and Application

Edited by Andrew C. Billings, W. Timothy Coombs, and Kenon A. Brown

Routledge
Taylor & Francis Group

NEW YORK AND LONDON

First published 2018
by Routledge
711 Third Avenue, New York, NY 10017

and by Routledge
2 Park Square, Milton Park, Abingdon, Oxon OX14 4RN

Routledge is an imprint of the Taylor & Francis Group, an informa business

© 2018 Taylor & Francis

The right of Andrew C. Billings, W. Timothy Coombs, and Kenon A. Brown to be identified as the authors of this work has been asserted by them in accordance with sections 77 and 78 of the Copyright, Designs and Patents Act 1988.

Library of Congress Cataloging in Publication Data
Names: Billings, Andrew C., editor. | Coombs, W. Timothy, editor. | Brown, Kenon A., editor.
Title: Reputational challenges in sport : theory and application / edited by Andrew Billings, W. Timothy Coombs and Kenon Brown.
Description: New York : Routledge, 2018. | Includes bibliographical references.
Identifiers: LCCN 2017056137 | ISBN 9781138055995 (hardback) | ISBN 9781138056008 (pbk.) | ISBN 9781315165608 (ebk)
Subjects: LCSH: Sports—Public relations. | Athletes—Public opinion.
Classification: LCC GV714 .R46 2018 | DDC 659.29796—dc23
LC record available at https://lccn.loc.gov/2017056137

ISBN: 978-1-138-05599-5 (hbk)
ISBN: 978-1-138-05600-8 (pbk)
ISBN: 978-1-315-16560-8 (ebk)

Typeset in Bembo Std
by Swales & Willis Ltd, Exeter, Devon, UK
Printed by CPI Group (UK) Ltd, Croydon CR0 4YY

CONTENTS

ABOUT THE EDITORS

Andrew C. Billings is the executive director of the Alabama Program in Sports Communication and Ronald Reagan Chair of Broadcasting in the Department of Journalism & Creative Media at The University of Alabama. He also serves on many editorial boards, including as an associate editor of the journals *Communication & Sport* and *Journal of Global Sport Management*.

W. Timothy Coombs is a full professor in the Department of Communication at Texas A&M University and an honorary professor at Aarhus University in Denmark. He is currently the editor of *Corporate Communications: An International Journal*.

Kenon A. Brown is an associate professor in the Department of Advertising and Public Relations at The University of Alabama. He is also the Programming Director for the Alabama Program in Sports Communication.

ABOUT THE CONTRIBUTORS

Rachel Allison is an assistant professor in the Department of Sociology at Mississippi State University.

William L. Benoit is a professor in the Department of Communication Studies at the University of Alabama-Birmingham.

Joseph R. Blaney is a professor and associate dean in the School of Communication at Illinois State University.

Natalie Brown-Devlin is an assistant professor in the Department of Advertising and Public Relations at the University of Texas-Austin.

James R. DiSanza is a professor in the Department of Communication, Media, and Persuasion at Idaho State University.

Melanie J. Formentin is an assistant professor in the Department of Public Relations at Towson State University.

Zac Gershberg is an assistant professor in the Department of Communication, Media, and Persuasion at Idaho State University.

Marion E. Hambrick is an associate professor in the Department of Health & Sport Sciences at the University of Louisville.

Jennifer L. Harker is an assistant professor in the Reed College of Media at the University of West Virginia.

Karen L. Hartman is an associate professor in the Department of Communication, Media, and Persuasion at Idaho State University.

Tom Isaacson is an assistant professor in the Department of Public Relations at Northern Michigan University.

Nancy J. Legge is a professor in the Department of Communication, Media, and Persuasion at Idaho State University.

Todd F. McDorman is a professor and associate dean in the Department of Rhetoric at Wabash College.

Ann Pegoraro is an associate professor in the Faculty of Management at Laurentian University.

Ryan S. Rigda is a doctoral student in the Department of Communication at Texas A&M University.

Lindsey A. Sherrill is a doctoral student in the College of Communication and Information Sciences at the University of Alabama.

Qingru Xu is a doctoral student in the College of Communication and Information Sciences at the University of Alabama.

Ziyuan Zhou is a doctoral student in the College of Communication and Information Sciences at the University of Alabama.

ACKNOWLEDGMENTS

This project has been quite enjoyable for us to execute. We each have different backgrounds and areas of expertise, yet those seemed to intersect in all of the right ways, creating an edited book that none of us could have accomplished on our own. We wish to thank Routledge for their steadfast support of the project, beginning with Linda Bathgate's initial commissioning of the project and then moving to Nicole Solano's steady hand as the effort slowly moved to fruition, and Kristina Ryan ensuring that all necessary parts of the project were accomplished. Having such a supportive publisher is always so key, and we were fortunate to have Routledge for this journey. We also wish to thank each of the contributors to this volume, as we were able to secure works from so many of the best and brightest in the burgeoning and connecting fields of sports communication and public relations. Finally, we must also send our gratitude to the DePaul University College of Communication for providing the space for us to hold a one-day event that became the nexus of this project.

In terms of individual thank-you notes, Andrew Billings must thank the administration at the University of Alabama as well as the Ronald Reagan Chair of Broadcasting endowment that helped to support this project. He also wishes to thank his wife, Angela, and two sons, Nathan and Noah, who are consistently understanding when this project necessitated a fair bit of time even after traditional business hours. Timothy Coombs wants to thank Sherry Holladay for her support during the project and Mugsy and Ash for not demanding too much attention. Kenon Brown must thank his wife, Amanda, and his daughter, Kensley, for their love, support, and understanding during the completion of this project.

When this project was initially conceived three years ago, we believed the time was right for a more sophisticated, in-depth examination of the interplay between sport and reputation management. We feel that purpose even more fervently today, and hope this volume contributes significantly to this inevitably growing subfield of sport communication.

INTRODUCTION
SPORTS CELEBRITY REPUTATION IN A MEDIATED WORLD OF SCANDAL

Reputation, Crisis, and the Presumed Power of Narrative Manipulation

Andrew C. Billings

> Up until a few years ago, if you were good at football, you could pretty much do crime and we were fine with it. Michael Vick. Ray Lewis. Ray Lewis tackled so many people that we were finally like, "You know, Ray, you get to murder one." If we like you enough, we will find a way to justify whatever it is you did. LeBron James could stab an old lady in public and everybody would be like "We all *talk* about stabbing old ladies. LeBron had the guts to *do* it. He's a leader." Michael Jordan could shoot up a shopping mall and people would be like "he's still got range from the outside."
>
> *Brennan, 2017*

In modern sports media, it is difficult to separate athlete from producer from consumer; for instance, the 2014 launch of the online *Players' Tribune* was heralded as an unfiltered voice of the modern athlete, yet ultimately represented the most curated and cultivated presentation of athletes to date (Bucholtz, 2015). It is equally indeterminate to declare a certain medium as having exemplary power; one may say they receive the majority of their sports information from "social media," yet Facebook and Twitter do not employ thousands of writers creating such massive content needs, as those are produced by everything from traditional journalism outlets to the proverbial basement blogger.

In the face of such a media maelstrom, one element of sports media has become clear: in terms of cultural influence, the power of sport and celebrity continues to expand. The 1986 film *Hoosiers* features a character, Myra Fleener, who argues that, in 1950s Indiana, "heroes come pretty cheap around here . . . if you can put a ball through a hoop, people treat you like a God." Decades later, the celebrity only escalates; Dallas Cowboys quarterback Troy Aikman once was featured on a box for Town House crackers and those boxes can now be found on eBay—sold as collectors' items. Even a bag of *air* from Kobe Bryant's last competitive game was once featured on the website. When Wenner published his book *Fallen Sports Heroes, Media, & Celebrity Culture* in 2013, the title was tacitly acknowledging an ancillary truism: the falls of athletes are so memorable because the perches in which they descend are so high. Wenner (2013) writes:

> Like a character in a Kris Kristofferson song, the sports hero is "partly truth" and "partly fiction." Ripe with contradiction, this construction presents a captivating conundrum. At a time when many wonder about where all the heroes have gone, ever-ready constructions of the sports hero fill the void.
>
> *p. ix*

The accolades have never been more prominent; the transgressions have never been more public. Some believe 2011 to be the pinnacle year of scandal in sports because of the lead story—Penn State child sex abuse—while others counter that 2014 constituted the pinnacle year of scandal with myriad stories of assault, including the most prominent case of a TMZ video of running back Ray Rice knocking out his girlfriend and dragging her out of an elevator. The truth is that each year is a year of scandal in the sports world, as the transgressions happen with seemingly clockwork regularity even as the magnitudes differ from case to case.

This book is an attempt to build a cohesive sense of where reputation is managed, discussed, and analyzed within these continual crises of the modern sports world. As discussed in the next section, theories have been advanced to understand conceptions of image and crisis in broader lenses. As discussed in the section beyond that, sport has often been the subject of analyses of said crises. However, this book asks core questions about the pairing, discerning what can be gleaned about sport through crisis, yet equally pertinently advancing what can be learned about crisis specifically through sport. In the end, reputation is bandied, discussed, and negotiated within many constituencies and, as this volume will show, the number of those groups continues to expand, as each feels some ownership as a stakeholder in the sports world.

The Evolution of Reputational Theories

The management of one's reputation is certainly not new; yet the stakes and prominence afforded within sport-based situations have never been more amplified. Apologia has millennia of origins, including the work of Aristotle, Plato, and Isocrates, who used it primarily as a source of legal defense of oneself. This strategy gradually morphed from one of self-defense to one of public figurative self-immolation, as people found apology to be the most expedient way to move on from crises and begin the process of rebuilding one's image. If "honesty is the best policy," apology surely was not far behind. Ware and Linkugel (1973) deconstructed apologia, finding four subgenres of investigation: absolutive, vindicative, explanative, and justificative. These genres became largely viewed as strategies that offered nuance to the reputational management construction—and the reception each strategy would receive in different contexts.

Enter Benoit's image restoration theory (IRT), which was later more commonly referred to as image repair theory, predominantly because many reputational crises were so severe as to render full restoration of one's image unreasonable to attain. Formulated in the 1980s and refined in the 1990s, Benoit (1995) outlines five core elements (denial, evading responsibility, reducing offensiveness, corrective action, and mortification) which provided more solution-based structures one could or would use to manage reputational crises. Based on interest in the contribution of image change in the public relations sector (Botan, 1993; Grunig, 1993) IRT was widely adopted (Benoit & Hanczor, 1994; Brown, Dickhaus, & Long, 2012; Dardis & Haigh, 2009), yet also was much more likely to be applied for individuals than entities, who may have a multitude of messages impeding any intended solution.

Coombs (2007) answered the call for more focus on management of reputation within/during a crisis rather than after one had already largely reached its zenith. There were two stages to diagnosing a reputational-altering situational strategy. The first came from Coombs and Holladay (2002), who contended that crisis type could be identified as one of three classifications: victim (minimal crisis responsibility), accident (low crisis responsibility), and preventable (strong crisis responsibility). After that type is identified, there were four postures in which strategies should unfurl: (a) denial (e.g., attack the accuser, scapegoat), (b) diminishment (e.g., excuse, justification), (c) bolstering (e.g., victimage, ingratiation), and (d) rebuilding (e.g., apology, compensation). Ancillary studies (Brown & Billings, 2013; Choi & Chung, 2013; Coombs & Holladay, 2008) followed that utilized such strategy postures and their relative impact to great effect.

Throughout the evolution of pinpointing the nebulous concept of crisis and responses to it—from apologia to IRT to SCCT (situational crisis communication theory)—all congregate around conceptions of reputation. All approaches seemingly move beyond the origins of strictly legal rhetoric to include various facets of society. Sports provide a unique vantage point, as sometimes the stakes are quite high (such as a Kobe Bryant or Ben Roethlisberger rape allegation), while others are fairly meager (such as an emphatic Richard Sherman tirade or a poorly worded tweet).

Sports, Heroes, and the Public Personae

After decades of being sidelined in academic pursuits because of its presumed unserious nature, sport now has become a useful and formative lens for examining how society functions and what it values. McDonald and Birrell (1999) forge a compelling case for reading sport critically, which is often difficult to do when fans use it as a central means for escape (Billings & Ruihley, 2013) and frequently combine in-person and sports media consumption with free-flowing alcohol (Wenner & Jackson, 2008). Nevertheless, insights can be gleaned from the youth to professional—and every part of the ladder between (see Billings, Butterworth, & Turman, 2017). A unique vantage point appears to be those whose stories rise to the level of media attention—whether adulation or notoriety. As Beal (2013) argues, "the structures and values embedded in narratives of sports celebrities provide insight into societal ideals of success and what attributes are associated with it" (p. 104).

As online media created a glut of expansive options for media content, coverage of such celebrities has magnified exponentially, with the need for public relations damage control rising along with it. When one's reputation is continually contested in a variety of media spaces—both legitimate and far less so—one's promotional "Q" score is apt to fluctuate far more dramatically as well. Hence, the need for persuasion, more formally unpacked as a "spin" one can provide in cases of potential image rehabilitation or crisis management. However, spin has forged into the lead in the creation, affirmation, and reinterpretation of one's reputation, leading Iyengar (1991, p. 1) to ask: "is anyone responsible?"

The answer to that question, particularly in the sports world, is that the athlete or team represents the nexus of such responsibility. The high economic and social capital reacts to form an area of privilege, one that is prone to high levels of scrutiny (see Rae, Billings, & Brown, 2017). As Wenner (2013) claims:

> When an athlete's actions go awry—on the field or off—we tend to blame the actor, rather than the structures and socialization of sport that may have wrought the problem of the forces of the media that encourage a certain kind of star "to be born."
>
> *p. 11*

Thus, with millions of dollars and one's career inevitably about to be curtailed by a combination of injury and Father Time, the result is the formation of safe, vanilla, athletic personas, perhaps manufactured, yet with the aim akin to the Hippocratic Oath of a medical doctor: first do no harm. Rick, Silk, and Andrews (2013) use the exemplar of David Beckham to illustrate the rise of "liquid celebrity" (p. 218), a function of the athlete in which commercial-driven reputation trumps personal authenticity and the underpinnings of activism.

As will be reviewed in this book, sports have consequently operated in a somewhat different persuasive space than other forms of reputation triage. For instance, non-sport organizations use ingratiation as a primary strategy, rarely—if ever—opting for apologies as a strategy (Allen & Caillouet, 1994). Yet, sports operate within a different realm, partly because of their entertainment function, but also because their success or failure is more evident for all to see: points, wins, championships.

In this equation, the celebrity of an athlete is laid to bare in a way quite dissimilar than other prominent CEOs, companies, or even entertainment stars. Each theoretical approach was ultimately adopted in the sphere of sport, with apologia first tied to athletics by Kruse (1981) and then reputation being uncovered in a multitude of contexts in the decades that followed. Isolated athlete cases appeared most predominant, with focus ranging from the deadly serious—ranging from athletes with guns (Glantz, 2013; Lavelle, 2013; Sheckels, 2013) to rape allegations (Griffin, 2013) to assault (Brown & Brown, 2014)—to the relatively minor—ranging from (re)building the legacy of LeBron James (Mocarski & Billings, 2014) to a picture of star Olympic swimmer Michael Phelps smoking pot (Troester & Johns, 2013; Walsh & McAllister-Spooner, 2011). Some studies represented deviance and affronts to the integrity of sport, such as Denham and Desormeaux's (2008) analysis of Zinedine Zidane's World Cup head-butt and Sanderson's (2008) examination of performance-enhancing drug accusations levied against baseball's Roger Clemens. Others pertained to moral crises without legal ramifications, such as Tiger Woods' infidelity and subsequent downfall (Sanderson, 2010) or the on-field antics of Terrell Owens (Brazeal, 2008) and on-court tirades of Serena Williams (Brazeal, 2013). Some transgressions crossed lines to become national and international stories outside the world of sports, including the 1994 figure skating controversy of Tonya Harding and Nancy Kerrigan (Benoit & Hanczor, 1994) and the Michael Vick dogfighting scandal (Smith, 2013). Some pertained more to teams and institutions, including the Duke lacrosse rape accusations (Fortunato, 2008) and arguably the greatest of all sports transgressions, the Penn State child molestation case (Brown, Brown, & Billings, 2015).

These studies collectively illustrate that reputation can alter how one perceives corporate social responsibility (Haigh & Brubaker, 2010) with the potential to alter endorsements (Jones & Schumann, 2004) and the entire economics of sport-based celebrity (Smart, 2005). Moreover, these cases are seemingly tinged by elements of gender (Compton, 2013; Mean, 2013) and race (Brown, Billings, & Devlin, 2016; Brown, Billings, Mastro, & Devlin, 2015; Mastro, Blecha, & Seate, 2011), highlighting the need to advance more evidence-based studies of reputation and crisis (see Coombs, 2010) in a sphere many regard as out of control in a number of ways (Butterworth, 2013). Hence, this book is intended to provide substantial layering to such multifaceted discussions.

Reputational Challenges in Sport: An Overview

This volume is divided into three main parts—the first pertaining to overarching frameworks of sport-based reputation management, and the latter two focusing on the application of these frameworks within various epistemologies and contexts.

The first three chapters form a Venn diagram of base knowledge. Chapter 1 is written by one of this volume's co-editors, W. Timothy Coombs, who situates his widely applied situational crisis communication theory (SCCT) with a laser-like focus on the elements most pertinent to sport. Coombs advances the Sato, Ko, Park, and Tao's (2015) concept of the Athlete Reputational Crisis (ARC), arguing that, while there are "unique contextual factors," sport becomes a ideal realm for exploring elements of effectiveness (or lack thereof) regarding SCCT. Part I then concludes with a piece from William L. Benoit, who then offers similar insight for his image repair theory (IRT) within Chapter 2, with an eye again on how sport shifts the elements within his theory, partly because of the entertainment-based context and partly because of the celebrity status that many 21st-century athletes enjoy, contending that "this adulation makes favored athletes into heroes," which makes image repair an "important option."

Part II is exclusively dedicated to the applications of Coombs's situational crisis communication theory. Chapter 3 opens with Natalie Brown-Devlin's examination of how empiricism has informed previous works in SCCT, creating a warrant for expanding "the theoretical understanding of crisis management while simultaneously providing sports organizations and athletes with practical crisis management plans." This piece is then followed by a research team (James R. DiSanza, Karen L. Hartman, Nancy J. Legge, and Zac Gershberg) who adopt a more humanistic approach to advancing SCCT within sport, making a case in Chapter 4 for "narrative management" as a key element of any crisis. The chapter incorporates two case studies, one regarding the NFL's Ray Rice's domestic abuse case and the other relating to the NBA's Donald Sterling's racist comments, utilizing core threads to form insight on a holistic level. The remaining chapters in Part II then offer singular applications of SCCT within differing and contrasting sports contexts. University needs are the focus of Chapter 5, as Lindsey Sherrill examines the University of Missouri race-relations crisis of 2015, which featured a football team walkout until both the President and Chancellor resigned. Sherrill concludes that SCCT represents "an excellent starting point for university leaders, but at this point may not fully address all their crisis communication needs." Chapter 6 is written by Jennifer L. Harker, who applies SCCT to the most popular sport in the United States, professional football, finding shortsighted decisions the norm for the National Football League, at least in part due to the high-profile nature of the crises within what is now best considered America's sport. "Had the league preemptively had a comprehensive policy and stuck with consistent disciplinary actions," Harker argues, "the league could have scapegoated blame attribution because the reputational challenges would have remained with the players." Chapter 7 is written by Ryan S. Rigda, who gazes to the event that is arguably the world's largest and most examined, the Olympics, to discern the multiplicity of voices and stakeholders that are seemingly part and parcel of Olympic-based crises, using the 2014 Sochi Winter Games as an exemplar for the importance of studying the "before" elements of a crisis before delving into the still-central "during" and "after" phases. Part II then concludes with a piece from Melanie J. Formentin, who uses Chapter 8 to explore SCCT in the context of the National Basketball Association lockout, concluding that "future SCCT research should consider investigating the role of stakeholder investment in the formation of beliefs and perceptions about an organization in crisis," an integral—and increasingly prevalent—variable in modern discussions of sport and reputation.

Part III offers a similar "deep dive" in regard to Benoit's image repair theory. Marion E. Hambrick begins the part in Chapter 9 by implementing IRT as a lens for examining how specific athlete reputations hold the potential to not only be restored but also sometimes enhanced in the process of overt repair strategies; his review of 43 cases from 38 studies is truly comprehensive. Chapter 10 then features a more rhetorical focus from Todd F. McDorman, who uses the seemingly ever-robust debate over the transgressions of baseball hit king Pete Rose to argue for a nostalgia-oriented approach to interpreting reputation of heroes of years (and decades) past, capitalizing on what he terms "a sense of comfort and security that can soothe uncertainties of the present" at a time of rebuilding for the Cincinnati Reds franchise. Book co-editor Kenon Brown (along with co-authors Ziyuan Zhou and Qingru Xu) then reviews empirical examinations of image repair in Chapter 11, finding clear preferences for certain strategies over others—yet with caveats that can be tinged by everything from gender, race, or celebrity status of the athlete or team involved. The next two chapters focus on how the role of "team" unfolds within sport-based reputation management. Chapter 12, written by Tom Isaacson, focuses on a case study of the Chicago White Sox, utilizing a successful rebuild of the team 20 years prior to foster trust in the organization when a similar rebuild could have potentially threatened the team brand and image, while Chapter 13 connects team- and fan-related issues as Joseph R. Blaney examines relationships between victories (or lack thereof) and ticket prices, concluding that "pointing to unfortunate situations beyond organizational control (defeasibility) does not result in a more positive audience response" within the realm of sport. The final offering in this book, Chapter 14, is co-authored by Rachel Allison and Ann Pegoraro, who show how IRT informs the mediated coverage of American Olympic soccer hero Abby Wambach, illustrating the double-edged sword that is presented for many A-list celebrity athletes seeking to manage their reputation in traditional and social media outlets. They find that "while Facebook became a site of fierce debate among users as to the meaning of Wambach's transgression, the predominant user message was one of acceptance and forgiveness."

In all, we believe this book represents a noteworthy and logical next step in understanding various interactions between sport, reputation, media, public relations, and culture. Whether this volume poses more questions than it answers is up to the reader; regardless, we believe the case is ably made for the need for future investigations of reputation to include some of the most prominent parts of societal conversations that emerge in the wide world of sport.

References

Allen, M. W., & Caillouet, R. H. (1994). Legitimation endeavors: Impression management strategies used by an organization in crisis. *Communication Monographs, 61*(1), 44–62.

Beal, B. (2013). The ups and downs of skating vertical: Christian Hosoi, crystal meth, and Christianity. In L. A. Wenner (Ed.), *Fallen sports heroes, media, & celebrity culture* (pp. 92–106). New York: Peter Lang.

Benoit, W. L. (1995). Accounts, accuses, and apologies: *A theory of image restoration strategies*. New York: SUNY Press.

Benoit, W. L., & Hanczor, R. (1994). The Tonya Harding controversy: An analysis of image restoration strategies. *Communication Quarterly, 42*, 416–433.

Billings, A., Butterworth, M., & Turman, P. (2017). *Communication and sport: Surveying the field*. Thousand Oaks, CA: Sage.

Billings, A. C., & Ruihley, B. J. (2013). Why we watch, why we play: The relationship between fantasy sport and fandom motivations. *Mass Communication & Society, 16*(1), 5–25.

Botan, C. (1993). A human nature approach to image and ethics in international public relations. *Journal of Public Relations Research, 5*, 71–82.

Brazeal, L. (2008). The image repair strategies of Terrell Owens. *Public Relations Review, 34*, 145–150.

Brazeal, L. (2013). Belated remorse: Serena Williams's image repair rhetoric at the 2009 U.S. Open. In J. R. Blaney, L. R. Lippert, & J. S. Smith (Eds.), *Repairing the athlete's image: Studies in sports image restoration* (pp. 239–252). Lanham, MD: Lexington Press.

Brennan, N. (2017). 3 Mics. *Netflix, Standup Special*.

Brown, K. A., Billings, A. C., & Devlin, M. B. (2016). Image repair across the racial spectrum: Experimentally exploring athlete transgression responses. *Communication Research Reports, 33*(1), 47–53.

Brown, K. A., Billings, A. C., Mastro, D., & Devlin, N. B. (2015). Changing the image repair equation: Impact of race and gender on sport-related transgressions. *Journalism & Mass Communication Quarterly, 92*(2), 487–506.

Brown, K. A., & Brown, N. (2014). Responding to criminal accusations: An experimental examination of Aqib Talib's 2011 aggravated assault case. In J. Blaney (Ed.), *Putting image repair to the test: Empirical approaches to image restoration strategies*.

Brown, K. A., Dickhaus, J., & Long, M. (2012). "The decision" and LeBron James: An empirical examination of image repair in sports. *Journal of Sports Media, 7*, 149–167.

Brown, N., & Billings, A. C. (2013). Sports fans as crisis communicators on social media websites. *Public Relations Review, 39*(1), 74–81.

Brown, N., Brown, K., & Billings, A. C. (2015). "May no act of ours bring shame": Fan enacted crisis communication surrounding the Penn State sex abuse scandal. *Communication & Sport, 3*(3), 288–311.

Bucholtz, A. (2015, Mar. 30). The *Players' Tribune* articles aren't written by the players, which creates a host of issues. *Awful Announcing*. Retrieved from: http://awfulannouncing.com/2015/players-tribune-articles-arent-written-by-the-players-which-creates-a-host-of-issues.html

Butterworth, M. L. (2013). Coaches gone wild: Media, masculinity, and morality in big time college football. In L. A. Wenner (Ed.), *Fallen sports heroes, media, and celebrity culture* (pp. 284–297). New York: Peter Lang.

Choi, J., & Chung, W. (2013). Analysis of the interactive relationship between apology and product involvement in crisis communication: An experimental study on the Toyota recall crisis. *Journal of Business and Technical Communication, 27*, 3–31.

Compton, J. L. (2013). Unsports(wo)manlike conduct: An image repair analysis of Elizabeth Lambert, the University of New Mexico, and the NCAA. In J. R. Blaney, L. R. Lippert, & J. S. Smith (Eds.), *Repairing the athlete's image: Studies in sports image restoration* (pp. 253–266). Lanham, MD: Lexington Press.

Coombs, W.T. (2007). Ongoing crisis communication: Planning, managing and responding (2nd ed.). Thousand Oaks, CA: Sage.

Coombs, W. T. (2010). Pursuing evidence-based crisis communication. In W. T. Coombs & S. Holladay (Eds.), *Handbook of crisis communication* (pp. 719–725). Malden, MA: Blackwell.

Coombs, W. T., & Holladay, S. J. (2002). Helping crisis managers protect reputational assets: Initial tests of the situational crisis communication theory. *Management Communication Quarterly, 16*(2), 165–186.

Coombs, W. T., & Holladay, S. J. (2008). Comparing apology to equivalent crisis response strategies: Clarifying apology's role and value in crisis communication. *Public Relations Review, 34*, 252–257.

Dardis, F., & Haigh, M. (2009). Prescribing versus describing: Testing image restoration strategies in a crisis situation. *Corporate Communications: An International Journal, 14*, 101–118.

Denham, B. E., & Desormeaux, M. (2008). Headlining the head-butt: Zinedine Zidane/Marco Materazzi portrayals in prominent English, Irish, and Scottish newspapers. *Media, Culture & Society, 30*, 375–392.

Fortunato, J. A. (2008). Restoring a reputation: The Duke University lacrosse scandal. *Public Relations Review, 34*, 116–123.

Glantz, M. (2013). Plaxico Burress takes his best shot. In J. R. Blaney, L. R. Lippert, & J. S. Smith (Eds.), *Repairing the athlete's image: Studies in sports image restoration* (pp. 187–202). Lanham, MD: Lexington Press.

Griffin, R. (2013). Power, privilege and the surprising absence of repair: Kobe Bryant and interest convergence. In J. R. Blaney, L. R. Lippert, & J. S. Smith (Eds.), *Repairing the athlete's image: Studies in sports image restoration* (pp. 97–122). Lanham, MD: Lexington Press.

Grunig, J. (1993). Image and substance: From symbolic to behavioral relationships. *Public Relations Review, 19*, 121–139.

Haigh, M., & Brubaker, P. (2010). Examining how image restoration strategy impacts perceptions of corporate social responsibility, organization-public relationships, and source credibility. *Corporate Communications: An International Journal, 15*, 453–468.

Iyengar, S. (1991). Is anyone responsible?: How television frames political issues. Chicago, IL: University of Chicago Press.

Jones, M., & Schumann, D. (2004). The strategic use of celebrity athlete endorsers in print media: A historical perspective. In L. Kahle & C. Riley (Eds.), *Sports marketing and the psychology of marketing communication* (pp. 107–132). Mahwah, NJ: Lawrence Erlbaum.

Kruse, N. (1981). Apologia in team sport. *Quarterly Journal of Speech, 67*, 270–283.

Lavelle, K .L. (2013). Guns are no joke: Framing Plaxico Burress, Gilbert Arenas, and gunplay in professional sports. In L. A. Wenner (Ed.), *Fallen sports heroes, media, and celebrity culture* (pp. 179–192). New York: Peter Lang.

McDonald, M. G., & Birrell, S. (1999). Reading sport critically: A methodology for interrogating power. *Sociology of Sport Journal, 16*(4), 283–300.

Mastro, D., Blecha, E., & Seate, A. (2011). Characterizations of criminal athletes: A systematic examination of sports news depictions of race and crime. *Journal of Broadcasting & Electronic Media, 55*, 526–542.

Mean, L. J. (2013). On track, off track, on Oprah: The framing of Marion Jones as golden girl and American fraud. In L. A. Wenner (Ed.), *Fallen sports heroes, media, and celebrity culture* (pp. 77–91). New York: Peter Lang.

Mocarski, R. A., & Billings, A. C. (2014). Manufacturing a messiah: How Nike and LeBron James co-constructed the legend of King James. *Communication & Sport, 2*, 3–23.

Rae, C., Billings, A. C., & Brown, K. A. (2017). On-field perceptions of off-field deviance: Exploring social and economic capital within sport-related transgressions. In A. C. Billings & K. A. Brown (Eds.), *Evolution of the modern sports fan: Communicative approaches* (pp. 147–166), Lanham, MD: Lexington Press.

Rick, O., Silk, M. L., & Andrews, D. L. (2013). Liquid Beckham: Inoculating a star against falls from grace. In L. A. Wenner (Ed.), *Fallen sports heroes, media, & celebrity culture* (pp. 208–221). New York: Peter Lang.

Sanderson, J. (2008). How do you prove a negative? Roger Clemens's image-repair strategies in response to the Mitchell Report. *International Journal of Sport Communication, 1*, 246–262.

Sanderson, J. (2010). Framing Tiger's troubles: Comparing traditional and social media. *International Journal of Sport Communication, 3*, 438–453.

Sato, S., Ko, Y. J., Park, C., & Tao, W. (2015). Athlete reputational crisis and consumer evaluation. *European Sport Management Quarterly, 15*(4), 434–453.

Sheckels, T. F. (2013). The failed comedy of the NBA's Gilbert Arenas: Image restoration in context. In J. R. Blaney, L. R. Lippert, & J. S. Smith (Eds.), *Repairing the athlete's image: Studies in sports image restoration* (pp. 169–186). Lanham, MD: Lexington Press.

Smart, B. (2005). *The sport star: Modern sport and the culture economy of sporting celebrity.* London, England: SAGE.

Smith, J. (2013). Bad Newz Kennels: Michael Vick and dogfighting. In J. R. Blaney, L. R. Lippert, & J. S. Smith (Eds.), *Repairing the athlete's image: Studies in sports image restoration* (pp. 151–168). Lanham, MD: Lexington Press.

Troester, R., & Johns, L. (2013). The Michael Phelps saga: From successful Olympian, to pot smoker caught on camera, to renewed role model and brand. In J. R. Blaney, L. R. Lippert, & J. S. Smith (Eds.), *Repairing the athlete's image: Studies in sports image restoration* (pp. 71–88). Lanham, MD: Lexington Press.

Walsh, J., & McAllister-Spooner, S. (2011). Analysis of the image repair discourse in the Michael Phelps controversy. *Public Relations Review, 37*, 157–162.

Ware, B. L., & Linkugel, W. A. (1973). They spoke in defense of themselves: On the generic criticism of apologia. *Quarterly Journal of Speech, 59*(3), 273–283.

Wenner, L. A. (Ed.) (2013). *Fallen sports heroes, media, & celebrity culture.* New York: Peter Lang.

Wenner, L. A., & Jackson, S. (Eds.) (2008). *Sport, beer, and gender: Promotional culture and contemporary social life.* New York: Peter Lang.

PART I
Theoretical Foundations

1

ATHLETE REPUTATIONAL CRISES: ONE POINT FOR LINKING

Situational Crisis Communication Theory and Sports Crises

W. Timothy Coombs

As evidenced by this project and other publications, there is a growing interest in applying crisis communication to sports crises. Globally, sports organizations are major businesses involving billions of dollars annually (Billings, Butterworth, & Turman, 2015) and we think of sport as an industry. Granted, sport is a diverse industry covering teams and individuals as well as professional and amateur. Sport has some unique features as an industry that separate it from typical corporations and create unique crisis communication demands. These unique features can influence how we adapt and apply crisis communication theory, developed for typical corporations, to sports crises. In this chapter, I posit that sport as an industry holds important modifiers when applying Situational Crisis Communication Theory (SCCT) (Coombs, 2007) to certain types of sports crises. The chapter is divided into three sections. The first section explains the context of crisis communication and the development of SCCT; the second section explores the reputational nature of sports crises through athlete reputational crises (ARC); while the final section considers the application of SCCT to athlete reputational crises.

The Context of Crisis Communication

Crisis communication emerged when developing interest in crisis management became a distinct area of interest for practitioners and researchers in the 1980s. Crisis communication was beneficial to organizations because it helped managers to survive and to recover from operational crises. Operational crises represent actual or potential disruptions to the functioning of a firm. Facility fires, toxic chemical releases, product harm recalls, and weather disruptions to airline traffic are all examples of operational crises. The early definitions of crises emphasize the focus on disruption/potential disruption of operations (e.g., Barton, 2001; Fink, 1986). Risk assessments, crisis plans, and training reflected the focus on operational crisis. A distinguishing feature of operational crises is that they frequently involve a risk to public safety (including employees). Consider how a product harm crisis places customers at risk, while toxic chemical releases pose threats to employees and community members living in close proximity to the facility.

As Barton (2001) noted, all crises present some reputational threat to a given organization. Other scholars have posited that reputational crises are a unique form of crisis. Booth (2000) argued that reputational crises do not have be event driven but can be the result of the organization being associated with "some other activity, entity, or incident" (p. 197). Sohn and Lariscy (2014) favor an event-based view, specifying that a reputational crisis is problematic because it indicates the organization has violated social norms or values. Thus, we can combine the two to define a reputational crisis as a situation or event where stakeholders perceive the organization has violated important social values and is acting irresponsibly.

Reputational crises involve some specific reputational damage to the organizations and generally lack the immediate concerns over public safety. That does not mean some entities will not be harmed by a reputational crisis but that the damage is limited and unlikely to spread as in an operational crisis. When a top manager is guilty of sexual harassment, there are victims but other stakeholders are no longer at risk when the manager is removed. When a toxic chemical cloud is released, employees are in immediate danger, as are those living in the path of the cloud. Reputational crises generally have a narrower set of victims and potential victims than do operational crises.

There are important differences between operational and reputational crises that affect what constitutes effective crisis communication. Operational crises are primarily event driven with tangible or concrete indicators such as a harmful product or a release of toxic chemicals. Reputational crises can be event driven or perception driven (stakeholders and organizations agree there is a crisis). The indicators for reputational crises can be intangible and abstract, such as concerns over whether or not an action is irresponsible or offensive, or something that a majority of stakeholders would consider inappropriate. Two examples can illustrate the range of concerns.

In 2010, Greenpeace posted a video mocking a Nestlé commercial. This commercial marked the beginning of Greenpeace's efforts to define Nestlé's palm oil sourcing as irresponsible. Not all stakeholders know about palm oil or care about its sourcing—there was room for interpretation. Greenpeace initiated a communication campaign to raise awareness and concern over palm oil sourcing by Nestlé. Nestlé hurt itself by trying to suppress Greenpeace's message, thereby turning a reputational risk (palm oil sourcing) into a reputational crisis (massive negative commentary in social media; Coombs, 2014). In 2016, a social media comment about a racist Red Cross pool safety poster escalated into a reputational crisis.

The poster showed right and wrong behaviors at a public pool. All the right behaviors involved children that were white, while most the wrong behaviors showed children that were black; social media sentiment about the Red Cross went from 10 percent to 80 percent negative. Most people who heard about the poster agreed it seemed racist. The palm oil sourcing concern was much more abstract and open to interpretation than the images in the pool poster.

We can locate a crisis on both operational and reputational continua, as a crisis can have both operational and reputational concerns. Typically, one of the two continua will dominate the crisis frame: how people are interpreting the crisis. The two continua are required to denote the connection between operational and reputational crises. Most of the extant writing on crisis communication derived from crisis management is based on the original notion of operational crises. The plans and warning signs were developed for operational crises, not reputational crises. That is why organizations often have trouble coping with reputational crises and paracrises (common precursors to a reputational crisis that involve the public management of a crisis risk; Coombs & Holladay, 2012). It could also be argued that crisis thinking itself was constrained by the operational emphasis. I would include SCCT's original writing as a victim of this operational constraint category. While SCCT does recognize some reputational crises, its central tenets reflect an operational focus. SCCT works best for event-driven crises and are defined primarily by the crisis situation.

In 2015, SCCT was expanded to address the need to address paracrises and reputational crises. A paracrisis occurs when organizations manage a crisis risk in full view of stakeholders—the public management of crisis risks (Coombs & Holladay, 2012, 2015. The expansion centered on locating a set of crisis response strategies fitting for paracrises and reputational crises, and identifying the salient factors influencing the communicative response selection decisions in such circumstances (see Table 1.1). There is a greater range of potentially effective options for paracrises and reputational crises due to the more ambiguous nature of these crises. Such crises are more open to multiple interpretations of events and what qualifies as appropriate behavior. You cannot reasonably contest that your facility exploded by choosing to ignore the carnage. You can, however, dispute if your sourcing of raw materials is responsible or choose to ignore activist stakeholders proclaiming your sourcing is irresponsible, such as the Nestlé case discussed earlier. Denial and silence are sub-optimal crisis response strategies for operational crises (Coombs, Holladay, & Claeys, 2016) but can be viable options in a reputational crisis. Reputational crises provide a bridge from SCCT to the discussion of sports crises because sports crises are predominantly reputational. The following sections link SCCT to sports crises by examining the types of crises common in sports and the contextual factors that help both to shape reactions to sports crises and to influence the effectiveness of various crisis response strategies during sports crises.

TABLE 1.1 Factors That Could Influence Response Selection to ARCs

Response	Relevant Factors Driving the Response Choice					
	Intentionality	Violation Domain	Violation Clarity	Fan Reaction	System Reaction	Career Risk
Denial						Ends
Justification or Minimization	Accidental	Non-performance (Minor)	Gray	Supportive	Supportive	
Apology	Intentional	Performance Non-performance (Severe)	Rule	Negative	Negative	
Apology plus Adjusting	Intentional	Performance Non-performance (Severe)	Rule	Negative	Negative	Interrupts

Sports and Crisis: A Reputational Focus

Sports reporters often use the term "optics" to refer to actions of a team, league, or individual that does not look good to stakeholders. This term captures the reality that most sports crises are reputational rather than operational, because most sports crises do not threaten the delivery of services. In *Communication and Sport: Surveying the Field*, the examples used in the chapter on crisis communication are predominantly reputational (Billings et al., 2015). Koerber and Zabara (2017) noted that sports crises rarely reach the level of serious damage or disruption of business, two common definitional characteristics of a crisis (Coombs, 2015). Riots, terror attacks, and other operational disruption do occur in sports, but reputational crises are far more common. Koerber and Zabara (2017) warn that the reputational bias in sports crises "should not be taken to mean that sports crises are inherently less significant than crises in other fields" (p. 194). Rather, there is simply a difference in the nature of crises in sports versus other organizations. This section refines the sports crisis focus of this chapter and the potential implications for adapting SCCT to sport.

Clarifying the Focus of Sports Crises

Sato, Ko, Park, and Tao (2015) developed the concept of athlete reputational crisis (ARC). An ARC is "an event caused by (un)intentional and on (off)field athlete behaviors that threaten to disrupt an athlete's reputation" (Sato et al., 2015, p. 435). An ARC can involve intentional or unintentional behaviors that can occur on or off the field, hence covering a variety of events. There are other types of sports crises, but the focus in this chapter is on ARCs. In crisis management there is the concept of spillover, when a crisis affects other related entities not directly involved with the crisis (Roehm & Tybout, 2006; Zavyalova, Pfarrer, Reger, & Shapiro, 2012). For instance, spillover occurs when a crisis with one product of a company has negative effects for the company's other products or a crisis for one company affects an entire industry. In 2011, Listeria in cantaloupe from one farm in Colorado killed 33 people and had a devastating effect on the entire cantaloupe industry, because people were afraid to eat any cantaloupe. Even two years later, the cantaloupe industry in Colorado was still suffering the spillover effects (Whitney, 2013). ARCs can have a spillover effect on teams, leagues/associations, and sponsors. If the athlete is involved in a team sport, his or her actions can negatively affect the team. Team sports belong to associations and ARCs can create reputational crises for those associations as well. The Ray Rice domestic abuse crisis created a spillover effect for the Baltimore Ravens (team) and the National Football League (association; Richards, Wilson, Boyle, & Mower, 2017). Some athletes are in individual sports such as tennis or golf. Still, there are associations overseeing these sports and an ARC can raise crisis risks for the association. Individual athletes using performance-enhancing drugs (PEDs) creates problems for various, including the International Olympic Committee.

The spillover potential of an ARC creates a coupling between the individual athlete and the larger system (teams, associations, and/or sponsors) that reflects a multivocal approach to crisis communication (Frandsen & Johansen, 2010, 2017), ARC communication should consider both the response of the athlete and the response of the larger system. I am not saying these responses are coordinated but they *will* affect one another; hence, it can be insightful to examine ARCs as crisis communication networks.

The ARCs and SCCT

This section explores the fit between SCCT and ARCs. The consistencies between ARCs and SCCT are developed along with ways SCCT needs modification for application to ARCs. Crisis types and contextual modifiers supply the guiding points for this section.

Crisis Types

Within the scope of ARC, there are a variety of crisis types. Consistent with the organizational crisis communication literature, ARC research found that crisis type does shape attributions and reactions of stakeholders (Sato et al., 2015). A 2 × 2 matrix of ARC types has been created using intentionality, and performance draws from Attribution Theory, as does SCCT. Performance is whether the event is related to athletic performance or off the field (non-performance related). Taking PEDs would be classified as performance, while domestic abuse more befits the non-performance domain. Attitudes toward an athlete were found to be more negative for intentional actions and performance-related actions. The reason for the difference is tied to the fact that performance actions result in people questioning the integrity of the game (Sato et al., 2015).

It should be noted the study used a low severity non-performance action (pushing an aggressive fan). Other studies have found highly negative reactions to high severity non-performance behaviors (physical abuse; Fink, Parker, Brett, & Higgins, 2009). I would argue that a non-performance ARC that has the potential to generate outrage (Salerno & Peter-Hagene, 2013) should be viewed as seriously as a performance ARC. Overall, there is consistency between how SCCT and ARC crisis types are conceptualized and their effects on stakeholders. Both hold that increased intentionality and severity create greater threats to reputations and other salient outcomes.

Another factor to consider for ARCs would be whether or not the event is a clear violation of the rules. Taking a banned substance in a sport is a clear violation of a rule. Some off-field behaviors may not be covered by specific rules, subsequently falling into a gray area. Treatment of spouses or family members and driving violations are examples of events that may not have a specific rule. Until the Ray Rice event, the NFL had not set rules about domestic abuse. A rules violation gives the individual athlete and the larger systems fewer options for a response because the response is bound by the rule violation. This is similar to the early conceptualizations of SCCT arguing that crisis responses differ when there is clear evidence of a problem (most operational crises) and when the evidence is disputable (reputational crises; Coombs, 1995). Overall, the discussion of crisis types for ARCs fits well with the discussions of crisis types in SCCT.

Contextual Factors

In SCCT, contextual modifiers are factors influencing how people attribute crisis responsibility and influence the crisis response selection. It is reasonable to assume an industry can create specific contextual modifiers and is, itself, a contextual modifier. I have identified three potentially robust contextual modifiers for ARCs: (a) fans, (b) economic factors, and (c) visibility of athletes. In business-to-consumer firms, the dream is to have customers that are fans. The reality is that only a few elite firms or brands have a significant fan base and that fans are a minority of customers. In contrast, sports teams are predicated upon devoted fans. Social identity theory (Tajfel & Turner, 1979) explains the strong bond between fans and teams. The team is part of the fan's identity and is a powerful force (Chien, Kelly, & Weeks, 2016). Consider how fans spend larger sums of money for team jerseys and even get tattoos to show their support and connection to a team and its players. Sports communication recognizes there are gradients of fans ranging from low to high identification and commitment to an athlete, team, or sport (e.g., Courtney & Wann, 2010). The focus in this section is on fans that identify strongly.

As strong supporters, fans can be assets during a crisis. Research has shown that people with strong connections to an organization react less negatively to a crisis. Fans are willing to disregard or ignore the negative signals generated by a crisis. Cognitive dissonance is a possible explanatory mechanism. The principle of cognitive consistency posits that people seek to maintain consistency in their beliefs and attitudes. Discomfort occurs when something arises that creates contradictions in beliefs or attitudes—cognitive dissonance is created. People then often wish to eliminate the cognitive dissonance and their actions might be dysfunctional. One of three courses of action for resolving cognitive dissonance is important for this discussion. People may choose to reduce the importance of the cognition creating the dissonance. For a fan, a crisis can create cognitive dissonance because there is negative information about something they like. By reducing the importance of the crisis, fans can reduce the cognitive dissonance created by the crisis.

The data do support that people who identify with an organization place less importance on the crisis information (Fink et al., 2009). Furthermore, fans can defend the team during reputational crises (e.g., Brown & Billings, 2013). Consider how some fans will defend controversial team names and mascots or how they justify their team's signing of a controversial player. Fans of the Cleveland Indians typically do not want the name to change nor clamor for the complete elimination of Chief Wahoo. Many Dallas Cowboy fans defended the signing of defense standout Greg Hardy even though he was linked and suspended for domestic abuse. Fans can discount reputational crises that other stakeholders perceive as salient and negative.

Zavyalova, Pfarrer, Reger, and Hubbard (2016) examined the effects of stakeholder identification on crisis reactions using NCAA violations. NCAA violations are a common form of reputational crises for universities and colleges. Identification was defined as a cognitive and emotional connections between the stakeholder and the organization. This definition is consistent with the early discussion of fans and social identity theory. Their data found that, for schools with positive reputations, high identification stakeholders increased their support after a crisis. Support was measured in terms of amount of money donated to the university. However, they argued that a threshold does exist. When there are multiple crises, even high identification stakeholders will eventually accept the negative information and decrease donations (Zavyalova et al., 2016). Another avenue for addressing cognitive dissonance is to change attitudes. Multiple crises may be enough to cause fans to rethink their support for a team. Unfortunately, there is not exact data on what the crisis threshold is—how many crises it might take to cause a fan to disengage from a team. Fink et al. (2009) found similar results in an experiment using college sports fans. High identification fans were more supportive during a crisis than low identification fans, to a point. However, once a crisis became very severe, the difference evaporated.

Revenue: Sponsorship

Sponsorship deals are extremely lucrative for individual athletes, teams, and associations. Individual athletes can secure more income annually from sponsorship deals than from salaries or winnings. Teams and associations generate millions of dollars in revenues by placing the names of sponsors on items such as jerseys, official cars or airlines, and placement in stadiums and arenas. Sponsors spend the money because the people who like the sports entity may then like the product or service. In other words, fans buy the products or services associated with their favorite athlete, team, or even association (Yoon & Shin, 2017). Sponsorship deals generate considerable revenues. Consider how LeBron James signed a $90 million deal with Nike while still in high school and then a lifetime contract with Nike in 2015 that could be worth as much as $1 billion (Badenhausen, 2016). Moreover, individual athletes contribute to ticket sales and television contracts. The presence or absence of an athlete can negatively affect associations and teams. Consider how the Professional Golf Association suffered financially when Tiger Woods did not play because of his off-field ARC in 2009. Teams can suffer revenue loss if a star player misses time because on an ARC. Sports are about winning because that attracts both fans and revenue. ARCs will be evaluated in part by the projected effect the situation has on the potential to generate revenues.

The revenue concerns vary from individual athlete to systems. For individual athletes, an ARC can be career-ending or, minimally, a disruption of revenue. An event can lead to a ban from competition and loss of sponsors. An event that simply interrupts a career is less threatening and may not even result in the loss of all sponsors. Tiger Woods and Maria Sharapova lost some sponsors during their ARCs but other sponsors stayed with them. Contrast that to Adrian Peterson, who immediately lost contracts with Nike, Castro Oil, and Mylan when charges of child abuse surfaced (Roberts & Snyder, 2014). It was very easy for these sponsors to find other professional football players to endorse their products. Woods and Sharapova, however, were both unique, powerful endorsers for their sports. The systems have to consider the value the athlete adds to revenues. If a tainted athlete is performing well and attracting fans, there is a greater incentive to minimize the ARC.

The structure of leagues and associations can serve to insulate the leagues and associations due to the lack of competition. Many leagues and associations are monopolies. In the United States, the National Football League is legally recognized as a monopoly. If there are no alternatives, it becomes difficult for fans to effectively hold a league or association accountable and to punish them. When FIFA was plagued by multiple corruption scandals, there was no mechanism for fans to hold FIFA accountable. FIFA knew fans would still watch, attend, and buy merchandise for its World Cups. Only when sponsors threatened to remove financial support did FIFA take precautions to correct its problems (Fortunato, 2017; Pielke, 2013). The monopolistic structure of leagues and associations can limit the negative effects of reputational crises by protecting financial assets. Teams have a greater vulnerability/accountability to fans than do the associations. Consider how a fan protest over proposed ticket price increases by Liverpool Football Club fans prompted the team to rethink the price hike (Hunter, 2016).

Media Interest in Athletes and Teams

The traditional and social media have a much greater interest in athletes and teams than most corporate personnel and firms. As Billings et al. (2015) noted, "sport's ability to generate media interest is almost unparalleled" (p. 5). The media interest creates an increased reputational threat. Scandals, when they are crises, are driven by media coverage (Entman, 2012). The media will be much more interested in the misconduct of a player than the misconduct of corporate leadership. Because media attention is a key driver in reputational crises, the media gravitation toward athletes, especially star athletes, creates special crisis concern for sports. The media interest creates pressure for both athletes and the systems to respond.

Implications for SCCT and ARCs

For an ARC, there is some event rendering denial a risky crisis communication choice. For athletes, an ARC that is intentional, performance related, or non-performance with a strong outrage factor warrants an apology because of the significance of the ARC. Adjusting information will be included if the ARC is simply an interruption of the career. If the ARC is career-ending, that is when athletes will use denial in an attempt to save a career. When denial fails, the athlete can apologize and exit the sport. Lance Armstrong and Marion Jones are examples of this pattern, as systems can facilitate the athletes' exit with bans from the sport and loss of sponsorships.

Unintentional and minor non-performance ARCs create minimal crises. Athletes can use minimization by reinforcing that the actions were not that bad and/or the behavior was accidental. Adjusting information can be used to emphasize the behavior will not be repeated. A similar pattern can be used when the ARC is performance related but unintentional. However, athletes can face great skepticism that their actions were unintentional. Fan support, favorable media coverage, and system reactions should be critical to denial of intention. If the fans and media support the unintentional claim, the athlete should stand a better chance of stakeholders accepting the response. System reactions can include sponsor support and association support. Sponsors can support the athlete's unintentional claim by retaining the athlete while associations can offer support by reducing the punishment for the athlete. Maria Sharapova's ARC reflected support for her claim of unintentionally violating the banned substance policy in tennis. There were many sympathetic fans and media stories while some sponsors kept her and her suspension was reduced (Mavromati, 2016).

Systems will generally react by distancing themselves from an athlete when there is a specific rule violation, because rule breakers must be punished. The rules also dictate if the suspension is temporary or permanent. There is room for leniency when the ARC is in a gray area or the athlete can make a case for unintentional actions, and it increases when the athlete has the potential to generate revenue. Both sponsors and associations want to retain athletes who still can generate revenue. Again, Maria Sharapova's ARC illustrates this inclusion of the revenue contextual factor. Furthermore, the athlete can reinforce that leniency was the right choice by performing at a high standard upon their return (Koerber & Zabara, 2017). There is an increased danger when the system and fans are non-supportive because of the negative voices those groups add to the rhetorical arena formed by the crisis.

Conclusion

ARCs are a specific type of sports crisis that fits well with SCCT. However, the unique contextual factors must be considered when applying SCCT to ARCs. There are patterns in ARC responses that can be explained by SCCT and the contextual factors. The more serious crises will result in systems rejecting the athletes and the best option being apology. The apology will be coupled with adjusting information when the ARC is a career interruption rather than career ending. We will see some athletes use denial in an effort to protect their revenue streams. Such denials are doomed to failure when the systems reject the denial and there is evidence of the athlete's guilt. Another option is to argue the ARC is unintentional. There is potential for minimization to work if fans, media, sponsors, and associations provide support for the response.

Sport is a major global industry, but has some unique contextual factors that seem to affect the selection and effectiveness of crisis response strategies. This chapter has just begun to identify and explore how the contextual factors of sports affect the application of SCCT to ARCs. Future research can extend this research by testing the factors articulated in the chapter, by identifying additional contextual factors, and by adapting SCCT to other types of sports crises.

References

Badenhausen, K. (2016). *LeBron James' net worth: $275 million in 2016.* Retrieved from: www.forbes.com/sites/kurtbadenhausen/2016/12/13/lebron-james-net-worth-275-million-in-2016/#240e91b64be9

Barton, L. (2001). *Crisis in organizations II* (2nd ed.). Cincinnati, OH: College Divisions South-Western.

Billings, A. C., Butterworth, M. L., & Turman, P. D. (2015). *Communication and sport: Surveying the field* (2nd ed.). Thousand Oaks, CA: Sage Publications.

Booth, S. A. (2000). How can organisations prepare for reputational crises?. *Journal of Contingencies and Crisis Management, 8*(4), 197–207.

Brown, N. A., & Billings, A. C. (2013). Sports fans as crisis communicators on social media websites. *Public Relations Review, 39*(1), 74–81.

Chien, P. M., Kelly, S. J., & Weeks, C. S. (2016). Sport scandal and sponsorship decisions: Team identification matters. *Journal of Sport Management, 30*(5), 490–505.

Coombs, T., & Holladay, S. (2015). CSR as crisis risk: Expanding how we conceptualize the relationship. *Corporate Communications: An International Journal, 20*(2), 144–162.

Coombs, W. T. (1995). Choosing the right words: The development of guidelines for the selection of the "appropriate" crisis response strategies. *Management Communication Quarterly, 8,* 447–476.

Coombs, W. T. (2007). Protecting organization reputations during a crisis: The development and application of Situational Crisis Communication Theory. *Corporate Reputation Review, 10*(3), 163–177.

Coombs, W. T. (2014). *Applied crisis communication and crisis management.* Thousand Oaks, CA: Sage Publications.

Coombs, W. T. (2015). *Ongoing crisis communication: Planning, managing, and responding* (4th ed.). Thousand Oaks, CA: Sage Publications.

Coombs, W. T., & Holladay, S. J. (2012). The paracrisis: The challenges created by publicly managing crisis prevention. *Public Relations Review, 38*(3), 408–415.

Coombs, W. T., Holladay, S. J., & Claeys, A. S. (2016). Debunking the myth of denial's effectiveness in crisis communication: context matters. *Journal of Communication Management, 20*(4), 381–395.

Courtney, J. J., & Wann, D. L. (2010). The relationship between sport fan dysfunction and bullying behaviors. *North American Journal of Psychology, 12*(1), 191–198.

Entman, R. M. (2012). *Scandal and silence: Media responses to presidential misconduct.* Malden, MA: Polity Pres.

Fink, S. (1986). *Crisis management: Planning for the inevitable.* New York: AMACOM.

Fink, J. S., Parker, H. M., Brett, M., & Higgins, J. (2009). Off-field behavior of athletes and team identification: Using social identity theory and balance theory to explain fan reactions. *Journal of Sport Management, 23*(2), 142–155.

Fortunato, J. A. (2017). The FIFA crisis: Examining sponsor response options. *Journal of Contingencies and Crisis Management, 25,* 68–78.

Frandsen, F., & Johansen, W. (2010). Crisis communication, complexity, and the cartoon affair: A case study. In W. T. Coombs & S. J. Holladay (Eds.), *Handbook of crisis communication* (pp. 425–448). Malden, MA: Blackwell Publishing.

Frandsen, F. & Johansen, W. (2017). *Organizational crisis communication: A multivocal approach.* London: Sage Publications.

Hunter, A. (2016, February 10). *Liverpool owner backs down on ticket prices and apologises to fans.* Retrieved from www.theguardian.com/football/2016/feb/10/liverpool-back-down-ticket-prices-77

Koerber, D., & Zabara, N. (2017). Preventing damage: The psychology of crisis communication buffers in organized sports. *Public Relations Review, 43*(1), 193–200.

Mavromati, Despina (2016, October 11), *Application of the 2015 WADA Code through the Example of a recent CAS Award (Sharapova v. ITF)*. Available at https://papers.ssrn.com/abstract=2850999

Pielke, R. (2013). How can FIFA be held accountable? *Sport Management Review, 16*(3), 255–267.

Richards, O., Jr., Wilson, C., Boyle, K., & Mower, J. (2017). A knockout to the NFL's reputation?: A case study of the NFL's crisis communications strategies in response to the Ray Rice scandal. *Public Relations Review, 43*(3), 615–623.

Roberts, D., & Snyder, B. (2014). *Ray Rice and 11 other athletes who lost their endorsements.* Retrieved from http://fortune.com/2014/09/20/ray-rice-adrian-peterson-tiger-woods-athletes-dropped-endorsements/

Roehm, M. L., & Tybout, A. M. (2006). When will a brand scandal spill over, and how should competitors respond? *Journal of Marketing Research, 43*(3), 366–373.

Salerno, J. M., & Peter-Hagene, L. C. (2013). The interactive effect of anger and disgust on moral outrage and judgments. *Psychological Science, 24*(10), 2069–2078.

Sato, S., Ko, Y. J., Park, C., & Tao, W. (2015). Athlete reputational crisis and consumer evaluation. *European Sport Management Quarterly, 15*(4), 434–453.

Sohn, Y. J., & Lariscy, R. W. (2014). Understanding reputational crisis: Definition, properties, and consequences. *Journal of Public Relations Research, 26*(1), 23–43.

Tajfel, H., & Turner, J. C. (1979). An integrative theory of intergroup conflict. In W. G. Austin & S. Worchel (Eds.), *The social psychology of intergroup relations* (pp. 33–47). Monterey, CA: Brooks/Cole.

Whitney, E. (2013). *Listeria outbreak still haunts Colorado's cantaloupe growers.* Retrieved from www.npr.org/sections/thesalt/2013/08/14/211784739/listeria-outbreak-still-haunts-colorados-cantaloupe-growers

Yoon, S.-W., & Shin, S. (2017). The role of negative publicity in consumer evaluations of sports stars and their sponsors. *Journal of Consumer Behaviour, 16*(4), 332–342.

Zavyalova, A., Pfarrer, M. D., Reger, R. K., & Hubbard, T. D. (2016). Reputation as a benefit and a burden? How stakeholders' organizational identification affects the role of reputation following a negative event. *Academy of Management Journal, 59*(1), 253–276.

Zavyalova, A., Pfarrer, M. D., Reger, R. K., & Shapiro, D. L. (2012). Managing the message: The effects of firm actions and industry spillovers on media coverage following wrongdoing. *Academy of Management Journal, 55*(5), 1079–1101.

2

IMAGE REPAIR THEORY AND SPORT

William L. Benoit

Sport is an extremely important part of society; competitive sports can be traced back to at least 776 BC, when the first Olympic Games were held in Olympia, Greece. People engage in sport casually, in leagues, in school, in colleges, and in professional leagues. Sport appears in a myriad of guises, including track, swimming, diving, miniature golf, archery, tennis, rugby, billiards, boxing, badminton, bowling, cycling, sailing, gymnastics, rowing, racing (including automobile, motorcycle, ATV, boats, horse, dog), pickleball, skateboarding, jujutsu, wrestling, handball, figure skating, squash, skiing (snow, water), roller derby, lacrosse, water polo, and bodybuilding. In the US in 2016, over 210 million people participated in sport (Physical Activity Report, 2016). From an international perspective, over 1 billion people watched the 2016 Rio Olympic Games. In the US, 33.6 million people watched the women's gymnastics finals (Berg, 2016). In addition, Dawson (2016) reported the number of fans for the most popular sports around the world (see Table 2.1).

TABLE 2.1 Number of Fans for Top Ten Sports Worldwide (Dawson, 2016)

Sport	Number of Fans
Soccer	3.5 billion
Cricket	2.5 billion
Field Hockey	2 billion
Tennis	1 billion
Volleyball	900 million
Table Tennis	850 million
Baseball	500 million
Golf	450 million
Basketball	400 million
Football	390 million

Accordingly, it should come as no surprise that sport represents a huge part of the economy. Statista (2017) reports that, in 2013, the global sports market was $76 billion. Market value of the global sports industry was $1.5 trillion in 2015.

Sport at any level can be extremely competitive. Multitudes look up to one athlete or another, considering them to be role models. This adulation makes favored athletes into heroes who can be, and are, attacked for a variety of reasons, including alleged cheating, poor performance while engaging in sport, unbecoming conduct while participating in sport, and private behavior. When heroes are attacked, whether fairly or unfairly, image repair becomes an important option. This chapter focuses on Image Repair Theory, explicating the theory and reviewing research on image repair in sport.

Image Repair Theory

Image repair theory (IRT) (Benoit, 1995, 2015) addresses the question of how to respond to accusations or suspicions of wrong-doing (see also Coombs, 2012; or Hearit, 2006). Burke (1970) is a key figure here, identifying two ways to address guilt: scapegoating (shifting blame) and mortification (confession). Ware and Linkugel (1973) proposed the rhetorical genre of *apologia*, with four strategies: denial, bolstering, differentiation, and transcendence. Benoit (1995, 2015), drawing on these works in rhetorical scholarship as well as on research on accounts in sociology (e.g., Scott & Lyman, 1968), articulated a more comprehensive list of options for repairing a damaged reputation. Three important assumptions undergird this theory, and each will be explained in turn.

Communication as Goal-Directed Activity

Communication generally can best be understood as an intentional act. Kenneth Burke declared that a rhetorical act "can be called an act in the full sense of the term only if it involves a purpose" (1968, p. 446). Of course, this observation requires several qualifications. First, it is possible that rhetors may have multiple goals that are not completely compatible. Second, an individual's goals can be vague, ill formed, or unclear. Third, human beings have limitations on their information processing ability. Accordingly, people do not accord the same amount of attention to all communicative encounters. Decisions about which goals to pursue can be made after thoughtful consideration of the situation, or they can be made on the spur of the moment. In situations that are important to us, we are more likely to plan our utterances carefully. Finally, even when a rhetor's goals are relatively clear, it can be difficult for others to discern rhetorical goals. Multiple goals and hidden agendas can complicate the situation. Furthermore, some artifacts (e.g., art, movies, TV shows) may have persuasive effects but do not possess a clearly identifiable persuasive purpose. Nevertheless, persuasion generally is best understood as an intentional activity. Communicators attempt to devise utterances that they believe will best achieve the goals that are most salient to them when they communicate (at reasonable cost).

Maintaining a Favorable Reputation as Key Goal of Communication

IRT posits that maintaining a favorable impression—particularly with key audiences—is an important goal. Image repair discourse is vital because human beings constantly engage in behavior that renders them susceptible to criticism for several reasons. First, we have limited resources—there is only so much time, money, office space, and so forth. When the allocation of scarce resources fails to satisfy an individual's desires—as it inevitably does—dissatisfaction occurs, prompting complaints. Second, events beyond our control (e.g., unanticipated traffic jams) can prevent us from meeting our obligations. Third, people are human beings and make mistakes, some honestly, and others guided by self-interest. Alcohol, drugs, or even sleep deprivation can impair our performance. Finally, people often seek different goals: Do we want the cheapest goods or the ones with the least environmental impact? These four factors—limited resources, external events, human error, and conflicting goals—ensure that actual or perceived wrong-doing is a recurring feature of human behavior.

Persuasive Messages Have the Potential to Repair or Protect an Image

This assumption, which has been confirmed in research (see, e.g., Benoit, 1995, 2015; Blaney, 2016), explains why communication is important to image repair. Of course, persuasive defenses do not invariably repair one's reputation. It is possible that an image repair effort could backfire, making things worse. Think of United Airlines CEO Munoz's flimsy defense after a customer was dragged off a United airplane:

> After video of the man being violently pulled out of his seat went viral Monday, United responded with a brief statement:
> "Flight 3411 from Chicago to Louisville was overbooked. After our team looked for volunteers, one customer refused to leave the aircraft voluntarily and law enforcement was asked to come to the gate. We apologize for the overbook situation."
> Later, United chief executive Oscar Munoz followed up with some remarks of his own:

"This is an upsetting event to all of us here at United," Munoz's statement read in part. "I apologize for having to re-accommodate these customers."

The combination of airline jargon and public relations spin didn't sit well with many people—especially when contrasted with the images of three officers yanking the man out of his seat and pulling his limp body by the wrists down the center aisle. Other videos showed the man pacing around the plane's cabin with blood dripping from his mouth. The Internet mocked United's responses mercilessly.

Hawkins, 2017

Nevertheless, when used intelligently, image repair discourse has the potential to help a damaged reputation.

Image Repair Discourse

These image repair strategies function to improve a damaged reputation; they can be understood by analyzing the nature of attacks, reproaches, or complaints (see Ryan, 1982). Fundamentally, an attack on a person's (or an organization's, or a group's) image, face, or reputation comprises two components (Pomerantz, 1978):

1. An act occurred which is considered undesirable.
2. The accused is responsible for that action.

The accused's image is at risk only if both of these conditions are believed to be true by a relevant audience.

First, for one's reputation to be threatened, a reprehensible act must have occurred. If nothing bad happened—or if the audience does not consider what happened to be offensive—then the rhetor's face is not threatened. Notice the importance of perceptions here at two levels: The *rhetor* must believe (perceive) that the *audience* thinks (perceives) an offensive act has occurred. The perceptions of the persuader and the audience are important for different reasons. The rhetor's perceptions matter because those perceptions motivate the persuader to engage in image repair and they can help shape image repair messages. The perceptions of the audience are important because those perceptions influence whether the audience is persuaded by the image repair message. Note that audiences are comprised of individuals, and members of the audience can have different perceptions of the rhetor and the offensive act, which complicate persuasion.

The concept of an offensive act should be construed broadly, to include words as well as deeds. "Offensive action" can also encompass failure to perform expected actions as well as performance of offensive actions (in other words, acts of omission as well as commission). One can also be criticized for performing an action poorly.

It seems reasonable that the more serious the offense—the more vile the action, the more people harmed by it, the longer or more widespread the negative effects, and so forth—the greater the damage to the accused's reputation (see Benoit, 2017; Benoit & Dorries, 1996; Benoit & Glantz, 2017; Benoit & Harthcock, 1999). In other words, offensiveness can be thought of as existing on a continuum: Actions vary in the degree of offensiveness attributed to them.

The second element of an accusation is that the audience must believe that the accused is responsible for the reprehensible act. No matter what happened or how terrible it was, it is not reasonable to form an unfavorable impression of a person who is not responsible for that act. Perceptions are vital here again: The idea here is not whether *in fact* the accused caused the damage, but whether the relevant audience *believes* (perceives) the accused should be blamed for the reprehensible act. Of course, whether the accused is actually innocent can be an important component of the defense; however, the point here is that perceived guilt is essential for an accusation to occur.

Responsibility for an act can appear in a variety of guises. The accused may have performed an action, permitted others to perform an act, encouraged others to act, or facilitated an action. Just as the offensiveness of the act exists on a continuum, blame may not be a simple question of truth or falsity. If several persons committed the offensive act together, we might not necessarily hold them all fully responsible; we could apportion the blame among them. Some (for example, leaders, instigators, ones who played a particularly important role in commission of the act) might be thought to be more responsible for the reprehensible act than others. Furthermore, we tend to hold people more accountable for the effects they intended—and less responsible for unintended or unexpected effects. It seems reasonable to assume that a person's reputation will suffer to the extent to which they are personally or individually held responsible for the undesirable act (including whether they are believed to have intended the act).

Typology of Image Repair Strategies

Image repair strategies can be organized into five broad categories (three with variants or subcategories): denial, evading responsibility, reducing offensiveness, corrective action, and mortification. Remember that the two elements of an attack (which provokes a defense) are blame and offensiveness.

Denial

The accused may deny performing the wrongful act (Ware & Linkugel, 1973). Whether the accused denies that the offensive act happened or denies that the act was really harmful or denies that he/she committed that act, these options could relieve the rhetor of blame. When denial is used, others might wonder, "Well if you didn't do it, who did?" Burke (1970) discusses victimage or shifting

TABLE 2.2 Sports Image Repair Strategies

Strategy	Key Characteristic	Example
Denial		
Simple denial	Did not perform act	Lance Armstrong denies doping
Shift the blame	Another performed act	Athlete says trainer gave drugs
Evasion of Responsibility		
Provocation	Responded to act of another	You fouled me, so I fouled you back
Defeasibility	Lack of information or ability	We didn't know the stadium roof leaked
Accident	Mishap	Fall during skating was an accident
Good intentions	Meant well	We wanted to help fans with new menu
Reducing Offensiveness of Event		
Bolstering	Stress good traits	Armstrong helped charitable donations
Minimization	Act not serious	Calling a person names is not as bad as a physical injury
Differentiation	Act less offensive than . . .	Point shaving is not as bad as throwing a game
Transcendence	More important values	It is OK to cheat if we help a child's confidence
Attack accuser	Reduce accuser's credibility	You can't believe my accuser; he/she just wants to keep me from participating
Compensation	Reimburse victim	If you don't report athlete's misdeeds, we will give you season tickets
Corrective Action	Plan to solve/prevent recurrence of problem	Athlete promises never to take performance-enhancing drugs again
Mortification	Apologize; express remorse	Armstrong sorry he lied about doping

the blame. This is a variant of denial—the accused cannot have committed the repugnant act if someone else actually did it.

Evasion of Responsibility

Those who cannot deny performing the offensive act might be able to evade their responsibility for it. Four versions of this strategy can be identified: provocation, defeasibility, accident, and good intentions.

Provocation argues that the accused performed the offensive act because he/she was harmed by someone else, provoking the offensive act in question (Scott & Lyman, 1968). For instance, a person might say, "Yes, I shoved you, but only because you shoved me first."

A second strategy for evading responsibility is defeasibility (Scott & Lyman, 1968), claiming a lack of information about or control over important factors in the situation. The persuader suggests that lack of information or ability means that he or she should not be held fully responsible for the act. For instance, when someone is late to a meeting, we may not hold them completely responsible if the employee had not been informed of the meeting's time change.

Third, the accused can proffer an excuse based on accident (Scott & Lyman, 1968). We usually hold others responsible only for factors they can reasonably be expected to control. Inadvertently missing (forgetting) a meeting is an example of an offensive act that occurred by accident.

A fourth possibility is for the rhetor to argue that an offensive act can be justified on the basis of the accused's good intentions (Ware & Linkugel, 1973). The audience is asked not to hold the accused fully responsible because the act was performed with good intentions. People who do bad while trying to do good are usually not blamed as much as those who intend to do bad.

Reducing Offensiveness of Event

A person or organization accused of committing an offensive act can try to reduce the offensiveness perceived by the audience. This strategy has six variants: bolstering, minimization, differentiation, transcendence, attacking one's accuser, and compensation.

Bolstering (Ware & Linkugel, 1973) may be used to mitigate the negative effects of the offensive act on the accused by strengthening the audience's positive affect for the rhetor. Here the accused might relate positive attributes they possess or positive actions they have performed in the past.

Second, one might be able to minimize the number of negative feelings evoked by the offensive act. If the source can convince the audience that the negative act is not as bad as it initially appeared, the amount of ill feeling associated with that act should be reduced (see Scott & Lyman, 1968).

A third way to reduce the offensiveness of an action is differentiation (Ware & Linkugel, 1973). Here the persuader tries to distinguish the act performed from other similar but less desirable actions. In comparison with other actions, the act may appear less offensive to the audience. One could say, "I'm not slow, I'm careful." This may reduce the audience's negative feelings toward the act and the accused.

Next, the accused can employ transcendence (Ware & Linkugel, 1973). This strategy works by placing the act in a different context. Ware and Linkugel specifically discuss placing the action in a broader context, but it can also be useful to simply suggest a different frame of reference. For example, Robin Hood might suggest that his actions (robbery) were meant to help the poor and downtrodden. Similarly, a person accused of wrong-doing might direct our attention to other, allegedly higher values, to justify the behavior in question (Scott & Lyman, 1968). Someone caught shoplifting food could claim that he or she was trying to help keep a child from starving.

One accused of wrong-doing can attack their accusers (Scott & Lyman, 1968). If the credibility of the source of accusations can be reduced, the damage to one's image from those accusations may be diminished. If the accuser is also the victim of the offensive act (rather than a third party), the apologist may create the impression that the victim deserved what happened, lessening the perceived unpleasantness of the action in question (Semin & Manstead, 1983). Finally, a strong attack could deflect attention away from the accused.

Compensation is the remaining strategy for reducing offensiveness (Schonbach, 1980). Here the accused offers to remunerate the victim to offset the negative feeling arising from the wrongful act. This redress may take the form of valued goods or services as well as monetary reimbursement. For example, I was on a Southwest Airlines flight that had a delayed departure; Southwest sent me coupon for future travel to help repair its image.

These six strategies of for offensiveness do not deny that the accused committed the objectionable act or attempt to diminish the accused's responsibility for that act. Instead, these strategies attempt to reduce the unfavorable feelings toward the accused by increasing the audience's esteem for the accused or by decreasing their negative feelings about the act.

Corrective Action

Here the accused promises to correct the problem. This approach can take the form of restoring the situation to the state of affairs before the objectionable action occurred, and/or a promise to make changes that will prevent recurrence of the undesirable act. The difference between this strategy and compensation is that corrective action addresses the actual source of injury (offering to rectify past damage and/or prevent its recurrence), whereas compensation consists of a gift designed to counterbalance, rather than correct, the injury.

Mortification

Mortification is Burke's (1970) term for apology. The accused may admit committing the wrongful act and ask for forgiveness, engaging in mortification. If the audience believes the apology is sincere, they might pardon the wrongful act. It may be advisable to couple this strategy with plans to correct (or prevent recurrence of) the problem, but these strategies can occur independently.

Mortification is a particularly complex image repair strategy. No universally agreed definition of "apology" stipulates the components of an apology. It can include an explicit acceptance of blame, expression of regret or remorse, or a request for forgiveness. Also, the phrase "I'm sorry" can be ambiguous. It can reflect an admission of guilt, as in "I'm sorry I hurt you," or it can be an expression of sympathy, as in "I'm sorry you have been hurt," without admitting guilt. However, a person who admits blame risks further damage to his or her reputation from this admission. This makes apology a dispreferred response in many cases.

Some people accused of wrong-doing can exploit ambiguity in language. They may hope that saying "I'm sorry" will get them off the hook without actually admitting guilt. Furthermore, people who do admit guilt can be vague regarding the offensive misdeed they are admitting. This vagueness could occur because it is embarrassing to rehash details of the offensive act and/or because persuaders try to avoid concrete admissions. It is also possible to offer a pseudo-apology: "I'm sorry if you were offended." This type of statement is not a real "apology," because the accused admits no wrong-doing and may suggest that the problem arises from the victim, who "misunderstood" an innocent action.

Image Repair in Sport

Research has applied image repair theory to a variety of sports-related situations. Benoit (2015) reviews the literature on sports image repair. While the majority of research on image repair in sport takes the form of case studies and applies the method of rhetorical criticism, some research on image repair in sport has adopted a quantitative approach, studying both the production of defensive strategies (Brown & Billings, 2013) and the reception (effects) of defensive strategies (Brown, 2014; Brown, Dickhaus, & Long, 2012).

One of the earliest treatments of image repair in sport was written by Kruse (1981), who argued that team sport is "a phenomenon of cultural import" (p. 270). "Athletes who attempt to repair their images must understand the "ethic of team sport," which "holds that the team is greater than any of its individual members" (p. 273). Kruse explains that

> In defending their characters, sport figures use the same strategies other apologists employ. However, it is incumbent upon those who have violated the sport ethic to assure fans that equilibrium has been restored, and a stable relationship exists between the team and the fates. Consequently, sport apologists assert their positive attitudes toward the game. For this reason, too, they express sorrow for their behaviors.
>
> *p. 283*

Several scholars developed the study of image repair in sports. For example, the revelation that Billie Jean King had been involved in an affair with her secretary threatened the tennis star's reputation. Nelson (1984) examined defenses by King and other sports figures after revelations that King had engaged in an affair with her former secretary; King used bolstering and differentiation. The surrogates employed strategies not used by King. Her peers used bolstering, but made different arguments; transcendence argued that this affair was a private choice.

Tonya Harding, an American figure skater, was accused of being involved in the assault on rival Nancy Kerrigan prior to the 1994 Winter Olympics (Benoit & Hanczor, 1994). Harding participated in an interview on *Eye to Eye with Connie Chung* in which the main strategies were bolstering, denial, and attacking accusers.

Sports-related image repair research exploded in 2008. Terrell Owens had been critical of his football team, the Philadelphia Eagles. Owens offered a vague apology without admitting any fault. His manager attacked Owens' accusers (the team had not supported him). The spokesperson bolstered Owens' image, claimed good intentions, and offered mortification for Owens (again without conceding any specific faults). This image repair effort was poorly conceived (Brazeal, 2008).

Jerome (2008) investigated image repair from NASCAR driver Tony Stewart after he assaulted a newspaper photographer. She employed the Rhetoric of Atonement (Koesten & Rowland, 2004), which has five potential elements: acknowledging wrong-doing and asking for forgiveness, promise to never to repeat the offense, reparation or restitution, mortification, and public confession. Jerome describes three phases of Stewart's defense and identifies several strategies (all but the first element).

The Canterbury Bulldogs (Australasian men's rugby team) were accused of cheating (Bruce & Tini, 2008). The Bulldogs began with denial, moving to scapegoating when their CEO resigned. Shifting the blame was employed again as the Bulldogs' entire Board resigned. The Rugby League entered the fray, using provocation and mortification, shifting to scapegoating the Bulldogs team first and then the Leagues Club spokesperson, who resigned. Bruce and Tini argue for a new strategy, diversion, as the Bulldogs tried to shift attention away from the scandal.

Three members of Duke University's lacrosse team were alleged to have sexually assaulted an exotic dancer hired for a party; eventually the charges were dropped and the athletes declared innocent (Fortunato, 2008). Based on Fortunato's (2008) rhetorical analysis of the public relations messages on this topic, the university employed mortification (accepting responsibility for the incident), bolstering (stressing positive traits of the university), and corrective action (working to prevent recurrence of the incident). Len-Ríos (2010) content-analyzed statements from Duke, as well as newspaper stories on the scandal. When discussing the athletes, the university used denial (of the rape allegation) and mortification (for a lapse in judgment in holding the party). When defending the university, Duke used bolstering, attacking accusers, corrective action, and separation (suggesting that the coach was in part to blame and that he would be replaced). The defense was more effective repairing the athletes' images with the local community (compared with other audiences).

Floyd Landis, world-renowned cyclist, was accused of using illegal performance-enhancing substances to win the Tour de France in 2006. Glantz (2009) explained that his use of denial and differentiation was inconsistent, his use of attacking the accuser was unpersuasive, and the supporters who offered third-party defenses lacked credibility. Thus, his image repair effort was ineffectual.

Multiple organizations engaged in image repair at the Indianapolis Motor Speedway (Pfahl & Bates, 2008). After two crashes during practice, Michelin asked the international racing organization, the Fédération Internationale de l'Automobile (FIA), to change the rules for the race. FIA employed transcendence (it is important to uphold the rules of the sport and apply them consistently) and attacking the accuser (blaming Michelin for problems and suggesting Michelin reimburse fans). Michelin used transcendence in a different way, arguing safety was the most important consideration. It shifted blame to FIA for not adopting any of Michelin's alternative solutions. The tire company also used corrective action, vowing to investigate and fix the problem. The Michelin-supported racing team shifted blame to Michelin and argued for the importance of safety (transcendence). Finally, the Indianapolis Motor Speedway also blamed Michelin and used defeasibility (the problems were beyond the Speedway's control).

Dick Cheney injured Harry Whittington while hunting in 2006. The Vice President was criticized for the accident as well as for maintaining a public silence about the incident for four days. Theye (2008) argued that his narrative defense for shooting his hunting partner was generally effective, but his attempt to respond to charges of his handling of the situation (remaining silent for days) was less successful.

Wen, Yu, and Benoit (2009) analyzed image repair for Taiwanese major league pitcher Chien-Ming Wang after lost games. They compared defenses made by Wang and by Taiwanese newspapers. They observed that the newspapers could utilize strategies such as blaming his teammates that Wang could not (or should not) employ.

Swimmer Michael Phelps had won more Olympic medals than anyone else in history. A photograph was published in a tabloid that showed him smoking marijuana from a pipe. Walsh and McAllister-Spooner (2011) found that this athlete effectively utilized mortification, bolstering, and corrective action to repair his image.

Husselbee and Stein (2012) used Stein's (2008) concept of *antapologia* (a critical response by the accused to an apology) to examine newspaper responses to Tiger Woods' 2010 apology for his infidelity. News coverage stressed Wood's character flaws, argued that he had not sufficiently accepted responsibility for his offense, and questioned his motive for apologizing.

Benoit (2013) investigated Tiger Woods' image repair after the revelations of his marital infidelity. He relied primarily on mortification and corrective action. He also using transcendence (right to privacy) and attacked his accusers for hounding his family. His choice of strategies was appropriate; some wondered why he waited so long to give his speech and questioned his sincerity. Blaney, Lippert, and Smith's (2013) book collects several other useful analyses of image repair in sports.

Benoit (2015) analyzed the New Orleans Saints' bounty program, which gave bonuses to Saints' players who knocked opposing players out of the game with intentional injuries. Head coach Sean Payton and general manager Mickey Loomis employed mortification, accepting full responsibility for this program. They were quick to deny that the Saints owner Tom Benson was involved in the bounty program. Payton and Loomis also made use of corrective action, promising that they would never allow this to occur again. Saints owner Tom Benson said his team had cooperated fully with the NFL's investigation.

This scandal also tarnished the National Football League's reputation. NFL Commissioner Roger Goodell also employed corrective action asserting that this sort of misconduct would not be tolerated. Goodell also suspended five players, former defensive coordinator for the Saints Gregg Williams, head coach Sean Payton, general manager Mickey Loomis, and assistant head coach Joe Vitt.

Lance Armstrong is a legendary cyclist (he won the Tour de France seven times after recovering from cancer). Some suspected he used performance-enhancing drugs; he denied this for years and sued accusers to silence the criticism. In 2012, the U.S. Anti-Doping Agency (USASA) issued a report condemning Armstrong for doping. He was interviewed on Oprah Winfrey's television show (Benoit, 2015). He enacted mortification in several ways (admitting his wrong-doing, acknowledging mistakes, apologizing for his actions, and expressing remorse). Then he made excuses, blaming the culture of cycling, justifying his use of testosterone (cancer left him with low levels of testosterone), differentiated his offenses as less offensive than the East German team, differentiated his comments that he never failed a test at the time of the test; some samples were reanalyzed later to show violations. His attempts to excuse and justify undermined his defense.

Conclusion

This chapter began by advancing arguments for the importance of sport and the image repair that arises in this context. Then it explicated the theory of image repair discourse. Key assumptions were outlined and a list of strategies for repairing a damaged reputation developed. An analysis of attacks as comprised of blame and offensiveness was advanced to explain how strategies function. The literature review showed that this perspective has proven useful in understanding image repair in sport; of course there are a variety of useful approaches to understanding defensive discourse in this realm.

References

Benoit, W. L. (1995). *Accounts, excuses, apologies: A theory of image restoration strategies.* Albany: State University of New York Press.

Benoit, W. L. (2013). Tiger Woods' image repair: Could he hit one out of the rough? In J. R. Blaney, L. R. Lippert, & J. S. Smith (Eds.), *Repairing the athlete's image: Studies in sports image restoration* (pp. 89–96). Lanham, MD: Lexington Books: Rowman & Littlefield.

Benoit, W. L. (2015). *Accounts, excuses, apologies: Image repair theory and research* (2nd ed.). Albany: State University of New York Press.

Benoit, W. L. (2017). Criticism of actions and character: Strategies for persuasive attack extended. *Relevant Rhetoric, 8 (Spring)*, 1–17. Retrieved from http://relevantrhetoric. com/CriticismofActionsandCharacter.pdf

Benoit, W. L., & Dorries, B. (1996). *Dateline NBC's* persuasive attack on Wal-Mart. *Communication Quarterly, 44*, 464–477.

Benoit, W. L., & Glantz, M. (2017). *Persuasive attack on Donald Trump in the 2016 Republican primaries.* Lanham, MD: Lexington Books.

Benoit, W. L., & Hanczor, R. (1994). The Tonya Harding controversy: An analysis of image repair strategies. *Communication Quarterly, 42*, 416–433.

Benoit, W. L., & Harthcock, A. (1999). Attacking the tobacco industry: A rhetorical analysis of advertisements by the Campaign for Tobacco-Free Kids. *Southern Communication Journal, 65*, 66–81.

Berg, M. (2016, August 10). The final five finally get Americans to watch the Olympics. *Forbes.* Retrieved November 7, 2017, from www.forbes.com/sites/maddieberg/2016/08/10/ the-final-five-finally-gets-americans-to-turn-on-tv/#56943ef42d23

Blaney, J. R. (Ed.). (2016). *Putting image repair to the test: Quantitative applications to image restoration strategies.* Lanham, MD: Lexington Books.

Blaney, J. R., Lippert, L. R., & Smith, J. S. (Eds.) (2013). *Repairing the athlete's image: Studies in sports image restoration.* Lanham, MD: Lexington Books/Rowman & Littlefield.

Brazeal, L. M. (2008). The image repair strategies of Terrell Owens. *Public Relations Review, 34*, 145–150.

Brown, K. A. (2014). Is apology the best policy? An experimental examination of the effectiveness of image repair strategies during criminal and noncriminal athlete transgressions. *Communication & Sport, 4*, 1–20.

Brown, K. A., Dickhaus, J., & Long, M. C. (2012). LeBron James and "The Decision: An empirical examination of image repair in sports." *Journal of Sports Media, 7*, 149–175.

Brown, N. A., & Billings, A. C. (2013). Sports fans as crisis communicators on social media websites. *Public Relations Review, 39*, 74–81.

Bruce, T., & Tini, T. (2008). Unique crisis response strategies in sports public relations: Rugby league and the case for diversion. *Public Relations Review, 34*, 108–115.

Burke, K. (1968). Dramatism. In D. L. Sills (Ed.), *International encyclopedia of the social sciences* (vol. 7, pp. 445–452). New York: Macmillan/Free Press.

Burke, K. (1970). *The rhetoric of religion.* Berkeley: University of California Press.

Coombs, W. T. (2012). *Ongoing crisis communication: Planning, managing, and responding* (3rd ed.). Los Angeles, CA: Sage.

Dawson, S. (2016, August 26). Top 10 most popular sports in the world. *Gazette Review.* Retrieved January 11, 2017, from http://gazettereview.com/2016/08/top-10-popular-sports-world/

Fortunato, J. A. (2008). Restoring a reputation: The Duke University lacrosse scandal. *Public Relations Review, 34*, 116–123.

Glantz. M. (2009). The Floyd Landis doping scandal: Implications for image repair discourse. *Public Relations Review, 30*, 157–163.

Hawkins, D. (2017, April 11). "Re-accommodate"? United ridiculed for corporate speak response to passenger dragging. *Washington Post*. Retrieved April 23, 2017, from www.washingtonpost.com/news/morning-mix/wp/2017/04/11/re-accommodate-united-gets-lampooned-for-its-awkward-response-to-passenger-dragging/?utm_term=.b5dc4530ea35

Hearit, K. M. (2006). *Crisis management by apology: Corporate response to allegations of wrong-doing*. Mahwah, NJ: Lawrence Erlbaum.

Husselbee, L. P., & Stein, K. A. (2012). Tiger Woods, apology, and newspapers' responses: A study of journalistic *antapologia*. *Journal of Sports Media*, 7, 59–87.

Jerome, A. M. (2008). Toward prescription: Testing the rhetoric of atonement's applicability in the athletic arena. *Public Relations Review*, *34*, 124–134.

Koesten, J., & Rowland, R. (2004) The rhetoric of atonement. *Communication Studies*, *55*(1), 68–87.

Kruse, N. W. (1981). Apologia in team sport. *Quarterly Journal of Speech*, *67*, 270–283.

Len-Ríos, M. E. (2010). Image repair strategies, local news portrayals and crisis state: A case study of Duke University's lacrosse team crisis. *International Journal of Strategic Communication*, *4*, 267–287.

Nelson, J. (1984). The defense of Billie Jean King. *Western Journal of Speech Communication*, *48*, 92–102.

Pfahl, M. E., & Bates, B. R. (2008). This is not a race, this is a farce: Formula One and the Indianapolis Motor Speedway tire crisis. *Public Relations Review*, *34*, 135–144.

Physical Activity Council. (2016). *2016 Participation Report: The Physical Activity Council's annual study tracking sports, fitness, and recreation participation in the US*. Retrieved from www.physicalactivitycouncil.com/pdfs/current.pdf

Pomerantz, A. (1978). Attributions of responsibility: Blamings. *Sociology*, *12*, 115–121.

Ryan, H. R. (1982). *Kategoria* and *apologia: On their rhetorical criticism as a speech set*. *Quarterly Journal of Speech*, *68*, 256–261.

Schonbach, P. (1980). A category system for account phases. *European Journal of Social Psychology*, *10*, 195–200.

Scott, M. H., & Lyman, S. M. (1968). Accounts. *American Sociological Review*, *33*, 46–62.

Semin, G. R., & Manstead, A. S. R. (1983). *The accountability of conduct: A social psychological analysis*. London: Academic Press.

Statista, (2017). *Global sports market—total revenue from 2005 to 2016 (in billion U.S. dollars)*. Retrieved January 14, 2017, from www.statista.com/statistics/370560/worldwide-sports-market-revenue/

Stein, K. A. (2008). Apologia, antapologia and the 1960 Soviet U-2 incident. *Communication Studies*, *59*, 19–34.

Theye, K. (2008). Shoot, I'm sorry: An examination of narrative functions and effectiveness within Dick Cheney's hunting accident *apologia*. *Southern Communication Journal*, *73*, 160–177.

Walsh, J., & McAllister-Spooner, S. M. (2011). Analysis of the image repair discourse in the Michael Phelps controversy. *Public Relations Review*, *37*, 157–162.

Ware, B. L., & Linkugel, W. A. (1973). They spoke in defense of themselves: On the generic criticism of apologia. *Quarterly Journal of Speech*, *59*, 273–283.

Wen, J., Yu, J., & Benoit, W. L. (2009). Our hero can't be wrong: A case study of collectivist image repair in Taiwan. *Chinese Journal of Communication*, *2*, 174–192.

PART II

Applications Using Situational Crisis Communication Theory (SCCT)

3

EXPERIMENTALLY EXAMINING CRISIS MANAGEMENT IN SPORTING ORGANIZATIONS

Natalie Brown-Devlin

Many sports media consumers may believe that the drama of sport is best summarized by Jim McKay's introduction to ABC's Wide World of Sports as he proclaimed that sports showcase "the thrill of victory . . . the agony of defeat." While it is true that sports media coverage is dominated by wins and losses, coverage has also been inundated with sports scandals. For instance, in November 2011, child sex abuse allegations were waged against Jerry Sandusky, a former coach associated with Penn State University. These allegations eventually led to the firing of head coach Joe Paterno. This scandal did not simply dominate sports-specific media coverage, but rather was the subject of 17 percent of *all* news coverage the week of November 7–13, 2011 (PEJ News Coverage Index, 2011). Additionally, the intense coverage of sports-related scandals is not simply relegated to traditional media; rather, these scandals are also heavily discussed online and are often featured on sports fans' social media websites. Former Stanford University swimmer Brock Turner was convicted of sexual assault in 2016 and faced up to 14 years in prison; however, he was given a short, six-month jail sentence and was released after serving only three months. The case incited much commentary online, and his quick release from jail prompted the hashtag #thingslongerthanBrockTurnersrapesentence to trend on Twitter (Haltiwanger, 2016).

Collegiate sports are not alone in facing sports scandals. Bradley (2016) noted "the surprising thing about each professional sports scandal isn't the scandal itself, but the fact that anyone is surprised" (p. 1). While Bradley's observation may initially appear cynical, the large number of scandals plaguing sport has also influenced how sport fans perceive the sport industry, itself. The *Guardian*, along with the strategic communications consultancy Brewery at Freuds, surveyed 2,000 people in Britain and discovered that one third reported their "trust in the sports industry has declined in the last 12 months" (Kelner, 2017). Similarly, Bialik (2014) noted that another poll conducted by Ipsos for Thomson Reuters reported that 21 percent of women and 23 percent of men viewed the NFL less favorably after their handling of domestic abuse allegations against Ray Rice (Richards, Wilson, Boyle, & Mower, 2017) and child abuse allegations against Adrian Peterson (O'Connor, 2014).

While sports scandals can negatively impact fans' perceptions, they can also threaten teams financially. In October 2017, a judge will determine if a lawsuit initially brought by 10 former National Hockey League (NHL) players will receive class action status. The players allege that the league downplayed concussion-related injuries, which have resulted in some players experiencing symptoms of chronic traumatic encephalopathy (CTE) (McIndoe, 2017). The lawsuit is similar to one that was brought against the National Football League (NFL) in which the League settled out of court with former players for $1 billion (McIndoe, 2017). If found at fault, such a large settlement could leave the NHL bankrupt (McIndoe, 2017).

Thus, when facing a scandal, sports organizations and athletes can experience negative media coverage, negative reactions and distrust from key stakeholders (fans), and negative financial implications that classify the event as a crisis facing their brand. Coombs (2007) defines a crisis as "the perception of an unpredictable event that threatens important expectancies of stakeholders and can seriously impact an organization's performance and generate negative outcomes" (pp. 2–3). Sports scholars have investigated such sports-related crises by exploring an athlete's response to crisis (Brown, Dickhaus, & Long, 2012), an organization's response to a crisis (Richards et al., 2017), a sponsor's response to a crisis (Walsh & McAllister-Spooner, 2011), and fan responses to a crisis (Brown et al., 2015).

While sports scholars have examined crises that befall athletes and organizations for decades (Benoit & Hanczor, 1994; Brazeal, 2008; Kahuni, Rowley, & Binsardi, 2009; Yoon & Shin, 2017), little scholarly attention has examined the effectiveness of their crisis response through the use of experiments. This area of research presents scholars with a long list of potential variables to explore that would allow for a better understanding of how athletes and sports organizations could effectively respond to mitigate the negative impact of a crisis. This chapter seeks to first provide an overview of Coombs's (2007) Situational Crisis Communication Theory (SCCT). Next, a review of previous literature that has examined sports-related crises (often through the theoretical lens of SCCT) is proffered to discuss how the variables addressed in previous works could be expanded in current scholarship. Last, some opportunities for theoretical advancement of SCCT to aid sports scholars as they experimentally examine sports-related crises are discussed. Overall, this chapter seeks to encourage continued, thorough exploration of the intersection of crisis communication and sports communication research. The unique nature of sport (individual athlete vs. organizational considerations, intense media scrutiny, etc.) provides an important context for crisis communication research that is ripe for scholarly examination. This research can expand the theoretical understanding of crisis management while simultaneously providing sports organizations and athletes with practical crisis management plans.

Crisis Communication Theory

How organizations should respond to a crisis situation has been explored thoroughly in scholarship (Benoit, 1995; Burke, 1973; Coombs, 2007; Rosenfield, 1968; Ware & Linkugel, 1973). Crisis communication is grounded in the idea that "human beings engage in recurrent patterns of communicative behavior designed to reduce, redress, or avoid damage to their reputation (face or image) from perceived wrongdoing" (Benoit, 1995, p. vii).

A prominent theory utilized by crisis communication scholars is Coombs's (2007) Situational Crisis Communication Theory (SCCT), which is primarily tested to determine which reputation repair strategies are most effective at improving an audience's perspective of a corporation. SCCT argues that crisis managers must select their reputation repair strategies according to the reputational threat that the crisis situation presents. As the reputational threat intensifies, a crisis manager must utilize more accommodating reputation repair strategies (Coombs, 2007). SCCT evolved from a call by Benson (1988) that urged scholars to address three key issues in order to advance crisis communication research: (1) the creation of a typology of crises that could negatively impact an organization, (2) a list of strategies for crisis response, and (3) a theoretical foundation that links the two lists.

In order to address the first issue, Coombs and Holladay (2002) created a typology of 10 crises that typically impact organizations. Along with listing the potential crises, they also determined the amount of crisis responsibly the public might attribute to an organization that is impacted by each type of crisis. This led to the creation of three clusters of varying level of attributed crisis responsibility—Victim Crises (natural disasters, rumors, workplace violence, product tampering/malevolence), which result in minimal crisis responsibility being attributed to the organization; Accident Crises (challenges, technical error accidents, technical error product harm), which result in a low level of crisis responsibility being attributed to the organization; and Preventable Crises (human-error accidents, human-error product harm, organizational misdeed), which result in a strong level of crisis responsibility being attributed to the organization.

After a crisis manager identifies the type of crisis their organization is facing, they must select a corresponding reputational repair strategy or combination of strategies to guide their crisis response. SCCT's list of reputation repair strategies includes 10 strategies that are organized into four postures: Denial Posture (attack the accuser, denial, scapegoat); Diminishment Posture (excuse, justification); Bolstering Posture (reminder, ingratiation, victimage); and Rebuilding Posture (compensation, apology). When determining which reputational repair strategy should be used during a crisis, Coombs (2007) recommends that organizations also consider the level of credibility they have with their stakeholders and their reputation prior to the offending action. When an organization either suffers from low credibility or has a history of committing similar offending actions, they will need to select accommodative strategies during crisis response.

Last, Heider's (1958) attribution theory provided the theoretical linkage between SCCT's crisis typology and its list of reputation repair strategies. Coombs (2007) argued that, when a crisis occurs, the sudden and negative nature of crises causes stakeholders to attribute blame and/or seek to punish who they deem responsible for committing the offending action. How stakeholders choose to attribute blame and responsibility for the crisis will have a large impact on how the public and the organization will interact during crisis response. Most often, when facing a crisis, stakeholders will place blame on either the organization or the crisis situation itself. When an organization is perceived by its stakeholders as being at fault, it is likely to result in reputational harm. In addition to harming the organization's reputation, Coombs and Holladay (2006) note that the negative impact of a crisis could also influence stakeholders to stop supporting the organization financially, which could result in decreased profits, and could encourage stakeholders to engage in negative word of mouth. For instance, following reports of Baylor University mishandling sexual assault complaints and the subsequent firing of head coach Art Briles, ticket prices for the 2016 football season dropped 62 percent on the secondary market (Solomon, 2016). A large amount of research has been dedicated to examining the linkage between the attribution of crisis responsibility and the resulting threat to organizational reputation (Claeys, Cauberghe, & Vyncke, 2010; Coombs, 2007; Coombs & Holladay, 1996, 2006; Sisco, 2012).

Evolution of Sports Crisis Response Research

The area of sport features several instances from which a crisis can develop, including in-game competitions, off-field situations, or broader reflections about issues of identity (Billings, Butterworth, & Turman, 2011). Some have previously cast aside sports image repair as a topic worthy of scholarly exploration (Kruse, 1981), suggesting that winning and team success was all that truly mattered to a sports organization's stakeholders rather than an athlete's character issues. While there is certainly evidence to support the idea that fans are primarily concerned with winning (Anderson, 2013; Arnold, 1992; McCloskey & Bailes, 2005), recent events have shown that crisis situations can still be quite detrimental for both athletes and sports organizations.

Such negative consequences that result from poorly managed crises inspired a new desire to protect sports organizations and athletes through proper image repair and crisis management (Wilson, Stavros, & Westberg, 2010). Issues such as the Penn State and Brock Turner scandals captured the headlines of primary news outlets and showcased the growing prominence of sports-related crises (Haltiwanger, 2016; PEJ News Coverage Index, 2011). Recent events and crises have shown that a negative image can impact sponsorship and bowl money, leading sports organizations and individuals to place a larger importance on defending their reputations with key stakeholders (Sanderson, 2008). Sports scholars have primarily analyzed crisis response in sport through the use of case studies, rhetorical analyses, and content analyses. These studies have established a strong foundational understanding of sports-related crises and identified numerous variables worthy of further inquiry utilizing experimental design.

Individual Athlete Crisis Research

Many sports studies examining crisis response in the context of sport analyzed the response strategies used by individual athletes. Perhaps sport provides a unique context to analyze crisis communication, because many crises do not necessarily impact the larger organization. For instance, during Michael Vick's dogfighting scandal, the public primarily blamed Vick for the problems before they blamed his team, the Atlanta Falcons. Benoit and Hanczor (1994) performed one of the initial image repair studies in the context of sport as they examined Tonya Harding's defense of her image on *Eye-to-Eye with Connie Chung* after the attack on her rival figure skater, Nancy Kerrigan. Prior to the 1994 U.S. Figure Skating Championships, Harding's ex-husband planned an attack on Kerrigan, resulting in Kerrigan's knee being injured and the elimination of Harding's competition. Benoit and Hanczor (1994) determined that Harding employed the bolstering, denial, and attacking the accuser strategies. Several important implications arose from this study. First, the authors noted that the selected image repair strategies must be consistent with the existing identity of the person engaging in it. Thus, it was ineffective when Harding attempted to transform her existing image from that of a "bad girl" to an apologetic, innocent victim during crisis response. Second, when an individual encounters a crisis, honesty and transparency are critical. Finally, the authors encouraged other crisis scholars to examine image repair in sports, citing an increase in media coverage being allocated to sports crises such as the O. J. Simpson double murder case and the New England Patriots harassing a female reporter in the 1990s.

Brazeal (2008) examined the image repair strategies Terrell Owens used when public sentiment about him suffered. A lack of public support is especially threatening to a professional athlete, as the "market value" of an athlete's image often hinges on their public reputation (Brazeal, 2008, p. 146). During contract negotiations with the Philadelphia Eagles, Owens was brash with the press and openly critical of his teammates, resulting in the Eagles deactivating him. This deactivation prompted Owens and his agent to engage in image repair. Brazeal (2008) analyzed the repair strategies used in Owens' press conference, which included both mortification and bolstering strategies. However, he also launched attacks against his accusers that reinforced his prior reputation of being self-centered and arrogant. Rather than accepting responsibility for his actions, Owens attempted cast himself as a victim by having his agent, Drew Rosenhaus, paint the Eagles organization as selfish and ungrateful for all Owens' sacrifices and accomplishments. Brazeal (2008) noted that image repair in sports must understand the nature of team sport, which "demands unity, commitment, and sacrifice" (p. 145). Owens' attempt at image repair failed to portray him as a "team player." Thus, the idea of examining the impact crises can potentially pose to both individual athletes and sports organizations was offered as a future area for research.

Brown et al. (2012) built upon Brazeal's (2008) study to experimentally test the effectiveness of image repair strategies. The study examined LeBron James' image when he announced on an hour-long ESPN special that he was leaving his hometown Cleveland Cavaliers to play for the Miami Heat. The program, known as "The Decision," also harmed James' image, because, similar to Owens, sports fans felt as though James' actions violated the "team culture" that sport possesses. Results from the study revealed that the mortification strategy improved James' image while both of the other strategies, shifting the blame and mortification, harmed James' image. This study provided an important evolution in sports crisis research, as it empirically tested the effectiveness of an athlete's use of image repair strategies.

Organizational Sports Crisis Research

While many sports-related crises are centered on individual athletes, others impact coaches, engulf the entire organization and potentially impact additional, external stakeholders. For example, Frandsen and Johansen (2007) analyzed the image repair strategy used by Anja Andersen, a Danish handball coach following an incident that occurred when Slagelse, Andersen's team, faced rival Aalborg DH in a match that was watched by hundreds of thousands of handball fans in Denmark. During the match, Andersen vehemently disagreed with calls made by two referees, and also received a "red card" for pulling the arm of a referee. Angered by the referees' actions, Andersen withdrew her team from the match. Slagelse stayed in the locker room before eventually returning and losing the match to Aalborg DH. While Andersen apologized the next day for her actions during the match, the Danish sports media questioned the sincerity of her apology. Thus, Frandsen and Johansen (2007) sought to evaluate the effectiveness of her apology to better determine what constitutes a "real" apology when a sports figure is attempting to recover from a crisis. While Andersen's apology was viewed as being truthful, the authors noted that she "could have expressed her apology in a more unambiguous and explicit way, just as she could have focused more on her stakeholders" (p. 102). The authors also stressed that future research should further examine how sports figures can effectively apologize in the era of globalization where communication technologies might bridge different nations with differing cultural norms, making it difficult to identify and appease the common sociocultural order that has been transgressed.

Kahuni et al. (2009) completed a case study to understand negative image transfer that can impact a company serving as a title sponsor of a sports team affected by a crisis. In 2006, the Vodafone Group entered into a sponsorship agreement with the McLaren-Mercedes Formula One team, forming the Vodafone McLaren-Mercedes team. One year later, the Vodafone McLaren-Mercedes team was found guilty of "spying" on a rival team, resulting in an organizational crisis. Results showed that, while Vodafone was tied to the scandal through the team's name, "the actions of key partners and effective 'bad' image crisis management minimized the extent and impact of the spill-over" (Kahuni et al., 2009, p. 60). Kahuni et al. (2009) called for future researchers to further investigate the relationship between organizations and sponsors by determining how team performance and team media coverage can impact sponsors.

Len-Ríos (2010) performed a content analysis of the strategies Duke University exercised after members of the men's lacrosse team were accused of raping a female dancer at an off-campus party, an accusation that the players were never found guilty of committing. Results showed that Duke used the simple denial and mortification strategies to defend the athletes. The university also used the bolstering, corrective action, separation, and attack the accuser strategies to defend its own reputation. While it was certainly useful to determine the preferred strategies that Duke University utilized, Len-Ríos's (2010) study also showed the value of content analysis research in examining crisis response from both an individual and organizational perspective. The results determined that the attack the accuser strategy resulted in the most positive media coverage. While content analysis research is typically limited by its inability to show the effects of a message, these results did lend support to the positive impact of that particular repair strategy and provide an important area for future experimental research. Len-Ríos (2010) also suggested an addition of a new category of response called "expression of disappointment," suggesting that the current list of response strategies included in SCCT might not fully encompass the issues encountered in sport and contributing new ideas for future SCCT research.

Williams and Olaniran (2002) used Coombs's (1995) response strategies to examine a crisis affecting both Texas Tech University and the city of Lubbock, Texas. In 1998, the Texas Tech Lady Raiders basketball team was scheduled to play Hampton University. Before the game, Lubbock police arrested Hampton University's head coach, assistant coach, and the head coach's husband, falsely accusing them of attempting a parking lot scam at the local Wal-Mart, resulting in allegations that racial profiling contributed to their arrest. Despite the fact that Texas Tech did not actually contribute to the crisis, the connection between the incident and the basketball team forced them to engage in crisis response. Texas Tech utilized Coombs's (1999) excuse strategy, claiming that the university had no control over the events that transpired. On the other hand, city officials provided conflicting crisis response strategies. In addition to utilizing Coombs's (1999) strategies, this study illustrated how sports crises can also be caused in a non-sports setting, obtaining national news coverage. This study also illustrates the unique connection that exists between a university, its sports teams, and the city in which it is located.

Brown et al. (2015) conducted a content analysis of fan reactions to the Penn State sex abuse scandal on Twitter. In 2011, authorities charged former Penn State coach Jerry Sandusky for sexually assault involving eight boys over 15 years. As previously discussed, the scandal both dominated media headlines and led to the firing of head coach Joe Paterno. Following Paterno's firing, Penn State fans were outraged and showcased a broad spectrum of reactions, ranging from riots to social media posts. Brown et al. (2015) analyzed Twitter posts of Penn State fans to determine how they utilized traditional reputation repair strategies as defined in SCCT. Results showed that fans utilized the ingratiation, reminder, and scapegoat strategies in an attempt to help mitigate the negative effects this crisis was having on their school's/team's reputation. While previous studies showed that fans will typically use traditional strategies to help their school/team (Brown & Billings, 2013), results from this study showed that fans rebelled against the Penn State administration and, instead, sided with Joe Paterno. Overall, this study showed that sports fans will also engage in traditional reputation repair strategies online, suggesting that future research should continue to explore both fan involvement and online crisis communication.

Richards et al. (2017) used SCCT as a theoretical framework to analyze the reputation repair strategies used by the Baltimore Ravens after running back Ray Rice was arrested for domestic violence. The authors found the Ravens utilized minimization, justification, and ingratiation strategies while they largely tried to support Rice and protect his status as a face of the franchise. This study highlighted the number of entities that could be affected by one single crisis event, as Rice, the NFL, the Ravens organization, and head coach John Harbaugh all had to engage in some form of crisis response. Thus, crisis managers must now address an even wider array of stakeholders during a crisis. Richards et al. (2017) also addressed the conflict of who is more to blame during a crisis: the sports organization or the individuals associated with it.

Experimental Research in SCCT

While previous sports–related research in SCCT has largely evaluated crisis response using methodological approaches such as case studies (Richards et al., 2017) and content analyses (Len Ríos, 2010), scholars (Brown, 2012; Hong & Len Ríos, 2015; Sato, Ko, Park, & Tao, 2015) have also employed experimental methodologies to investigate a number of variables (crisis type, crisis responsibility, organizational reputation, organizational crisis history, etc.).

Brown (2014) examined the effectiveness of sports fans utilizing traditional reputational repair strategies on behalf of their preferred team during a time of crisis. Using SCCT, the study investigated how an online environment has changed the role of a sports organization's stakeholders by giving them more power to comment during times of crisis by using social media websites. The study employed a 3 (crisis response strategy) × 2 (crisis type) × 3 (fan association) factorial design. Several dependent variables were included in the study to measure participants' attitude and behavioral intentions toward the organization such as organizational reputation, crisis responsibility, positive word of mouth, and potential fan-enacted crisis communication behavior.

Through the use of experimental design, Brown (2014) investigated how different types of crises (individual athlete vs. organizational) impacted stakeholders' evaluation of crisis responsibility. Results showed that stakeholders attribute a higher degree of crisis responsibility to organizations that are dealing with organizational mismanagement as compared to those dealing with a crisis involving individual athletes. However, the type of crisis response strategy did not impact any of the four dependent variables. These results support additional empirical testing of the use of SCCT's response strategies in a social media environment.

Experimentally examining crises facing sports organization allows researchers to study a unique group of stakeholders, fans. Brown (2014) found that the organizational reputation scores of an organization would suffer most among its fans, whereas those who were rivals of or neutral towards the organization would not be as affected. Last, a participant's willingness to engage in either positive word of mouth or potential fan-enacted crisis communication behaviors was in accordance to his/her fan association. Therefore, participants were most likely to engage in these behaviors on behalf of their preferred team and least likely to engage in these practices on behalf of their rival team.

Hong and Len Ríos (2015) used a 2 (race of spokesperson: black/white) × 2 (crisis type: sport vs. product recall) × 2 (performance history: prior incidents vs. no prior incidents) within-subjects experiment to investigate the impact of these variables on evaluations of source credibility and crisis severity. The authors found that black spokesmen were rated as being more credible during university sports-related crises. Additionally, they found that "in sports crises with no history, they are stereotyped more and the crises are seen as more severe" (p. 76). Not only did this study provide important revelations about crisis response, it also uncovered deeper findings about the role of race in crisis evaluations.

SCCT also provided the theoretical framework for Brown (2012), explored how different types of crises that featured an individual athlete (team-related/not team-related) impacted the amount of crisis responsibility attributed to a sport team. Brown (2012) found that stakeholders would attribute a higher degree of responsibility on a sports organization when an offending action involving an athlete occurred during team-related activities rather than activities that were not team-related. This finding suggests that stakeholders do not hold the team responsible for every offending action that involves one of the team's athletes.

Brown (2012) also tested Coombs's (2007) recommendation that organizations that suffer from low credibility or have a history of committing similar offending actions will face a higher degree of responsibility attributed to them for a transgression. Brown (2012) found that stakeholders will attribute more responsibility to teams with a history of athlete transgressions. Thus, sports organizations should still be wary of signing athletes that have a history of committing such offending actions.

Sato et al. (2015) utilized a 2 (performance relatedness: related vs. unrelated) × 2 (intentionality: intentional vs. unintentional) × 2 (involvement: high vs. low) between-subjects experiment to determine how crises affected fans' evaluations of an athlete's reputation. Sato et al. (2015) found that the intentionality and performance relatedness of the athlete's crisis negatively impacted fans' evaluations of the athlete. Highly involved fans were found to be especially critical of athletes involved in scandals that were both intentional (e.g., PED usage) and performance-related. In addition to exploring these new variables in a sports-related context, Sato et al. (2015) also called for future research to include additional variables such as consumer culture and fan identification.

Yoon and Shin (2017) did incorporate fan identification into their design as they examined how a sports-related crisis involving an athlete could also impact fans' evaluation of the athlete's sponsors. The authors utilized a 2 (negative information type: immoral or incompetent) × 2 (game-relevant information: game, non-game) × 2 (fan identification: low, high) factorial design and explored how these variables impacted participants' evaluations of the athlete involved in the crisis and the athlete's sponsor. Yoon and Shin (2017) found that a negative event involving an athlete (especially events involving an athlete's incompetence) can influence a consumer's opinion of the athlete's sponsor. Also, the authors showed that a crisis involving an athlete will have a more negative impact on lowly identified fans' evaluations of the athlete's sponsor rather than highly identified fans. This study revealed many important implications for future sports-related crisis research, such as the examination of how crises impact sponsors and the importance of fan identification as a variable. Yoon and Shin (2017) encouraged future researchers to replicate their study in a variety of sporting contexts, investigate the impact of gender, and analyze the impact of athlete attractiveness. Overall, previous scholarship that has examined sports-related crises using experimental designs have helped to better scholarly understanding of SCCT, provide crisis managers with better crisis management plans, and propose ideas for future studies.

Future Directions for Sports-Related Research Using SCCT

This chapter serves as a call for researchers to design experiments that build upon the foundation and recommendations from previous case studies, content analyses, textual analyses, and other experiments that have examined sports-related crises. Utilizing experimental research provides scholars with three important advantages, as defined by Wimmer and Dominick (2011). First, and most important, experimental research provides evidence of causality, establishing a cause and effect relationship between variables. This ability is critical in SCCT crisis communication research. It is imperative that scholars determine the causal relationship between selected reputation repair strategies and an organization's reputation during a sports-related crisis. A better understanding of this relationship would broaden both the theoretical understanding of SCCT and provide sports practitioners with more effective crisis management strategies. Additionally, the use of experiments allows researchers to test whether the attribution of crisis responsibility matches the expected outcomes in SCCT, as Sisco (2012) determined was the case for non-profit organizations, which the author felt "reinforces the applicability of the SCCT to this sector" (p. 12).

The second advantage to experimental research is the potential for replication. Through thorough scholarly description of the instrumentation and procedures utilized in this study, future scholars will be able to confirm the initial results crisis experiments. The final advantage to experimental research is control. The aspect of control will help sports crisis scholars better understand the impact of a variety of variables that influence crisis response.

Sports-Specific Crisis Typology

In order to properly examine sports-related crises through the lens of SCCT, a crisis typology that classifies sports-related crises should be created to properly evaluate the level of crisis responsibility stakeholders attribute to an organization during a crisis event. Sato (2015) claimed that "careful, systematic categorization and accumulation of sport crises has yet to be accomplished" (p. 106), and advocated for sports scholars to create a crisis typology to effectively categorize sports crises.

Wilson, Stavros, and Westberg (2010) provided an important first step, as they adapted crisis types created by Coombs and Holladay (1996) (accident, faux pas, transgression, terrorism) and identified sports-related incidents that fit the existing categories. The authors hoped this exercise would build toward a sports-related typology while simultaneously encouraging further sports-related crisis research that utilized experimental design. Wilson et al. (2010) noted a need for further experimental research that tests a variety of stakeholder groups (sponsors, fans, etc.), tests for gender differences, and tests the impact of culture by examining "mega-sporting" events such as the Olympics. Despite the advances this typology made, Sato (2015) still claimed their typology was "not able to incorporate all the unique characteristics of sport crises" (p. 106). Thus, the creation of a typology that fully classifies the unique crises that impact athletes and sports organizations is crucial to help advance the use SSCT in a sporting context.

Variables Warranting Additional Experimental Testing

Given the limited number of studies that currently use experiments to ana-lyze sports-related crises, it is clear that this area is ripe for scholarly inquiry and presents scholars with a rich and diverse context for crisis communication research. There are a number of variables that, when explored, will broaden sports scholars' theoretical understanding in SCCT.

First, scholars should continue to examine how the tenets of SCCT can be properly applied in a sporting context. Sports-related scandals and crises can potentially be caused by organizations, coaches, and the individual athletes that play for those organizations. Thus, scholars must determine how the person/group that committed the offending action will impact crisis response.

Sports also hae a unique group of stakeholders that have a strong, personal tie to the organization: sports fans. Wann (2006) describes this relationship through the concept of fan identification, which is defined as "the extent to which a fan feels a psychological connection to a team and the team's perfor-mances are viewed as self-relevant" (p. 332). Brown and Billings (2013) noted that fans will attempt to help their team salvage its reputation, and are likely to avoid cognitive dissonance between their strong ties to the institution and the offending action that has occurred. Consequently, scholars should continue to investigate the degree to which a stakeholder's level of fandom impacts their evaluation of crises.

The role of sponsors also presents a unique variable for continued experimen-tal testing. Westberg, Stavros, and Wilson (2011) note that "negative incidents involving athletes representing the sport entity may threaten the brands of both the sport and sponsor and can weaken or even dissolve the partnership" (p. 603). Walsh and McAllister-Spooner (2011) performed a content analysis to assess the role Michael Phelps' sponsors played in his image repair process after he was caught smoking marijuana. The authors noted that Phelps' spon-sors were largely supportive of him during his crisis, and recommended that researchers conduct future research to further study the relationship between athletes/sports organizations and sponsors during times of crisis. Overall, exper-imentally testing the relationship between sponsors and sporting organizations during times of crisis could "provide significant managerial utility in sponsor-ship planning by creating more solid sponsorship crisis plans at the tactical level" (Wilson et al., 2010, p. 29).

Overall, communication scholars can be encouraged by the research possi-bilities found in sports-related crisis communication research. This research area presents scholars with the opportunity to provide important theoretical contri-butions as SCCT continues to be applied to a sporting context. Moreover, this research can have practical significance, as well, as crisis managers will have a bet-ter understanding of how to properly and effectively engage in reputation repair.

References

Anderson, M. (2013). "Winning takes care of everything": Tiger Woods ad under fire. *Huffington Post*. Retrieved from www.huffingtonpost.com/2013/03/26/winning-takes-care-of-everything-tiger-woods-ad_n_2957004.html

Arnold, P. J. (1992). Sport as a valued human practice: A basis for the consideration of some moral issues in sport. *Journal of Philosophy of Education, 26*(2), 237–255.

Benoit, W. (1995). *Accounts, excuses, and apologies: A theory of image restoration strategies*. Albany, NY: State University of New York Press.

Benoit, W. L., & Hanczor, R. S. (1994). The Tonya Harding controversy: An analysis of image restoration strategies. *Communication Quarterly, 42*(4), 416–433.

Benson, J. A. (1988). Crisis revisited: An analysis of strategies used by Tylenol in the second tampering episode. *Central States Speech Journal, 39*(1), 49–66.

Bialik, C. (2014). Have Ray Rice and Roger Goodell hurt NFL ratings? *FiveThirtyEight*. Retrieved from https://fivethirtyeight.com/datalab/have-ray-rice-and-roger-goodell-hurt-nfl-ratings/

Billings, A. C., Butterworth, M. L., & Turman, P. (2011). *Communication and sport: Surveying the field*. Thousand Oaks, CA: Sage Publications.

Bradley, M. (2016). We can't handle the idea that sport is no longer just sport. *ABC. net*. Retrieved from www.abc.net.au/news/2016-01-21/bradley-corruption-in-pro fessional-sport-should-be-no-surprise/7101508

Brazeal, L. M. (2008). The image repair strategies of Terrell Owens. *Public Relations Review, 34*(2), 145–150.

Brown, K. A. (2012). Off the field: An empirical examination of the impact of athlete transgressions and response strategy on the image repair and crisis communication process. Doctoral dissertation, University of Alabama, Tuscaloosa.

Brown, K. A., Dickhaus, J., & Long, M. C. (2012). LeBron James and "The Decision": An empirical examination of image repair in sports. *Journal of Sports Media, 7*(1), 149–175.

Brown, N. A. (2014). The convergence of situational crisis communication theory and social media: Empirically testing the effectiveness of sports fan-enacted crisis commu- nication. Doctoral dissertation, University of Alabama, Tuscaloosa.

Brown, N. A., Brown, K. A., & Billings, A. C. (2015). "May no act of ours bring shame": Fan-enacted crisis communication surrounding the Penn State sex abuse scandal. *Communication & Sport, 3*(3), 288–311.

Brown, N. A., & Billings, A. C. (2013). Sports fans as crisis communicators on social media websites. *Public Relations Review, 39*(1), 74–81.

Burke, K. (1973). *The philosophy of literary form* (3rd ed.). Berkeley, CA: University of California Press.

Claeys, A. S., Cauberghe, V., & Vyncke, P. (2010). Restoring reputations in times of crises: An experimental study of the situational crisis communication theory and the moderating effects of locus of control. *Public Relations Review, 36*(3), 256–262.

Coombs, W. T. (1995). Choosing the right words: The development of guidelines for the selection of the "appropriate" crisis response strategies. *Management Communication Quarterly, 8*(4), 447–476.

Coombs, W. T. (1999). *Ongoing crisis communication: Planning, managing and responding*. Thousand Oaks, CA: Sage Publications.

Coombs, W. (2007). *Ongoing crisis communication: Planning, managing and responding* (2nd ed.). Thousand Oaks, CA: Sage Publications.

Coombs, W. T., & Holladay, S. J. (2006). Unpacking the halo effect: Reputation and crisis management. *Journal of Communication Management, 10*(2), 123–137.

Coombs, W. T., & Holladay, S. J. (2002). Helping crisis managers protect reputational assets: Initial tests of the situational crisis communication theory. *Management Communication Quarterly, 16*(2), 165–186.

Coombs, W. T., & Holladay, S. J. (1996). Communication and attributions in a crisis: An experimental study in crisis communication. *Journal of Public Relations Research, 8*(4), 279–295.

Frandsen, F., & Johansen, W. (2007). The apology of a sports icon: Crisis communication and apologetic ethics. *HERMES—Journal of Language and Communication in Business, 20*(38), 85–104.

Haltiwanger, J. (2016). Twitter slams Brock Turner's short sentence with ridiculously long hashtag. *Elite Daily*. Retrieved from http://elitedaily.com/news/politics/twitter-slams-brock-turner-hashtag/1606843/

Heider, F. (1958). *The psychology of interpersonal relations*. New York: Wiley.

Hong, S., & Len-Ríos, M. E. (2015). Does race matter? Implicit and explicit measures of the effect of the PR spokesman's race on evaluations of spokesman source credibility and perceptions of a PR crisis' severity. *Journal of Public Relations Research, 27*(1), 63–80.

Kahuni, A. T., Rowley, J., & Binsardi, A. (2009). Guilty by association: image "spillover" in corporate co-branding. *Corporate Reputation Review, 12*(1), 52–63.

Kelner, M. (2017). General public is losing faith in scandal-ridden sports, survey claims. *Guardian*. Retrieved from www.theguardian.com/sport/2017/jul/05/public-faith-sport-low-corruption-doping-sacndals-survey

Kruse, N. W. (1981). Apologia in team sport. *Quarterly Journal of Speech, 67*, 270–283.

Len-Ríos, M. E. (2010). Image repair strategies, local news portrayals and crisis stage: A case study of Duke University's lacrosse team crisis. *International Journal of Strategic Communication, 4*(4), 267–287.

McCloskey, J., & Bailes, J. (2005). *When winning costs too much: Steroids, supplements, and scandal in today's sports*. Lanham, MD: Taylor Trade.

McIndoe, S. (2017). How the NHL concussion lawsuit could threaten the future of the league. *Guardian*. Retrieved from www.theguardian.com/sport/2017/apr/05/nhl-concussion-lawsuit-could-threaten-future-of-league

O'Connor, I. (2014). Visuals sealed Adrian Peterson's fate. *ESPN.com*. Retrieved from www.espn.com/nfl/story/_/id/11897549/minnesota-vikings-rb-adrian-peterson-was-done-horrific-visuals-child-abuse-case

PEJ News Coverage Index. (2011). Two explosive scandals top the news. Pew Research Center Journalism and Media. Retrieved from www.journalism.org/2011/11/13/pej-news-coverage-index-november-713-2011/

Richards, O., Jr., Wilson, C., Boyle, K., & Mower, J. (2017). A knockout to the NFL's reputation? A case study of the NFL's crisis communications strategies in response to the Ray Rice scandal. *Public Relations Review, 43*(3), 615–623.

Rosenfield, L. W. (1968). A case study in speech criticism: The Nixon-Truman analog. *Speech Monographs, 35*, 435–450.

Sanderson, J. (2008). "You are the type of person that children should look up to as a hero": Parasocial interaction on 38pitches.com. *International Journal of Sport Communication, 1*(3), 337–360.

Sato, S. (2015). Negative information in sport: Minimizing crisis damage. In K. Kanosue, K. Kogiso, D. Oshimi, & M. Harada (Eds.), *Sports management and sports humanities* (pp. 103–111). Tokyo, Japan: Springer.

Sato, S., Ko, Y. J., Park, C., & Tao, W. (2015). Athlete reputational crisis and consumer evaluation. *European Sport Management Quarterly*, *15*(4), 434–453.

Sisco, H. F. (2012). Nonprofit in crisis: An examination of the applicability of situational crisis communication theory. *Journal of Public Relations Research*, *24*(1), 1–17.

Solomon, J. (2016). Baylor ticket prices plunge on secondary market in wake of scandal. *CBS Sports.com*. Retrieved from www.cbssports.com/college-football/news/baylor-ticket-prices-plunge-on-secondary-market-in-wake-of-scandal/

Walsh, J., & McAllister-Spooner, S. M. (2011). Analysis of the image repair discourse in the Michael Phelps controversy. *Public Relations Review*, *37*(2), 157–162.

Wann, D. L. (2006). The causes and consequences of sport team identification. In A. Raney & J. Bryant (Eds.), *Handbook of sport and media* (pp. 331–352). Mahwah, NJ: LEA.

Ware, B. L., & Linkugel, W. A. (1973). They spoke in defense of themselves: On the generic criticism of apologia. *Quarterly Journal of Speech*, *59*(3), 273–283.

Westberg, K., Stavros, C., & Wilson, B. (2011). The impact of degenerative episodes on the sponsorship B2B relationship: Implications for brand management. *Industrial Marketing Management*, *40*(4), 603–611.

Williams, D., & Olaniran, B. (2002). Crisis communication in racial issues. *Journal of Applied Communication Research*, *30*(4), 293–313.

Wilson, B., Stavros, C., & Westberg, K. (2010). A sport crisis typology: Establishing a pathway for future research. *International Journal of Sport Management and Marketing*, *7*(1–2), 21–32.

Wimmer, R., & Dominick, J. (2011). *Mass media research: An introduction*. Boston, MA: Wadsworth.

Yoon, S. W., & Shin, S. (2017). The role of negative publicity in consumer evaluations of sports stars and their sponsors. *Journal of Consumer Behaviour*, *16*, 332–342.

4

ADDING NARRATIVE TO THE SITUATIONAL CRISIS COMMUNICATION THEORY

The Case for Crisis "Narrative Management" in Sport

James R. DiSanza, Karen L. Hartman, Nancy J. Legge, and Zac Gershberg

Crisis communication scholars and managers "must accept that no organization is immune from a crisis anywhere in the world even if that organization is vigilant and actively seeks to prevent crises" (Coombs, 2010, p. 17). Textbooks and journal articles provide strategies, tips, and tactics so crisis managers can be as proactive as possible (e.g., Kelleher, 2018; Wilcox, Cameron, & Reber, 2015). Nevertheless, many organizations are unprepared to handle a crisis. According to a 2013 study conducted by the communications firm Burson-Marsteller, 80 percent of business leaders believe their companies will face a crisis within a year, but only 54 percent of the companies had a crisis plan, and about half of those were perceived as insufficient ("Prepared for a crisis?" 2013).

There also appears to be a gap between what crisis communication researchers suggest and what crisis communication managers actually do in these stressful situations (e.g., Coombs, 2017). Research by Kim, Avery, and Lariscy (2009) analyzed 18 years of crisis communication research across 11 journals and found that organizations heavily rely on the denial strategy and the authors concluded that the link between prescriptions and practice is not as direct as one would expect, despite decades of extensive crisis research.

The Situational Crisis Communication Theory (SCCT) represents one attempt to provide proscriptive guidance to crisis managers (Coombs, 2007). The SCCT provides a set of guidelines for protecting victims and the organization's image from the consequences of serious calamities. The theory now serves as the leading theoretical framework in crisis communication research (e.g., Avery, Lariscy, Kim, & Hocke, 2010; Fediuk, Pace, & Botero, 2010; Ma & Zhan, 2016).

In this chapter, we analyze SCCT in relation to the theory's emphasis on the communicative and ethical considerations managers must make in the immediate moments following a crisis. According to Coombs (2007), when a crisis hits, two types of communication are needed: instructing and adapting. Instructing information identifies what stakeholders must do to protect themselves from any physical threat a crisis can cause. Adapting information helps alleviate the psychological threat a crisis produces. Because crises create uncertainty, and uncertainty creates stress, utilizing adapting information helps stakeholders cope. Coombs identifies three topics covered by adapting messages: first, identify what happened; second, identify what is going to be done to protect stakeholders from a similar crisis in the future; and third, express concern for any victims. The authors believe that adapting information is usually presented in the form of a narrative, and we therefore suggest that the concept of *narrative management* be added to the SCCT. Relying on two case studies—the National Football League's (NFL) Ray Rice domestic violence case and the National Basketball Association's (NBA) Donald Sterling race crisis—the authors identify how narrative management provides a framework that explains why some adapting messages succeed where others fail, and prescriptions for creating successful adapting narratives.

The chapter also addresses an identified gap within sport communication research. Wenner (2015) characterizes sport communication as an umbrella field that includes three distinct research dispositions. The first area is the Media, Sports, and Society disposition, which largely concerns itself with "the social and cultural dynamics at play in the media and sport intermix" (p. 251); the second is the Sport Communication as Profession disposition, which is anchored in the professional practice of sport communication typically surrounding public relations, broadcasting, sports reporting, etc.; and the third is the Communication Studies and Sport disposition, which focuses on non-mediated aspects of sport such as "interpersonal, group, and organizational communication dynamics" (p. 255). Wenner cautions the dispositions to "not [speak] past each other" (p. 259) but instead to engage one another in order to advance the field. This chapter, by suggesting practitioners could benefit from narrative in crisis situations, hopes to merge strategic communication studies (Sport Communication as Profession) with rhetorical studies (Media, Sports, and Society) to present a broader approach to communication and sport research that "talks to one another."

Crisis and Narrative

Situational Crisis Communication Theory

A crisis is defined as "the perception of an unpredictable event that threatens important expectancies of stakeholders related to health, safety, environmental, and economic issues, and can seriously impact an organization's performance and generate negative outcomes" (Coombs, 2015, p. 3). Coombs's (2007) SCCT helps organizations minimize reputational threat and, unlike previous crisis response theories, provides a "conceptual link between crisis response strategies and the crisis situation's characteristics, which enables practitioners to more effectively manage crisis responses" (Liu, 2010, p. 338). The theory involves specific steps. First, when a crisis hits, practitioners must identify and protect the physical and psychological needs of the stakeholders. Communication in this first stage must include instructing information (which tells stakeholders what they must do to protect themselves from any physical threat) and adapting information (which helps stakeholders understand what happened, what will be done to protect them from a similar crisis in the future, and expresses concern for the victims). Once these preliminary needs are met, practitioners should then move to the second step, which identifies and assesses any reputational threat a crisis poses. The SCCT offers a two-step process for assessing this reputational threat, which then determines the appropriate response. First, identify the type of crisis, based on a number of factors that shape stakeholder attributions, and then select response strategies appropriate to that crisis type. Coombs's model offers several types of response strategies, split into three groups: denial, diminish, and/or rebuild.

The model has received considerable attention within scholarly writing and serves to address a wide range of industries and crisis situations. For example, research on non-profits (e.g., Sisco, 2012; Sisco, Collins, & Zoch, 2010), social media (e.g., Brummette & Sisco, 2015; Cooley & Jones, 2013), and race (e.g., Liu, 2010), among several other areas, have been examined with this theoretical model. However, the application of the model to sport and athletes is still very limited (e.g., Brown, 2015; Jordan & Smith, 2013).

Narrative

The role and power of narrative have been examined by rhetoricians and rhetorical critics going back to Corax of Syracuse in 467 BCE. Carrying on this tradition, Fisher (1984, 1985, 1987) argued that humans are "homo narrans," the storytelling person. Stories are an essential element of the human experience and Fisher's narrative paradigm argues that symbolic language organized into stories creates communities and meaning. According to Fisher (1984), "symbols are created and communicated ultimately as stories meant to give order to human experience" (p. 4). Fisher (1987) argued that narrative is essential in defining the human experience and suggested the aesthetic power of narrative should challenge the more traditional, rationalist focus of argument. By viewing all human discourse as the product of the storytelling person, or homo narrans, Fisher sought to synthesize rhetorical and persuasive discourse on the one hand, and literary and aesthetic values on the other. Effective rhetoric within the narrative paradigm requires achieving narrative probability by suturing two interlocking components, coherence and fidelity. Coherence refers to whether the structure of the story makes sense to the audience, from the credibility of the characters to the style of delivery. Narrative fidelity speaks to whether the values of the story are consistent with the experience of the audience and the degree to which the narrative transcends mere story and persuades the audience to exercise judgment.

Narrative Management

To illustrate the possibilities of taking a narrative approach to examining and critiquing various "adapting" messages, we apply Fisher's (1985) concepts of coherence and fidelity to two case studies. The first illustrates an unsuccessful effort by the NFL's commissioner, Roger Goodell, in the Ray Rice domestic violence case. The second case explores a more successful use of an adapting narrative by NBA commissioner Adam Silver, who responded to racist comments from Clippers owner Donald Sterling.

Case Study #1: NFL's Ray Rice Domestic Violence Crisis

Former Baltimore Ravens running back Ray Rice and his then-fiancée, Janay Palmer, made headlines when a video surfaced in February of 2014 showing Rice dragging Palmer's unconscious body out of an Atlantic City hotel elevator after he assaulted her. Goodell suspended Rice for two games, a penalty that was heavily criticized for its leniency. In September, the celebrity news source TMZ released the in-elevator video that showed Rice punching Palmer in the face. The NFL, already reeling from public criticism, needed to craft a new narrative and Goodell suspended Rice indefinitely. He did several interviews and press conferences to explain the new decision. To illustrate, consider the extensive interview with Norah O'Donnell of CBS News on September 9 (*Roger Goodell,* 2014). O'Donnell opened by asking whether anyone at the NFL had seen the in-elevator video prior to the TMZ release, to which to Goodell said, "No" (para. 6). O'Donnell reiterated by asking, "No one in the NFL?" (para. 7). Goodell replied:

> No one in the NFL, to my knowledge, and I had been asked that same question and the answer to that is no. We were not granted that. We were told that was not something we would have access to. On multiple occasions, we asked for it. And on multiple occasions we were told no.
>
> *para. 8*

O'Donnell continued to press and ask how a website like TMZ could get hold of it when the NFL could not. Goodell said:

> Well, I don't know how TMZ or any other website gets their information. We are particularly reliant on law enforcement. That's the most reliable. It's the most credible. And we don't seek to get that information from sources that are not credible.
>
> *para. 12*

Goodell said that he wished he had seen the tape because, when he met with Ray Rice and his representatives, "It was ambiguous about what actually happened" (para. 14). O'Donnell then asked what was ambiguous about an unconscious woman being dragged out of an elevator by her feet. Goodell's reply:

> There was nothing ambiguous about that. That was the result that we saw. We did not know what led up to that. We did not know the details of that. We asked for that on several occasions. It was unacceptable in and of itself what we saw on the first tape. And that's why we took action, albeit insufficient action. And we acknowledge that, we took responsibility for that—I did personally—and I take responsibility for that now. But what we saw yesterday was extremely clear and graphic and was absolutely necessary for us to take the action we did . . . It was extremely graphic, and it was sickening.
>
> *paras. 16, 18*

When asked if the NFL had a larger problem with domestic abuse, Goodell began to highlight the NFL's plan for response—a commitment to redemption: "What we have is young men that are going to be unfortunately involved in this if we don't provide the right resources . . . We have to change our training and our education to try and eliminate that issue." Goodell went on to say:

> We're saying we have a problem. We have one incident, that's a problem. And what we want to do is by the policy that we implemented two weeks ago and say, "We haven't done this right." We have had lots of conversations, lots of listening and learning right here in this room with experts not just in the last two weeks or three weeks or month, but over the last couple of years to say, "How can we deal with this issue better? How can we prevent the cases from happening?" . . . People expect a lot from the NFL. We accept that. We embrace that. That's our opportunity to make a difference not just in the NFL, but in society in general. We have that ability. We have that influence. And we have to do that. And every day, that's what we're going to strive to do.
>
> *paras. 28–30*

To summarize, the Goodell narrative fulfilled two of the three objectives of adapting information. It describes what happened, especially in focusing on the in-elevator video: how they tried to get it, failed, and how that failure led to their poor decision-making. The narrative then went on to describe how the NFL is working to prevent this from happening again. However, the third element of adaptive information, expressing sympathy for the victim, either Janay Palmer herself or battered women in general, was entirely absent in this interview. Examining the Goodell narrative through the lens of coherence and fidelity provides us with useful insights into why it failed with the public and the media.

First, consider Goodell's narrative by focusing on coherence. According to Hart and Daughton (2005), narrative coherence involves an evaluation of the qualities of a story, including completeness, believability, followability, and the degree to which the story's structure and characters hang together. From this point of view, Goodell's narrative failed in almost every way. The opening tale about the NFL's failure to get the tape was poorly told and lacked detail, specificity, and character development. We were not told who tried to get the video, how they tried to get the video, how many times they tried to get the video, whom they contacted in law enforcement, and little about why these persons refused the request. The lack of development does not bolster the story's credibility, especially given that the NFL, the planet's most powerful sports organization, could not get the video, while TMZ, a paparazzo-style media outlet, obtained the video simply by asking the hotel. Because the story of the NFL's efforts are poorly structured, developed, and told, it is less than believable.

In contrast to Goodell's narrative, Baltimore Ravens owner Steve Bisciotti told a much more coherent story regarding his team's attempts to get the video.

> We contacted the casino management and asked if there was video of the incident from inside the elevator that we could see. The casino would not share such video. We asked the local New Jersey police and the police refused as well. We asked the prosecutor's office and that office refused. It was our understanding at that time that Ray's attorney had not yet seen the video. NFL officials had been informed, and we know they were also trying to retrieve and/or see the video.
>
> *Gatto, 2014, para. 9*

This narrative is a more fleshed-out telling, perhaps even in chronological order, of the specific agents from whom they sought the video and that each time they were rebuffed. The structure, detail, and consistency of this narrative made it more believable.

Goodell's narrative then moved to an important second act, wherein he blames his earlier suspension on limited information. O'Donnell appears to recognize incoherence in this story and asks Goodell why he needed anything more than the outside-elevator video of Rice dragging the unconscious Palmer to make the right decision. Goodell's only response is that the first video was the reason he took action. Even his attempts to accept responsibility are denied by other elements of the narrative where he scapegoats law enforcement for failing to provide the video and Rice for not being honest. His narrative remains incoherent and, when Goodell began to describe the solutions to the problem, his explanations appeared cynical rather than redemptive.

Second, consider Goodell's story in light of narrative fidelity, with attention to narrative truthfulness—how well it captures what is known and how well it reflects the audience's morals and values (Hart & Daughton, 2005).

Goodell repeatedly emphasized the necessity of having all the information, including the in-elevator video, to make a correct decision. Although "having all the facts" is certainly a value of American jurisprudence, appealing to this value is tenuous, at best, when justifying delayed discipline of apparent spousal abuse by an employee in a professional sports league where participation is perceived to be a privilege. The failure to express sympathy toward Palmer only reinforced the fact that Goodell was appealing to the wrong values in his narrative. O'Donnell calls Goodell out for this contradiction by asking:

> But what changed? I mean, on the first tape she was lying unconscious on the ground, being dragged out by her feet. Did you really need to see a videotape of Ray Rice punching her in the face to make this decision?
>
> *Roger Goodell, 2014, para. 17*

In asking this, O'Donnell is proposing a second, more important value: concern and sympathy for the victim of this abuse and the safety for women everywhere if a popular figure like Rice gets off with a minor penalty on the excuse that there was no clear evidence of actual violence. O'Donnell interrogated the values Goodell expressed in his narrative and prioritized the safety of women over Goodell's abstract formulation.

Even worse, Goodell implied that, in order to act, he needed to know what happened prior to the assault that might explain it: "That was the result of what we saw. We did not know what led up to that. We did not know the details of that" (para. 16). Here, Goodell's narrative continued to focus on the value of full discovery, apparently including what Palmer may have done to cause the assault. He quickly pulled back from this "victim blaming" inference, but he suggested that Rice was only partly responsible for the attack. Suggesting that the victim may have done something to cause the beating invites victim blaming and rationalizes violent conduct against women.

This analysis suggests that Goodell's crisis narrative lacked coherence and fidelity and would do little to convince people of the NFL's sincerity. Indeed, Goodell faced significant pushback from various sources, including the National Organization for Women and several ESPN analysts. Of his performance during the interview, noted sports columnist Mike Lupica said, "When you looked at him Tuesday night with Norah O'Donnell, you really did start to imagine the NFL commissioner bleeding from both eyes in the late rounds of a fight he lost on points long ago" (Lupica, 2014, para. 13).

Case Study #2: NBA's Donald Sterling Race Crisis

In April 2014, the NBA faced a crisis when TMZ released audio of Donald Sterling, the owner of the Los Angeles Clippers, making racist comments about

African-Americans. On the recording Sterling tells his girlfriend at the time, V. Stiviano, that he did not want her to bring black people to games or pose with them on Instagram (Goyette, 2014). The release of the audio immediately became a national story, with many calling on the commissioner to act. For example, civil rights activist Jesse Jackson commented: "The first burden is upon the commissioner, Adam Silver, to act decisively because we don't want this to drag on throughout the playoffs" (as cited in *Alleged Sterling*, 2014, para. 12). LeBron James, at that time a member of the Miami Heat, also directed comments to Silver: "As commissioner of our league, you have to make a stand and you have to be very aggressive with it" (as cited in *Alleged Sterling*, 2014, para. 25).

The NBA conducted a relatively quick investigation and, on April 29, Silver delivered a press conference announcing that the investigation was complete and that Sterling was immediately banned from the league and would be fined $2.5 million, the maximum fine under the NBA constitution. Further, Silver planned to force Sterling to sell the Clippers franchise (*Full transcript*, 2014).

Silver's narrative differed from Roger Goodell's in many ways. First, Silver started with a brief discussion of the process he went through to arrive at his judgment—in other words, he told his audience what happened.

> Shortly after the release of an audio recording this past Saturday of a conversation that allegedly included Clippers owner Donald Sterling, the NBA commenced an investigation, which, among other things, included an interview of Mr. Sterling. That investigation is now complete. The central findings of the investigation are that the man whose voice is heard on the recording and on a second recording from the same conversation that was released on Sunday is Mr. Sterling and that the hateful opinions voiced by that man are those of Mr. Sterling.
>
> *Full transcript, 2014, para 1*

Silver completed a simple narrative that explained the process by which the investigation was conducted and concluded that Sterling was the voice on the tape making racist comments.

Following those comments, Silver stated: "The views expressed by Mr. Sterling are deeply offensive and harmful; that they came from an NBA owner only heightens the damage and my personal outrage" (*Full transcript*, 2014, para. 3). In this portion of the narrative, Silver expressed sympathy to those who took offense at the comments. Silver went further in these sympathetic expressions:

> Sentiments of this kind are contrary to the principles of inclusion and respect that form the foundation of our diverse, multicultural and multiethnic league. I am personally distraught that the views expressed by Mr. Sterling came from within an institution that has historically taken

such a leadership role in matters of race relations and caused current and former players, coaches, fans and partners of the NBA to question their very association with the league.

(Full transcript, 2014, para. 4)

In these comments, Silver suggested that many people associated with the NBA were distraught by Sterling's views, which, from Silver's point of view, makes sense given that diversity and multiculturalism represent the very foundations of the league.

Before issuing his judgment, Silver connected his current narrative to the league's founding narrative: "To them, and pioneers of the game like Earl Lloyd, Chuck Cooper, Sweetwater Clifton, the great Bill Russell, and particularly Magic Johnson, I apologize" *(Full transcript,* 2014, para. 6). Singling out these African-American pioneers reinforced Silver's claims that the league is, and always has been, a diverse one.

Finally, Silver announced his decision—his prevention statement:

> Accordingly, effective immediately, I am banning Mr. Sterling for life from any association with the Clippers organization or the NBA. Mr. Sterling may not attend any NBA games or practices . . . He will also be barred from attending NBA Board of Governors meetings or participating in any other league activity. I am also fining Mr. Sterling $2.5 million, the maximum amount allowed under the NBA constitution. These funds will be donated to organizations dedicated to anti-discrimination and tolerance efforts that will be jointly selected by the NBA and its Players Association. As for Mr. Sterling's ownership interest in the Clippers, I will urge the Board of Governors to exercise its authority to force a sale of the team and will do everything in my power to ensure that that happens.
>
> *Full transcript,* 2014, para. 6

Silver closed by thanking the players, the players' union leadership, and others for supporting the NBA process in this matter. Unlike Goodell's adapting communication, Silver's included all three elements cited in the SCCT model, including a description of what happened, the corrective measures he employed to solve the problem, and extensive expressions of sympathy for those who may have been hurt or taken offense.

As recounted above, narrative coherence involves an evaluation of the qualities of a story, including completeness, believability, followability, and the degree to which the story's structure and characters hang together. Silver's opening, which described the processes the NBA followed to arrive at their conclusion, is brief, linear, complete, and believable—in short, a coherently structured narrative. The story had a clear beginning, when the audio recording was released; a middle, which is the investigation itself, including an interview with Sterling;

and a conclusion, which led to the action taken. The coherence of the narrative reinforced the fairness of the process, especially the inclusion of Sterling in that process. This contrasts with the lack of coherence in Goodell's narrative, which included backtracking to express apologies for the earlier, botched, decision. Silver's story was communicated without any qualifications, backtracking, or apology. The story's coherence established that justice was served and likely reinforced the audience's confidence in its truth.

The coherence of the process narrative also gave Silver leeway to express sympathy with those who are offended and outraged. Because the process story was coherent, the outrage that he then expressed appeared to be a natural outgrowth of the investigation. Goodell, as you recall, said what he saw in the in-elevator video was "sickening" and merited an additional suspension. However, as Nora O'Donnell reminded Goodell, he shouldn't have needed the in-elevator video to be sickened. In other words, Goodell's outrage did not flow naturally from a coherent narrative and appeared to be insincere. Silver's process narrative was clear and his outrage flowed from an honest source.

Silver inserted himself into the narrative he was constructing in a much more personal way than Goodell. In other words, Silver owned the narrative he told by expressing his personal outrage in several places. He frequently used the personal pronoun "I" to describe his distress and outrage and emphasized that the decisions were his. He said, "I am banning Mr. Sterling for life . . ."; "I apologize" to the pioneers of the game; "I am also fining Mr. Sterling . . ."; and "I will urge the Board of governors to . . ." By inserting himself into the narrative of past punishments and those yet applied, he projected strength and confidence. Although Goodell did use the personal pronoun "I" when he admitted he made a mistake in his early penalty assessment, he employed the corporate "we" through most of the story. The emphasis on the corporate "we" diminished Goodell as a sympathetic protagonist and suggested he was evading responsibility for decisions made and blaming other parties for his inability to acquire evidence. On the other hand, Silver's use of the "I" made himself and, by extension, the NBA, into sympathetic protagonists who were upended by a bigoted and misanthropic owner. The entire narrative suggests Silver was committed to redemption through decisions he was willing (and proud) to own, inviting publics to believe that the process was fair, that his outrage was justified, and the punishments were appropriate. By locating himself at the center of the outrage, apology, and punishment, Silver assumed full responsibility for the decision, which further reinforced the coherence of the story.

Narrative fidelity focuses on the story's truthfulness—how well it captures what is known, how well it reflects the audience's morals and values, and the degree to which those values are transcended. In this case, the fidelity of the story was established and reinforced by the discussion of the process. Silver confirmed that the voice on the two recordings was Sterling's—which was confirmed by Sterling himself. Thus, the story started out by stating the truth. Then, Silver isolated Sterling from the shared values that he and the rest of the NBA profess, which he also assumed are reflected in the general public. Silver said that the NBA is based on "inclusion" and "respect," "diversity," and "multiculturalism," which were not Sterling's values. Silver then connected these values to the pioneers of the NBA, and suggested that Sterling was not only in violation of the league and its fans' values, but values going back to the NBA's earliest days. This highlighted the seriousness of Sterling's breach. Commissioner Silver also created identification with his audience by contrasting the NBA's values with those of Sterling, by using words like "offensive" and "harmful" to describe Sterling's behavior.

Goodell, on the other hand, repeatedly separated himself from the values espoused by the American public on spousal abuse by suggesting he didn't have enough information to render an effective judgment, and saying that he needed to know what happened prior to the punch because it was important to know "what led up to that." These statements do not align with the audience's values.

Finally, Silver reinforced his connection to audience values by apologizing to the people who might have been harmed by the incident—the pioneers of the game, the players, and fans of the league. Despite the fact that Silver did not commit the wrongful act, his apology reinforced his claim that he shares the audience's values of diversity and inclusion. Goodell did apologize for making a poor decision when he suspended Rice for only two games, but he was mute on the harm his original decision caused and the possibility that Rice's light sentence might enable would-be abusers.

To summarize, Silver's narrative regarding Sterling demonstrated far more coherence and fidelity than Goodell's narrative around Rice. The reactions to this narrative were also more favorable. For example, LeBron James wrote on Twitter, "Commissioner Silver thank you for protecting our beautiful and powerful league!! Great leader!! #BiggerThanBasketball #StriveForGreatness" (as cited in Schwartz, 2014, para. 5). Several teams released official statements supporting Silver, and numerous people affiliated with the league expressed "pretty much universal appreciation" (Young, 2014, para. 2).

Conclusion

This chapter emphasized the importance of including narrative management techniques in Coombs's (2007) SCCT, specifically in the adapting communication stage of a crisis. Adapting messages help alleviate the psychological stress of a crisis and should identify what happened, explain what is going to be done to protect stakeholders from a future similar crisis, and express concern for any victims (Coombs, 2007). These two case studies suggest that adapting messages are inherently laid out as narratives and that thinking of adapting messages in terms of narrative management will help practitioners create stories that reflect coherence and fidelity (Fisher, 1985). Coherence focuses on the logical structure of a narrative and fidelity ensures that the values expressed in the narrative are consistent with stakeholder values.

Our two case studies, while limited, do suggest several specific suggestions for practitioners to incorporate *narrative management* during the adjusting communication phase of a crisis.

Managing Coherence

When managing coherence, practitioners can do four things. First, the adapting narrative should include all of the elements from SCCT (Coombs, 2007): what happened, how similar events will be prevented, and showing sympathy for victims. Goodell's narrative did not include any expressions of sympathy for the victim of the assault, Janay Palmer, or survivors of domestic violence in general. This, combined with his insistence that he needed something more than an unconscious woman being dragged out of an elevator to make the correct decision, made Goodell appear uncaring, evasive, and deceptive. In contrast, Commissioner Silver's narrative addressed the people hurt by Donald Sterling's remarks, specifically the "players, coaches, fans and partners of the NBA" who might be questioning their association with the league, as well as the African-American pioneers of the sport. As such, Silver's narrative was more coherent in its discussion of what happened because it included expressions of sympathy to those hurt by the crisis.

Second, the adapting narrative should be appropriately detailed and complete, preferably including a beginning, a middle, and an end that discusses specific people, events, dates, and places. Goodell's adapting narrative was incomplete in terms of the detail provided about the NFL's attempts to get the in-elevator videotape. The lack of detail made his claim that the most powerful sports league on earth could not get a video that TMZ obtained with apparent ease look insincere. Goodell was equally lacking in details when he discussed what he planned to do to prevent the problems going forward. The lack of detail throughout his adjusting narrative hurt his believability. Conversely, Silver's narrative described his investigation into the situation briefly, but thoroughly. The narrative had a clear beginning, middle, and end. The narrative also had the advantage of needing no backtracking and/or apology for previous missteps.

For the third and fourth steps, the adapting narrative should insert the commissioner (or player or team owner) into the story with "I" statements that "own" the description of the problem, the solutions, and especially the statements of sympathy. Likewise, the adapting narrative should avoid statements that focus on the corporate "we," which in the Goodell case study highlighted a lack of authoritative action and moral leadership on the part of the commissioner. Sterling used "I" frequently in his adjusting narrative, whereas Goodell frequently used the corporate "we," diminishing him as a sympathetic protagonist and suggesting he was evading responsibility. By locating oneself at the center of the story—making decisions and taking responsibility—the crisis manager owns the narrative and increases the audience's perceptions of credibility, confidence, and leadership.

Managing Fidelity

When managing fidelity, there are additional considerations for practitioners. First, the adapting narrative should explain how the precipitating event represented a violation of norms and values shared by the organization and audience. Goodell failed this criterion in a number of instances and Goodell's explanation for the crisis did not match the values espoused by his audience. On the other hand, Silver's discussion of what happened reinforced the values of his audience. In labeling the statements of Sterling as "hateful," the Commissioner reinforced the values that the NBA and most of his audience share. When discussing what happened to create the crisis, an explanation must be offered identifying how the crisis was precipitated by a violation of the norms and values shared by both the organization and the public.

Second, the adapting narrative should explain what will be done to prevent the problem in the future. The preventative action must flow from the shared norms and values and should clearly explain how the actions will restore the norms and values to their proper place. Here, too, Silver outperformed Goodell. The NFL Commissioner spent an extensive amount of time talking about preventative measures such as "conversations," "listening," and "learning," but there were no specific policies proposed to solve the problem of domestic abuse among players in the NFL. He never spoke of a program that would reinforce or restore the values he or Ray Rice violated. Adam Silver's performance was made somewhat easier by the nature of this crisis. To restore the norms and values he claimed the NBA shared with its fans, sponsors, and audience members, he had only to get rid of Donald Sterling, which is what he did. It was easy for the audience to see that this solution flowed naturally from the problem or breach and that this solution would redeem the NBA in the eyes of many people. For Silver, the scapegoat was obvious and his removal redemptive.

Finally, the third element of managing narrative fidelity suggests that all expressions of sympathy must clearly explain how the violation or crisis harmed people by connecting this harm to the violation of basic shared values and principles. Goodell failed to include any expressions of sympathy in his narrative. Silver's expression of sympathy was clearly connected to the NBA's shared values, saying that Sterling's comments were "contrary to the principles of inclusion and respect that form the foundation of our diverse, multicultural and multiethnic league." He went on to say that Sterling's comments, inexplicably, contradict the historical pattern of the NBA taking a leadership role in race relations. Silver's multiple expressions of sympathy were directly connected to the values of multiculturalism and racial inclusion that both the league and, presumably, America accepted. This made the anger he expressed about Sterling's comments appear genuine and the punishment fitting. Thus, his narrative met this criterion of fidelity.

This case study analysis suggests that the comments made by sports commissioners during the adjusting phase of a crisis can easily and naturally be viewed as a narrative. The case studies suggest there is value to be found in adding the concept of *narrative management* to SCCT's understanding of adapting information that organizations communicate during a crisis. Further case studies might be useful in examining the narrative coherence and fidelity of other organizations in the adapting phase of a crisis, with the eventual aim of isolating testable variables for quantitative study.

References

Alleged Sterling talk being probed (2014, April 27). Retrieved from www.espn.com/ los-angeles/nba/story/_/id/10843525/nba-investigating-offensive-audio-recording-allegedly-los-angeles-clippers-owner-donald-sterling

Avery, E. J., Lariscy, R. W., Kim, S., & Hocke, T. (2010). A quantitative review of crisis communication research in public relations from 1991 to 2009. *Journal of Public Relations Research*, *36*, 190–192.

Brown, N. A. (2015). The convergence of situational crisis communication theory and social media: Empirically testing the effectiveness of sports fan-enacted crisis communication. Unpublished doctoral dissertation, University of Alabama, Tuscaloosa.

Brummette, J., & Sisco, H. F. (2015). Using Twitter as a means of coping with emotions and uncontrollable crisis. *Public Relations Review*, *41*, 89–96.

Cooley, S., & Jones, A. (2013). A forgotten tweet: Somalia and social media. *Ecquid Novi: African Journalism Studies*, *34*(1), 68–82.

Coombs, W. T. (2007). Protecting organization reputations during a crisis: The development and application of situational crisis communication theory. *Corporate Reputation Review*, *10*(3). 163–176.

Coombs, W. T. (2010). Parameters for crisis communication. In W. T. Coombs & S. J. Holladay (Eds.), *The handbook of crisis communication* (pp. 17–53). Oxford, UK: Wiley-Blackwell.

Coombs, W. T. (2015). *Ongoing crisis communication* (4th ed.). Los Angeles: Sage.

Coombs, W. T. (2017). Revising situational crisis communication theory: The influences of social media on crisis communication on theory and practice. In L. L. Austin & Y. Jin (Eds.), *Social media and crisis communication* (pp. 21–37). New York: Routledge.

Fediuk, T. A., Pace, K. M., & Botero, I. C. (2010). Crisis response effectiveness: Methodological considerations for the advancement in empirical investigation into response impact. In W. T. Coombs & S. J. Holladay (Eds.), *The handbook of crisis communication* (pp. 221–242). Oxford, UK: Wiley-Blackwell.

Fisher, W. R. (1984). Narration as a human communication paradigm: The case of public moral argument. *Communication Monographs*, *51*(1), 1–22.

Fisher, W. R. (1985). The narrative paradigm: An elaboration. *Communication Monographs*, *52*, 347–367.

Fisher, W. (1987). Human communication as a narration: Toward a philosophy of reason, value, and action. Columbia, SC: University of South Carolina Press.

Full transcript of Adam Silver on Donald Sterling ban. (2014, April 29). Retrieved from usatoday.com/story/sports/nba/2014/04/29/adam-silver-commissioner-opening-statement-donald-sterling/8467947/

Gatto, T. (2014, September 9). *Roger Goodell interview: I didn't see video of Rice punch until Monday.* Retrieved from www.sportingnews.com/nfl/news/roger-goodell-interview-cbs-ray-rice-video-norah-o-donnell/e3zyhccrdi5k159sbg2qkuv6b

Goyette, B. (2014, April 26). *L.A. Clippers owner Donald Sterling's racist rant caught on tape*. Retrieved from www.huffingtonpost.com/2014/04/26/donald-sterling-racist_n_5218572.html

Hart, R. P., & Daughton, S. (2005). *Modern rhetorical criticism* (3rd ed.). Upper Saddle River, NJ: Pearson Education.

Jordan, T., & Smith, D. (2013). Crisis communication in sport management: Research aides crisis response selection. *KAHPERD Journal, 51*(1), 26–33.

Kelleher, T. (2018). *Public relations.* New York: Oxford University Press.

Kim, S., Avery, E. J., & Lariscy, R. W. (2009). Are crisis communicators practicing what we preach? An evaluation of crisis response strategy analyzed in public relations research from 1991 to 2009. *Public Relations Review, 35*(4), 446–448.

Liu, B. F. (2010). Effective public relations in racially charged crises: Not black or white. In W. T. Coombs & S. J. Holladay (Eds.), *The handbook of crisis communication* (pp. 335–358). Oxford, UK: Wiley-Blackwell.

Lupica, M. (2014, September 9). *In his TV defense of NFL's handling of Ray Rice, commissioner Roger Goodell looks like he's guilty*. Retrieved from www.nydailynews.com/sports/football/lupica-television-interview-roger-goodell-guilty-defense-article-1.1934271

Ma, L., & Zhan, M. (2016). Effects of attributed responsibility and response strategies on organizational reputation: A meta-analysis of situational crisis communication theory research. *Journal of Public Relations Research, 28*(2), 102–119.

Prepared for a crisis? (2013, April). *Tone at the Top Newsletter, 61*. Retrieved from https://global.theiia.org/knowledge/Public%20Documents/TaT_April_2013.pdf

Roger Goodell discusses Ray Rice tape on CBS. (2014, September 9). Retrieved from www.nfl.com/news/story/0ap3000000392302/article/roger-go—ell-discusses-ray-rice-tape-on-cbs?campaign=Twitter_atn

Schwartz, N. (2014, April 29). *NBA community reacts to Donald Sterling's lifetime ban.* Retrieved from http://ftw.usatoday.com/2014/04/donald-sterling-lifetime-ban-nba-clippers-reaction

Sisco, H. F. (2012). The ACORN story: An analysis of crisis response strategies in a nonprofit organization. *Public Relations Review, 38*(1), 89–96.

Sisco, H. F., Collins, E. L., & Zoch, L. M. (2010). Through the looking glass: A decade of Red Cross crisis response and situational crisis communication theory. *Public Relations Review, 36*(1), 21–27.

Wenner, L. (2015). Communication and sport, where art thou? Epistemological reflections on the moment and field(s) of play. *Communication & Sport, 3*(3), 247–260.

Wilcox, D. L., Cameron, G. T., & Reber, B. H. (2015). *Public relations: Strategies and tactics* (11th ed.). Boston: Pearson.

Young, R. (2014, April 29). *Reactions to the NBA's lifetime ban of Donald Sterling.* Retrieved from www.cbssports.com/nba/news/reactions-to-the-nbas-lifetime-ban-of-donald-sterling/

5

APPLYING SITUATIONAL CRISIS COMMUNICATION THEORY TO UNIVERSITY NEEDS

A Case Study of the 2015 University of Missouri Crisis

Lindsey A. Sherrill

In the fall of 2015, 32 Black members of the University of Missouri (Mizzou) football team seized national attention when they announced via Twitter that they would boycott the remainder of the season. On November 7, Mizzou defensive back Anthony Sherrils posted:

> The athletes of color on the University of Missouri football team truly believe "Injustice Anywhere is a threat to Justice Everywhere." We will no longer participate in any football related activities until president Tim Wolfe resigns or is removed due to his negligence toward marginalized students' experiences. WE ARE UNITED!!!!!!
>
> *Eppstein & Kisska-Schulze, 2016, p. 71*

The boycott followed racial tensions on the Columbia campus, protests, a student hunger strike, intense media scrutiny, and, ultimately, led to the resignation of the president of the university system and the chancellor of the Columbia campus ("Before protests," 2015; Niesen, 2015; Nocera, 2015). The Mizzou case illustrates a virtual perfect storm of crisis factors, including allegations of institutional racism, leadership ineptitude, and poor community relations (Nocera, 2015), as well the power of student-athlete protest. Edwards, who calls Mizzou a "textbook case" of university response to Black student and student-athlete activism (2016, p. 8), argues that universities, particularly in a social-media-driven world, will continue to face this dual crisis. He writes "if these struggles most legitimately do not take place on our campuses, and particularly within the racism-afflicted cultures and structures of our institutions of higher education—then where?" (p. 11).

Because the crisis faced by Mizzou is reflective of many crises that institutions of higher education face, it was chosen to study the concerns inherent in application of Situational Crisis Communication Theory (SCCT) to university settings. While SCCT has been applied in numerous case and empirical studies to corporate and nonprofit settings (Claeys, Cauberghe, & Vyncke, 2010; Jeong, 2009; Schultz, Utz, & Goritz, 2011), there is limited research on its application in crises at institutions of higher education (Brown, Brown, & Billings, 2015; Effiong, 2014). The purpose of this chapter is to examine Mizzou's institutional response through the lens of SCCT. It will address the concerns of organizational reputation, university identity, and stakeholder needs that are specific to colleges and universities.

Literature Review

Situational Crisis Communication Theory

While each organization and crisis has unique considerations, SCCT presents an empirically tested set of strategies for organizations facing reputational threats (Coombs, 2007). The precrisis period of organizational prevention and preparation was traditionally a private, internal, organizational function. Today the prevalence of social media has allowed stakeholders to publicize allegations of organizational misconduct before the organization itself may even be aware of an issue. This has led to the rise of the *paracrisis*, a publicly managed crisis risk that may evolve into a full-blown crisis as public awareness of issues spreads. SCCT identifies three types of paracrises: the challenge crisis, organizational faux pas, and angry customers (Coombs, 2017). This chapter will focus on the challenge crisis type.

Rather than stemming from one traumatic triggering event, a challenge develops as a reputational crisis as stakeholders communicate the organization's real or perceived failure to live up to its responsibilities (Coombs & Holladay, 2015). The challenge will be exacerbated based on the salience of the involved stakeholders. Salience is based on stakeholders' urgency, legitimacy, and power over the organization. Urgency is both the time pressure stakeholders can exert and their commitment to forcing organizational change. Legitimacy is the ability of the challenging stakeholders to convince others that their claims are important and should be supported. Legitimacy can be supported by using strategic messaging, acquiring resources such as endorsements from more powerful stakeholders, and the use of evidence-based or emotional appeals. Power is the ability of the challenging stakeholders to force change. Power-wielding "definitive stakeholders" use social media messaging to increase their power (Coombs, 2017; Coombs & Holladay, 2015).

Organizations facing challenge crises may respond in six strategic ways: refusal, refutation, repression, recognition/reception, revision, or reform. Refusal involves ignoring the challenge completely, and is best employed against illegitimate challenges. Refutation is used against a challenge that is factually false or that is brought by non-salient stakeholders. Repression attempts to stop the challenge from spreading on the basis that the challenge is falsely damaging to the organization. Repression must be used cautiously to avoid backlash over perceived silencing of critics. Recognition/reception involves addressing the challengers and the legitimacy of their claims, but does not act upon the demands for change. Revision strategy will make small modifications to the organization, but may not acknowledge the challengers' demands as the impetus for change. Finally, reform involves acknowledging the challengers' claims and working with stakeholders to make the necessary organizational changes (Coombs, 2017; Coombs & Holladay, 2015).

Reputation Management and Attribution Theory

Paracrisis challenge strategies are different than the responses organizations may use in an actual crisis, such as a manufacturing disaster, where ethical considerations to reduce physical harm or express sympathy for victims may preclude concern for reputational damage. In either case, crisis managers should assess the situation to determine the level of reputational threat. Coombs (2007) writes that damage to the organization's reputation is one of the foremost considerations in crisis situations and that protecting reputational assets must be paramount in any strategy selection. Reputation is part of an organization's image and is created through media representations of an organization, interpersonal communications both between stakeholders and between stakeholders and outside individuals, and through messages from the organization itself. A threat to reputation occurs when the organization fails to live up to its reputational image, creating an expectation gap. The reputational threat from a crisis is influenced by three factors: initial crisis responsibility, crisis history, and prior relational reputation (Coombs, 2007).

Initial crisis responsibility assessment is driven by attribution theory, which states that perceived causality affects the emotions of those affected by a situation. The more stakeholders attribute control of the creation of a crisis to an organization, the greater the reputational threat (Coombs, 2007). Crisis history of the organization and relationship history with the stakeholders are *intensifiers* to reputational threat, and in combination may lead directly to even greater damage to reputation than attribution (Coombs, 2006). In situations with a strong negative emotional response by stakeholders, more *secondary crisis communication* will occur; that is, individuals outside of the organization will be more likely to share negative information in person or through social media (Coombs, 2007; Schultz et al., 2011).

Strategy consideration must also be given to the *boundary conditions* (such as financial constraints) of the crisis. Perhaps the most important boundary condition is media framing. Information content in a news story may be presented in a straightforward way, but a headline or lead may completely change how the audience interprets the information, such as attribution of responsibility for the crisis. Cultural context is also part of the frame. If an organization is perceived as powerful or in control of its environment, the audience may interpret the organization as having more control over a crisis (Tewksbury & Scheufele, 2009). Secondary crisis communication online will also affect the crisis frames.

Image and Organizational Identity

While image and identity are similar constructs, they have different roles that are especially apparent in controlling reputation for universities. Image is an individual construct comprised of organizational messages, personal experience, interpersonal interaction, media framing, and the interactions of each factor. In the realm of reputation management, a single negative image projection can cancel all prior positive images (Kazoleas, Kim, & Moffitt, 2001). Organizational identity is different than image. Albert and Whetten (1985) posit that identity is tripartite. Identity in organizations consist of the *ideational* ("who are we as a whole?"), the *definitional* ("what kind of organization are we?"), and the *phenomenological* ("who have we been over time?"). Identity in the context of image is *ideational* and relates to both internal and external images of an organization (Whetten, 2006).

Gilpin and Miller (2013) studied identity in the context of nonprofit organizations, such as schools, and introduced the Model of Identity Brokerage. In organizations that depend on a community of stakeholders, boundaries of the organization are loosely defined, and the organization is best viewed as an open system in which all components of image are dynamic and may be individual or systemic and defined by an ongoing process of identity construction (Gilpin & Miller, 2013; Weerts, Freed, & Morphew, 2013). Part one of the model, *intramural identity brokerage*, states that stakeholders within an organization have different individual perceptions. Part two, *external identity brokerage*, involves creating ties with non-members and community relationships. In the context of universities, external identity brokerage depends upon the recruitment, representation, and liaison functions of the organization (Gilpin & Miller, 2013). Kazoleas et al. (2001) also found that community and customer relations had greater impacts on external image than official marketing campaigns, and that interpersonal relationships were more important to image framing than media portrayals. This effect decreases with distance, and media frames will more directly affect image for individuals who only have secondary contact with an institution.

University Identity and Albert and Whetten's Metaphor

In applying SCCT to higher education settings, there are special considerations regarding identity that affect how reputation can and should be managed. Organizations have both an *organizational identity* as a single collective actor and *collective identity* as a consortium of actors. The modern research university has been presented as a metaphor of dual identity as both a church and business (Albert & Whetten, 1985). These two identities are *normative* (e.g., the "missionary work" of the "trinity of missions," of teaching, research, and service; 1985, p. 285) and *utilitarian* (e.g., marketing and fundraising). Universities have diverse groups of stakeholders that exist in each identity. Stakeholders include students, staff, administrators, faculty, parents, alumni, and the communities in which the universities reside (Kazoleas et al., 2001). Each stakeholder has a part in both or either the normative and utilitarian identities. Faculty and students exist in the normative identity of the academic disciplines, while administrators are primarily utilitarian, but must work within the normative framework (Albert & Whetten, 1985). Further complicating this system is the concept of stakeholder loyalty within the normative frame (e.g., faculty members may feel more loyalty to their department or academic discipline than to the institution; Weerts et al., 2013). Reputation management for universities cannot be achieved without understanding the complexities of this ideographic multiplicity (Albert & Whetten, 1985; Gilpin & Miller, 2013; Kazoleas et al., 2001).

Precedent for Student-Athlete Protest

Collegiate athletics occupy a unique position in the study of organizational identity and reputation and thus to crisis reputation management. Student athletes are neither normative nor utilitarian; they are both. As students of the university they are a part of the academic, normative framework. Athletes are representative of the almost spiritual zeal that alumni and fans associate with the rituals of athletic competition. At Mizzou, associated with the monolithic Southeastern Conference (SEC), they are also utilitarian (the football program revenue for 2012–2013 was over $15 million; Brasier, 2015). The apex of Mizzou's challenge was reached only after student athletes lent their voices to the protests.

The Mizzou football team's stand is one in a long history of protests in sports, particularly in college football. In 1934, University of Michigan football players threatened to quit the team rather than play Georgia Tech after Tech demanded that Willis Ward, a Black player, not be allowed to play. Howard University players went on strike over housing conditions and tuition in 1927, 1936, 1968, and in the 1980s. In 1969, the Wyoming Cowboys "Black 14" players were expelled for attempting to protest before their game with Brigham Young University (BYU) in opposition to BYU's racial discrimination. The protest led to a failed lawsuit, but may have been the catalyst for BYU's and the Mormon church's reevaluation of their policies on race. More recent cases include protests at Grambling State in 2013, the University of Alabama at Birmingham in 2014, the University of Illinois in 2015, and Northwestern University in 2015. The Mizzou case is important because "the Missouri football team's 2015 activist effort was not the first of its kind in college sports, but marked one of the most effective and passionate mobilization campaigns in recent college sports history" (Eppstein & Kisska-Schulze, 2016, p. 72).

A 2010 exploratory study of Black college athletes' attitudes toward race and their role as students identified striking differences in student activism before and after the Civil Rights movement. Earlier protests had focused on overt racism and overcoming legal boundaries, while more recent action was geared toward fighting imbedded attitudes. Current Black student athletes expressed a knowledge of prior activism and feelings of responsibility to use their social status to effect change. At the same time, the athletes noted that their sense of responsibility was secondary to personal concerns about their current sports and education duties and future careers (Agyemang, Singer, & Delorme, 2010). This context makes the willingness of the Mizzou team to take a stand even more notable. The players were aware of the risk they were taking and of the public (and permanent!) nature of using social media to announce their boycott.

Applying SCCT: Mizzou's Challenge and Response

The issues at Mizzou leading up to the boycott and Wolfe's resignation illustrate how institutional failure to act strategically can exacerbate a challenge. A lack of coherent messaging from administrative leadership allowed multiple voices to shape the dialogue for the university and its stakeholders. By failing to address issues early, Mizzou allowed the paracrisis to build and took on the attribution for the events that followed. The following sections explore the issues that Mizzou's leadership should have considered to create a strategic response plan.

Challenge Responsibility and History

Administrative Failure

The 2015 challenge escalated through a combination of increasingly frequent campus incidents and failures at the highest levels of administration. The *Wall Street Journal* called racism at Mizzou "the tip of the iceberg" (Korn, Peters, & Belkin, 2015, para. 1). Both Columbia campus chancellor R. Bowen Loftin and university system president Tim Wolfe were unpopular and viewed as inept by faculty long before the football boycott. Wolfe came to Mizzou in 2012 with no experience in higher education leadership. Within three months of his hire, he announced the end of funding to the 50-year-old University of Missouri Press, an action that led to a petition in opposition with over 5,000 signatures. A few months later, Wolfe agreed to reinstate the subsidy, calling the original move "miscalculated" (Korn et al., 2015). The *New York Times* called Wolfe a "command and control" executive (Nocera, 2015, para. 13) who did not understand the compromises required in academia.

Loftin was no more popular. After the 2014 Ferguson, Missouri, riots, Loftin facilitated a campus forum on race issues, but students described the program as uncomfortable and insincere. Even with escalating campus incidents, Loftin called Mizzou's anti-hate and anti-bias programs "robust" (Korn et al., 2015, para. 10). In August of 2015, the administration notified graduate students of changes to their health insurance 13 hours before the cuts would be effective, leading to threats of a graduate student walkout and a campus rally. Loftin also ended a longstanding internship agreement between the medical school and Planned Parenthood. Again, students and faculty were not consulted prior to the action, leading to a campus rally in September against Loftin. Faculty were particularly outspoken against Wolfe and Loftin. They accused Wolfe of refusing to build bridges or to actively engage with faculty and staff, and saw Loftin as bending to outside political pressures or using Wolfe as a scapegoat (Korn et al., 2015). By October, the local off-campus newspaper was publishing editorials and almost daily reports of displeasure with the administration, and on October 31, staff and graduate student unions picketed the football game over labor disputes (*Columbia Daily Tribune online archive*, 2015). In early November, Missouri State Representative Steve Cookson of the Higher Education Committee called for Wolfe to resign over ongoing campus problems beyond the racial incidents (Korn et al., 2015).

Growing Race-Related Tension

Racial tensions were not new at Mizzou. In 1935, Black student Lloyd Gaines was denied admission, leading to a 1938 Supreme Court case. Later, Mizzou formed a separate law school in an abandoned beauty shop rather than allowing Black law students into the main law school. The first Black students were admitted to the university in 1950. During Black History Month 2010, two White students were charged for scattering cotton balls in front of the Black Culture Center (Staples, 2015). In 2011, Mizzou again faced questions of racial bias over the suicide of Black swimmer Sasha Menu Courey after her alleged rape by members of the football team ("Before protests," 2015; MU News Bureau, 2016). Anonymous social media threats were made, presumably by students, to burn down the Black Culture Center in December of 2014. Early in 2015, a Black professor reported being called racial slurs and spat upon while jogging, and other faculty said they too had been the recipients of slurs, even from fellow faculty and staff (Staples, 2015).

By the 2015 fall semester racial problems could no longer be ignored. On September 12, student body president Payton Head reported being harassed on campus. Another student reported a similar incident on October 5. On October 6, the Legion of Black Collegians' homecoming Royalty Court rehearsal was interrupted by several White students who used racial slurs and threatened members of the court. Lofton issued an official press release on October 8 announcing development of mandatory diversity training for faculty and students beginning January

2016, but made no mention of the incidents. During the homecoming parade on October 10, a group of mostly Black students calling themselves Concerned Student 1950 (CS1950) protested, blocking Wolfe's car on the parade route and demanding administrative action. The *Columbia Daily Tribune* reported on October 19 that Wolfe would not address faculty, students, and the public about the homecoming protest and would only respond via email through a spokesperson. This refusal response only increased stakeholder anger. On October 24, a swastika was found smeared in feces in a campus bathroom. On October 27, members of CS1950 met privately with Wolfe, but were unappeased by his response. On November 2, graduate student Jonathan Butler publicly announced that he would be on a hunger strike until Wolfe was removed, stating the purpose of specifically drawing administrative attention to campus racism and homophobia (*Columbia Daily Tribune online archive*, 2015; MU News Bureau, 2016; Niesen, 2015; Nocera, 2015).

Butler's hunger strike marked the beginning of serious national media attention to the situation. Students and faculty, including members of the Mizzou football team, began posting on social media with the hashtag #ConcernedStudent1950 (Eppstein & Kisska-Schulze, 2016). On November 3, the English department faculty voted no-confidence in Loftin and, within a few days, nine deans of other departments signed a letter asking for his dismissal (*Columbia Daily Tribune online archive*, 2015; Korn et al., 2015). The same week, the Missouri Legislative Black Caucus met with CS1950 and called the issues at Mizzou "systemic," and nearly 40 on- and off-campus organizations publicly condemned Loftin for a lack of response to the swastika incident ("Before protests," 2015). Perhaps most damning for the administration was a viral video recorded by a student as Wolfe spoke to those camped out in support of Butler's strike. When asked about the issue of institutional racism, Wolfe said, "I'll give you an answer, and I'm sure it will be the wrong answer. Systematic oppression is because you don't believe you have the equal opportunity for success" (Bajaj, Dietrich, & Marvin, 2016; Nocera, 2015, para. 14). After this refutation of the challengers, onlookers accused Wolfe of blaming students for the administration's failures. By this time, major donors had begun expressing concerns about Mizzou's leadership (Korn et al., 2015). A teleconference was held with CS1950 and alumni leaders who voiced support for the hunger strike, specific protester demands, and the removal of Tim Wolfe. Alumni leaders also suggested that CS1950 speak to members of the athletic department to garner support. On the morning of November 7, CS1950 met with the Alumnae Women's Leadership Group and proclaimed "Racism lives at the University of Missouri and SO DO WE" (Bajaj et al., 2016).

National Attention and Financial Threat

Early on the morning on November 7, a group of Mizzou football players quietly came to the CS1950 campout to express their solidarity with the protesters hours before the official tweet. On film, they issued a statement to the students:

As the football team, we're here to support the movement and use our platform. Let this be a testament to all the other athletes across the country that you do have power. It started with a few individuals on our team and look what it's become. This has become nationally known, but it started with just a few

Bijaj et al., 2016

Later that day, Wolfe issued a public apology for not getting out of his car to face the homecoming protesters and publicly acknowledged the racial strife on campus (*Columbia Daily Tribune online archive*, 2015), but his apology (a recognition/reception response) came too late. By that evening the official boycott statement was on Twitter, and the next day the entire athletics staff pledged their support. Head football coach Gary Pinkel tweeted, "The Mizzou family stands as one. We are united behind our players" (Niesen, 2015). It is important to note that the official Twitter statement was released during the University of Alabama-Louisiana State University rivalry game, insuring that national sports media attention was focused on SEC teams, including Mizzou, at the time of release.

The economic implications of the boycott for Mizzou were impossible to ignore. What had been easy to dismiss as disgruntled students and academics days earlier now had a price tag. The next game versus BYU, less than a week away, would cost the school $1 million if Mizzou was forced to forfeit.

TABLE 5.1 Timeline of the Missouri Paracrisis

2010	Black Culture Center Vandalized
2011	Rape and suicide of Sasha Menu Courey
2012	Wolfe becomes President
2014	Michael Brown shooting and Ferguson, Missouri, riots
12/2014	Social media threats to Black Culture Center
02/2015	Black faculty harassed
08/2015	Graduate student walkouts and rally
09/2015	Rally for Planned Parenthood and against Loftin
09/12/2015	Student body president harassed
10/05/2015	More students report harassment
10/06/2015	*Columbia Daily Tribune* attacks Wolfe and Loftin
10/08/2015	Loftin announces diversity training program
10/10/2015	CS1950 protests homecoming parade
10/19/2015	Local media attacks Wolfe's lack of responsiveness
10/24/2015	Swastikas found on campus
10/27/2015	CS1950 mobilizes protest and campout
11/02/2015	Hunger strike begins
11/03–08/2015	40 organizations, plus Missouri legislature, condemn administration
11/07/2015	Black football players and athletic staff boycott
11/09/2015	Wolfe resigns; Loftin steps down

Forfeiting the next SEC game in two weeks would make Mizzou liable for a portion of the $55 million CBS pad the SEC for yearly television rights. Economist Andy Swartz said, "The issues at Missouri are far more important than college football, but the Missouri athletes showed that the color that matters most is green" (Nocera, 2015, para. 8). In an emergency meeting with the Mizzou Board of Curators on November 9, Wolfe resigned. Within six hours of Wolfe's resignation, Loftin agreed to step down from his role as chancellor (*Columbia Daily Tribune online archive*, 2015).

Reputation, Stakeholders, and Identity

Mizzou entered this challenge with negative reputational assets in race relations. Prior relational history gave stakeholders an expectation that the administration would not handle the situation well and intensified negative emotions. By showing no willingness to change communication or leadership style, Loftin and Wolfe created an expectation of continuing strife stemming from the administration, which further damaged Mizzou's reputation for mishandling systemic issues. Acting quickly with a recognition, revision, or reform challenge response strategy (Coombs, 2017; Coombs & Holladay, 2015) could have slowed or lessened the reputational threat. Schultz et al. (2011) found that simply sharing more information, even without an apology, had positive reputational effects. Official blogs and social media posts were shown to "humanize" an organization and lead to higher reputation and perceived credibility than press releases. During the Loftin-Wolfe tenure, official press releases were infrequent, ignored important issues, and usually only issued for research awards or special events (MU News Bureau, 2016). While it is possible that posts were removed from social media after the crisis, the official Mizzou Facebook account shows no mention of campus troubles until after the resignations (Mizzou, 2015).

In the months prior to and during the challenge, Mizzou's leadership also failed at a vital part of organizational communication—internal communication. The rallies and outcry from graduate students and staff over insurance cuts, the Missouri Press kerfuffle, the issues with the medical school, and even the early incidents of racism may have been smoothed over or completely avoided if leadership had a robust dialogue within the university system. Empirical research on university leaders' communications during a crisis found that "the expectations of key stakeholders dictate that college and university executives not only fulfill a diverse array of roles, but perform each of them graciously and expertly" (Lucas, Linsenmeyer, & O'Brien, 2015). While messaging should not be contradictory, speaking directly to different groups with tailored messages should be a vital part of reputation and crisis management, yet Mizzou's leadership chose to act unilaterally, thus alienating members within the institution.

Mizzou's case is a prime example of the complexity of the stakeholder relationships for universities. As noted in research by Kazoleas et al. (2001), universities expand the corporate owner-employee-customer stakeholder model to one that includes staff, faculty, administrators, students, parents, alumni, and the community. The large-scale nature of the Mizzou case stretches this model even farther. In addition to the stakeholders above, donors, Planned Parenthood of Missouri, and the Missouri State Legislature were involved. Once the boycott was announced, the SEC and its other 13 member institutions were impacted both monetarily (by the possible loss of CBS television revenue from the November 20 game) and strategically (what would a forfeit by the back-to-back SEC East Champion Mizzou mean for rankings and playoff berths?). Mizzou's fans (both alumni and general football fans) were affected by the possible change to the season's hopes and the money lost on tickets to games that might never be played (Brasier, 2015). It is possible to speculate, too, that schools throughout the NCAA (National Collegiate Athletic Association) became stakeholders not only through the ripple effects of changes in football rankings, but also by the precedent that a small group of athletes could band together again in the future to enact such monumental changes to an institution's leadership.

Albert and Whetten (1985) encouraged universities to think of identity as a "self-reflective question" (p. 264). Weerts et al. (2013) explained that, while the post-1980 narrative of university identity focuses on strategy and market responsiveness, stakeholders still attach "special, even spiritual significance to campus ethos, traditions, values, symbols, places, and events" (p. 236). Albert and Whetten wrote: "Educational traditions, symbols, and rituals provide members a much-needed representation of stability and security in their otherwise chaotic life. They enable individuals to periodically reaffirm what they feel are society's core values" (1985, p. 283). This normative significance of ethos and values made perceived institutional racism even more salient, as it was viewed as antithetical to the mission of the university. The challenge created unity against the leadership between the normative (students, alumni, faculty), utilitarian (staff and community), and dual normative-utilitarian (athletics) branches of Mizzou's identity. The boycott proved that, though administrators might be able to ignore demands from young students and minority members, athletics has both symbolic and economic power (Nocera, 2015).

The salience of the diverse stakeholders in this case is noteworthy. Students and faculty had legitimacy, as their complaints were based on daily, lived experience, but they lacked the power to force change. Alumni and donors had monetary power to injure the university, but they lacked urgency, as their withdrawal of support might take years to hurt an institution of Mizzou's size. By far the most salient stakeholders were the football players and athletics staff. They had the legitimacy of being part of the normative framework as students and staff as well as a utilitarian, revenue-generating purpose. They had power through high-profile media exposure and their ability to affect financial harm. The football team also had urgency, as their boycott would cause both financial harm and media attention within six days of challenging the administration. Finally, by endorsing the challenges from other stakeholders, the football team increased the legitimacy of those challengers.

Framing, Secondary and Post-Crisis Communication

While Mizzou could not control how the news media represented the events on campus, Wolfe and Loftin seem to have ignored basic strategic principles for shaping the crisis frames (Coombs, 2007). As noted in the *Columbia Daily Tribune*, Wolfe refused to speak directly with local press, issuing only generic email statements through a spokesperson for his office. In video of his interactions with students both at the homecoming parade and during the hunger strike, Wolfe appeared to enhance the cultural context (Tewksbury & Scheufele, 2009) that Mizzou could control what was happening but was unwilling to do so. When refusal strategy was no longer possible, the administration turned to revision strategies by announcing diversity training and apologizing for only certain incidents (*Columbia Daily Tribune online archive*, 2015). In the days immediately preceding the boycott, Mizzou faced harsh criticism for what was framed as student protesters "whining" about a need for "safe spaces." Students and faculty blocked media from the campout around the hunger strike and refused to give interviews. A mass media instructor, Melissa Click (since fired from Mizzou), was seen in a viral video threatening a journalist, leading to negative national exposure. However, unlike the administration, the student and faculty protesters realized that their refusal to speak was hurting public perceptions. Soon after Wolfe's resignation, students and faculty agreed to speak to the media, citing the need to control their own narrative (Bajaj et al., 2016; Moyer, Miller, & Holley, 2015).

Coombs (2007) and Schultz et al. (2011) state that secondary crisis communication through unofficial channels, such as word of mouth and social media, must be incorporated into crisis strategy. The Mizzou case provides an example of the power of secondary crisis communication for a university. Mizzou's crisis was deemed an "unparalleled social media extravaganza," with over 20,000 tweets mentioning Wolfe's name going out within one hour of his resignation (Eppstein & Kisska-Schulze, 2016, p. 99). While Mizzou's official social media ignored the incidents, students and alumni peppered the comment sections with notes and videos about what was occurring on campus (Mizzou, 2015). There was a flood of *audience-enacted crisis response* (Brown et al., 2015) from stakeholders both within and outside the university attempting to frame the crisis publicly. CS1950 member Imani Simmons-Elloie explained, "We criticize Mizzou because we love it" (Bajaj et al., 2016). Stakeholders outside of the official administration used their external and internal identity brokerage (Gilpin & Miller, 2013) to present a public face of Mizzou through social media and interpersonal communication. This is particularly relevant to the criticism of student "safe spaces." While national media criticized the students, local outlets (like the *Columbia Daily Tribune*) that had personal relationships with people involved were more likely to avoid negative depictions of students.

Aftermath and Ongoing Crisis Communication

After Loftin's demotion, new Columbia Chancellor Hank Foley immediately shifted to reform strategies. Official press releases became an almost daily occurrence, and on November 10 an Interim Vice Chancellor for Inclusion, Diversity, and Equity was appointed to immediately begin addressing the causes and consequences of the crisis (MU News Bureau, 2016). During the next week, when the Black Culture Center sign was defaced and social media threats were made against Black students, the new administration publicly addressed and investigated the issues and reaffirmed their commitment to the safety and emotional wellbeing of all students (Bajaj et al., 2016; MU News Bureau, 2016). Foley released a statement fully explaining the changes to the medical school's partnership with Planned Parenthood, which Loftin had refused to address, and Mizzou created the Office for Civil Rights and Title IX. On December 15, Foley publicly addressed the vandalism and social media threats and subsequent arrests of the previous month. "It is imperative that our students, faculty, staff, and visitors know that when they visit Mizzou, we are doing everything possible to ensure a campus that is welcoming and safe" (MU News Bureau, 2016).

It seems clear that Mizzou's administration should continue using SCCT strategies in the aftermath of the 2015 challenge. In May of 2016, the softball team publicly mobilized against the athletic department, stating, "The administration was completely incompetent in handling the fall football scandal and they are doing a worse job at this" (Eppstein & Kisska-Schulze, 2016, p. 99). Earlier in 2016, several Asian students reported being the targets of racial slurs and discrimination, but claimed the incidents were never fully investigated (Na, 2016). A letter was sent to Interim President Mike Middleton in May 2016 from Jewish student groups claiming anti-Semitism had been ignored during the protests and citing four instances of anti-Semitic graffiti on campus over several months (Suhr, 2016). In September 2016, another racial incident on campus led to the suspension of the Delta Upsilon fraternity, an action that some described as being taken without enough evidence or discussion (Williams, 2016). The fraternity suspension points to the necessity for institutions not to go to overly accommodating strategies (Coombs, 2007) as a knee-jerk reaction in the aftermath of a crisis.

Implications for Theory and Practice

The SCCT framework offers universities many of the same benefits that it gives corporations and nonprofits. SCCT outlines a specific, tested formula for evaluating and acting pre-, during, and post-crisis. However, it is apparent that universities must focus on specific parts of the theory to appropriately handle their unique needs. Universities are open systems, comprised of multiple stakeholder constituencies, each having both a function and a voice in university identity. To manage their reputations, universities must address each of these constituencies. Identity is paramount to university reputation. The normative function of the university creates an almost religious fervor for stakeholders that enhances the emotional components of attribution and may build legitimacy for challengers. Gilpin and Miller's (2013) research on identity brokerage should be a part of strategic planning for universities, as well as more focus on influencing secondary crisis communications. Schultz et al. (2011) found that short Twitter and Facebook posts are the most useful way for institutions to initiate positive secondary crisis communication, and should be posted regularly as part of a strategic communication plan.

Later research by Coombs (2014) suggests adding an evaluation step to SCCT. This step is part of ongoing crisis communication and is vital for institutions to understand and prevent future crises. Coombs offers the idea of a strategic plan of data collection to help organizations understand the needs of their stakeholders. This data should include news and social media monitoring of internal and external stakeholders to identify issues as they develop, internal performance measures for administration, and listening to stakeholders directly (Coombs, 2014).

Finally, colleges and universities must remain aware of the issues that face student athletes and of the power those athletes wield when motivated and organized. As athletic departments continue to hold monetary and symbolic power within universities, they will continue to be salient stakeholders. The Mizzou case and many other examples suggest that universities still fail to recognize this power until forced into confrontation. Edwards (2016) wrote:

> Only time will tell if . . . the University of Missouri and other campuses today will approach the challenges they face with more wisdom, vision, and efficacy—and whether, in the end, they will have longitudinal effects with (or without) leveraging the power potential of Black athletes.
>
> *p. 11*

Identifying Future Theoretical Insights

Future research is still needed to determine how best to apply the principles of SCCT for institutions of higher education. An empirical study of social media responses by stakeholders to crisis strategies at multiple universities could help support the assumptions of secondary crisis communication applicability. More research into the particular dynamics of universities through organizational behavior and systems theory may enable leaders to apply better strategy to reputation and identity management. Finally, this chapter agrees with Effiong's (2014) suggestion that SCCT does not focus enough on communication across the internal and external relationship networks of universities. The interconnecting stakeholder relationships force universities to carefully plan communication strategies and to consider the potential salience of each member of those networks. This complicated relationship suggests a need for more analysis of how stakeholders utilize collective identity and power to build salience, and how organizations may best respond to multifaceted challenges. SCCT is an excellent starting point for university leaders, but at this point may not fully address all their crisis communication needs.

References

Agyemang, K., Singer, J., & Delorme, J. (2010). An exploratory study of black male college athletes' perceptions on race and athlete activism. *International Review for the Sociology of Sport, 45*(4), 419–435.

Albert, S., & Whetten, D. (1985). Organizational identity. In L. L. Cummings & B. Staw (Eds.), *Research in organizational behavior* (vol. 7, pp. 263–295). Greenwich, CN: JAI Press Inc.

Bajaj, V., Dietrich, A., & Marvin, K. (Dir.). (2016) *Concerned Student 1950 [short film]*. United States: Method M Films. Retrieved from https://fieldofvision.org/concerned-student-1950

Before protests, University of Missouri saw decades of race tension. (2015, November 15). *CBS News*. Retrieved from www.cbsnews.com/news/beforeprotestsuniversity ofmissourisawdecadesofracetension/

Brasier, J. (2015, November 9). What's the effect of the Mizzou walkout? *Saturday Down South*. Retrieved from www.saturdaydownsouth.com/sec-football/whats-stake-mizzou-walkout/

Brown, N., Brown, K., & Billings, A. (2015). "May no act of ours bring shame": Fan-enacted crisis communication surrounding the Penn State sex abuse scandal. *Communication & Sport, 3*(3), 288–311.

Claeys, A., Cauberghe, V., & Vyncke, P. (2010). Restoring reputations in times of crisis: An experimental study of the Situational Crisis Communication Theory and the moderating effects of locus of control. *Public Relations Review, 36*(3), 256–262.

Columbia Daily Tribune online archive. (2015, September 1–November 30). Retrieved from: http://archive.columbiatribune.com/

Coombs, W. T. (2006). The protective powers of crisis response strategies: Managing reputational assets during a crisis. *Journal of Promotion Management, 12*(3–4), 241–260.

Coombs, W. T. (2007). Protecting organization reputations during a crisis: The development and application of situational crisis communication theory. *Corporate Reputation Review, 10*(3), 163–176.

Coombs, W. T. (2014). *Ongoing crisis communication: Planning, managing, and responding* (4th ed.). Los Angeles, CA: Sage Publications.

Coombs, W. T. (2017). Revising situational crisis communication theory: The influences of social media on crisis communication theory and practice. In L. Austin & Y. Jin (Eds.), *Social media and crisis communication* (pp. 21–37). New York: Routledge.

Coombs, T., & Holladay, S. (2015). CSR as crisis risk: Expanding how we conceptualize the relationship. *Corporate Communications: An International Journal, 20*(2), 144–162.

Edwards, H. (2016). The promise and limits of leveraging Black athlete power potential to compel campus change. *Journal of Higher Education Athletics & Innovation, 1*(1), 4–13.

Effiong, A. (2014). Managing reputation risk and situational crisis in higher institutions of learning. *Independent Journal of Management & Production, 5*(2), 458–479.

Eppstein, A., & Kisska-Schulze, K. (2016). Northwestern University, the University of Missouri, and the "student-athlete": Mobilization efforts and the future. *Journal of the Legal Aspects of Sport, 26*(2), 71–105.

Gilpin, D., & Miller, N. (2013). Identity brokerage and nonprofit community building. *Journal of Nonprofit & Public Sector Marketing, 25*(4), 354–373.

Jeong, S. (2009). Public's responses to an oil spill accident: A test of the attribution theory and situational crisis communication theory. *Public Relations Review, 35*(3), 307–309.

Kazoleas, D., Kim, Y., & Moffitt, M.A. (2001). Institutional image: A case study. *Corporate Communications: An International Journal, 6*(4), 205–216.

Korn, M., Peters, M., & Belkin, D. (2015, November 10). Race wasn't the only issue at the University of Missouri. *Wall Street Journal.* Retrieved from www.wsj.com/articles/race-not-only-mizzou-issue-1447206995

Lucas, T., Linsenmeyer, W., & O'Brien, K. (2015). Crisis management: An assessment of college and university executive communications prior to the Darren Wilson grand jury decision. *Western Journal of Black Studies, 39*(4), 300–311.

Mizzou. (2015, October 1–November 10). In *Facebook* [official page]. Retrieved October 15, 2016, from www.facebook.com/Mizzou/?fref=ts

Moyer, J., Miller, M., & Holley, P. (2015, November 10). Mass media professor under fire for confronting video journalist at Mizzou. *Washington Post.* Retrieved from www.washingtonpost.com/news/morning-mix/wp/2015/11/10/video-shows-u-of-missouri-protesters-and-journalism-professor-barring-media-coverage/

MU News Bureau. (2016, October 6). *News releases.* Retrieved from http://munews.missouri.edu/news-releases/

Na, S. (2016, February 3). MU's Asian students reluctant to report episodes of discrimination, racism. *Columbia Missourian.* Retrieved from www.columbiamissourian.com/news/higher_education/mu-s-asian-students-reluctant-to-report-episodes-of-discrimination/article_e384936e-963b-11e5-8813-c34632bd9101.html

Niesen, J. (2015, November 16). Power play. *Sports Illustrated*, 14–15.

Nocera, J. (2015, November 10). Athletes' potential realized in resignations. *New York Times*, B10.

Schultz, F., Utz, S., & Goritz, A. (2011). Is the medium the message? Perceptions of and reactions to crisis communication via twitter, blogs and traditional media. *Public Relations Review, 37*(1), 20–27.

Staples, B. (2015, November 10). A history of racism at the University of Missouri. *New York Times.* Retrieved from http://takingnote.blogs.nytimes.com/2015/11/10/a-history-of-racism-at-the-university-of-missouri/

Suhr, J. (2016, May 5). Jewish group faults MU's anti-Semitism response. *Columbia Missourian.* Retrieved from www.columbiamissourian.com/news/higher_education/jewishgroupfaultsmusantisemitismresponse/article_0e3c76b1aed355ddae1b0ca67c56e879.html

Tewksbury, D., & Scheufele, D. A. (2009). News framing theory and research. In J. Bryant & M. B. Oliver (Eds.), *Media effects: Advances in theory and research* (pp. 17–34). New York/London: Routledge.

Weerts, D., Freed, G., & Morphew, C. (2013). Organizational identity in higher education: Conceptual and empirical perspectives. In M. Paulsen (Ed.), *Higher education: Handbook of theory and research* (pp. 229–278). New York: Springer.

Whetten, D. (2006). Albert and Whetten revisited. *Journal of Management Inquiry, 5*(3), 219–234.

Williams, M. R. (2016, September 29). Some University of Missouri students want campus hate speech punished. *Kansas City Star.* Retrieved from www.kansascity.com/news/local/article105048746.html

6

KNEE-JERK POLICYMAKING IN CRISIS RESPONSE

A Fumbled Play by the NFL

Jennifer L. Harker

The National Football League (NFL) endures reputational challenges regularly. Numerous off-field accounts of personnel and player indiscretions trigger many of these reputational challenges. The league, as an organization, continues to explore ways to address and eliminate these types of controversies from harming the reputation of the organization. Unfortunately, the league's response to deviant off-field behaviors only adds to the growing controversy. In fact, the league's actions have resulted in increasingly significant public outcry from fans, lawmakers, and a variety of other stakeholders. This chapter focuses on the NFL's reactive conduct policies and the long-lasting, challenging stakeholder reactions to those policies. This chapter focuses in particular on the 2014/2015 NFL season, when the league was embattled with an onslaught of societal and moral transgressions committed by NFL players. The 2014/2015 policy update is examined via the conceptual framework of crisis assessment offered within Situational Crisis Communication Theory (SCCT). In sum, this chapter explores the organizational crisis communication efforts extended by the NFL during times of reputational challenge and how the subsequent stakeholder response to those efforts further amplified reputational challenges.

Inside the NFL

The American Professional Football Association (APFA) formed in 1920. On June 24, 1922, the name of the APFA was changed to the National Football League (NFL). The commissioner oversees all operations of the NFL and holds the governing authority over the organization. Each of the 32 member teams of the league is an individually owned, for-profit entity (with the exception of the Green Bay Packers, which is citizen-owned). The teams pay annual membership dues to the NFL, which runs off of an annual budget of more than $326 million, according to the organization's 2012 fiscal year Form 990.

The NFLeague Players Association (NFLPA) was established in 1956 to protect the rights of NFL players in matters ranging from salary to health insurance. In 1977, the NFLPA and the NFL management council created and agreed upon a collective bargaining agreement (CBA). The CBA was ratified to protect the respective interests of players and the league. Before the CBA, much unrest had occurred concerning college drafts, player strikes, unfair compensation, pension payouts, and numerous other matters. The CBA was updated and/or extended in 1982, 1993, 1998, 2001, 2002, 2006, 2007, 2011, and 2012. The NFL Foundation was established in 2012 as a result of the 2012 agreement. The 2012 CBA also "reaffirmed the NFL Commissioner's disciplinary authority" ("NFL record & fact book," 2013, p. 362).

Historic Deviance and Reactive Policymaking in the NFL

The Commissioner's role in policing disciplinary action spiked in the 1990s with an uptick in player off-field deviance. For example, between the 1996 and 1997 seasons, the league reportedly recorded a 1-in-5 rate, or 20 percent tendency, for crime (Benedict & Yaeger, 1999). In fact, the NFL demonstrates higher-than-average crime rate among American athletes.

The lack of regulation in professional sport correlates with consistently high crime rates among professional athletes (Berry & Smith, 2000). Under Commissioner Paul Tagliabue, the league's 10,000th regular season game was played in 1997 and with it came the NFL's first version of a conduct policy ("NFL record & fact book," 2013). The purpose of the Violent Crime Policy was to supplement what was lacking in the NFL's CBAs. Denard Walker, who was drafted in 1997 and played as a cornerback for the Tennessee Oilers, was the first player disciplined under Tagliabue's new policy (Fainaru-Wada & Fainaru, 2014). Walker was arrested during the off-season in 1999 for threatening, punching, and attempting to strangle the mother of his son. Although the incident occurred in July 1999, the incident was not reported publicly until January 2000, when the Tennessee team played in the playoffs and ultimately went on to compete in that season's Super Bowl ("Walker probation," 2000). News reports stated that Walker's coach was aware when the arrest occurred (Murray-Garrigan, 2000), but no NFL-mandated punishment was handed down until the next season ("Titan Sidney," 2000).

The policy was later renamed the Personal Conduct Policy when updated in 2007, shortly after Roger Goodell assumed the Commissioner position and following the 2006 season, when yet another sharp increase in NFL personnel arrests occurred (Barrabi, 2014; "Goodell suspends Pacman," 2007; Schrotenboer, 2015). For instance, during that season nine Cincinnati Bengals players were arrested for various reasons. Adam "Pacman" Jones was among the most mediated reputational challenges for the league at that time. Jones was involved in a series of alleged crimes, including a fight and shooting at a strip club in Las Vegas, Nevada. Goodell reportedly wrote to the players, "Your conduct has brought embarrassment and ridicule upon yourself, your club, and the NFL, and has damaged the reputation of players throughout the league," ("Goodell suspends Pacman," 2007, para. 5). Goodell's updated and renamed policy featured longer suspension and stricter penalties than Tagliabue's Violent Crime Policy.

This chapter focuses on Goodell's third update of the policy, which occurred during the 2014/2015 season. Following is an overview and analysis of Goodell's latest reactive policy targeted to counter reputational challenges during yet another NFL season riddled with player misconduct.

NFL Communications Announces Policy Updates

The NFL's media releases pertaining to any incidences of an NFL-related perceived transgression, personnel misconduct, unlawful behavior, or any other reputational challenge involving a player, coach, coordinator, owner, or administrator employed or otherwise professionally associated with the NFL, were collected. The timeframe of collected materials are representative of the duration of the off-season leading to the 2014/2015 season, including the entirety of the 2014/2015 season, the playoff season, and the Super Bowl. Therefore, the time period studied in this chapter includes February 1, 2014 to February 28, 2015.

All NFL media releases were gathered directly from the communication and media relations websites of the NFL via NFL.com, NFLCommunications.com, and NFLMedia.com. All press releases, media releases, statements, infographics, publications, and announcements were saved electronically. Any release that strictly focused on the statistics of football players and games, the scheduling of NFL games, announcements concerning the availability of games watched via online sources (e.g., NFL.com, etc.), the deciphering of opponents in an upcoming season, new NFL products, NFL product placement, NFL Films announcements, and, finally, new online NFL apps or other unrelated online or mobile resource announcements (e.g., the NFL Now app), were eliminated from study.

All "From the Commissioner" transcripts, which recorded five Roger Goodell press conferences, were also collected and included in this analysis. In total, 52 documents were identified as pertinent and usable. The releases were categorized as corrective action strategies (n = 34) and ingratiation strategies (n = 18).

SCCT and Crisis Assessment

This chapter's focus rests within the conceptual framework of crisis assessment and blame placement concerning reputational threats, as noted within Situational Crisis Communication Theory (SCCT). Three factors assess the reputational challenges inherent in crisis: crisis responsibility (who is to blame), crisis history (how often the crisis has occurred), and prior reputation and relationship (Coombs, 2007). Crisis assessments are also shaped by the amount of observable evidence, meaning each crisis can range from ambiguous evidence to a veracity of evidence. Adjusting information is both an ethical response (Coombs, 1995) and a prescriptive strategy to redirect the affective and behavioral responses to a crisis. Corrective action is one form of adjusting information, and the coupling of a secondary strategy such as ingratiation can aid in the increased stakeholder acceptance of that primary remediation attempt.

The NFL's reaction to the reputational challenges during the 2014/2015 season necessitated corrective action due to the social and moral wrong-doings repeatedly carried out by the league's players. To explain, crisis responsibility eventually shifted from the players who carried out the wrongful acts onto the league due to mounting crisis history, or repeated offenses, that occurred throughout the season. In other words, the NFL's stakeholders looked to the league to provide the adjustments necessary to halt such repeated unacceptable acts by its players.

Stakeholders

Stakeholders must be accepting of the corrective action in order for the adjusted information to be successful in remediating the crisis situation (Coombs & Holladay, 2008). Stakeholder perceptions are key considerations because they trigger reputational assessment and subsequent behavioral reactions (Coombs, 2007). A stakeholder is defined as any associated person or group who effects or is affected by the organization's actions. Stakeholders include the media, government, employees, local community, suppliers, competitors, special interest groups, stockholders, consumers, and unions. For the NFL, stakeholders include the past and present players and staff of the 32 individual teams, the NFL Players Association, fans, all NFL conglomerate business partners, sponsors, advertisers, and partnered and at-large mass media outlets, to name a few. Stakeholders also include all 32 cities in which each NFL teams exists—including the residents, city governments, media outlets in each of those cities, all fans, and even nonfans.

The NFL's 2014/2015 Season

Brent Schrotenboer, a *USA Today* sports reporter, compiled a database during the 2014/2015 season of NFL arrests dating back to 2000. Schrotenboer conducted extensive research on the NFL and its players in response to the multitude of reports about the NFL's reputational challenges due to player deviant behaviors. The *USA Today* database reported a total of 783 arrests, charges, or citations involving NFL players between January 1, 2000 and March 1, 2015. The four most common charges, according to that database, include DUI, drug use or possession, assault, and domestic violence (Schrotenboer, 2015). Schrotenboer's articles and database listed 50 cases of domestic violence involving NFL players that occurred since Goodell took the Commissioner's office in 2006 until the completion of the 2014/2015 season. The domestic violence incidents involving players resulted in 16 that received no suspension, 14 resulted in a one-game suspension, and 15 received "grandstand justice" and were suspended for long periods of time or dropped completely from playing in the league (Schrotenboer, 2014, para. 5). Schrotenboer argued those dropped from the league were not "high status" players and were simply "grandstanded" as an act of social justice on behalf of Goodell and the NFL (Schrotenboer, 2014, para. 5).

The remainder of this chapter focuses on the domestic violence reputational challenges the NFL faced in 2014/2015. The Personal Conduct Policy (henceforth "PCP") and related materials issued by the NFL is analyzed. Please note, however, that other policies were rereleased in 2014, such as an updated drug policy and a "re-emphasized" sportsmanship policy ("Joint NFL-NFLPA statement on changes," 2014; "Joint NFL-NFLPA statement on wide-ranging," 2014). SCCT's reputational threats typology, coupled with observable evidence, guides this analysis (Coombs, 2007). Finally, strategies are categorized under corrective action and ingratiation.

Domestic Violence During the NFL's 2014/2015 Season

In 2014, nine arrests occurred for physically aggressive behavior and six additional arrests for physically aggressive acts against a child, spouse, or family member. Six highly mediated domestic violence incidents involving NFL players occurred throughout the 2014/2015 season. The players involved were Ray McDonald, Quincy Enunwa, Jonathan Dwyer, Greg Hardy, Ray Rice, and Adrian Peterson. Each of their cases is briefly explained in this section.

On August 30, 2014, Ray McDonald, a defensive end with the San Francisco 49ers, was arrested for physical violence against his pregnant fiancée at a party at their shared residence (Schrotenboer, 2015). The arresting officer on the scene moonlighted as a security guard for the 49ers (Aleaziz & Sernoffsky, 2014). Prosecutors dropped the case in November 2014 due to insufficient information, even though McDonald's pregnant fiancée had visible bruises (Aleaziz & Sernoffsky, 2014). The NFL took no disciplinary action against McDonald, such as the policy's stated minimum two-game suspension, throughout the duration of the investigation, nor thereafter.

Following, on September 4, 2014, Quincy Enunwa, a wide receiver on the practice squad for the New York Jets, was arrested and charged with simple assault after an incident with his girlfriend at a hotel in Florida. She dropped the charges in exchange for a 90-day restraint order. Because all charges against Enunwa were dropped, neither his team nor the NFL disciplined him for the incident (Slater, 2014).

Another account of domestic violence occurred on September 17, 2014, when Jonathan Dwyer, an Arizona Cardinals running back, was arrested for aggravated assault when he head-butted his wife and broke her nose in front of their 18-month-old son. He pled guilty to disorderly conduct and was sentenced to perform community service and serve 18 months of probation. The team deactivated him for the remainder of the season. By the end of February 2015, Dwyer was listed as a free agent.

Greg Hardy, a defensive end for the Carolina Panthers, was arrested on May 13, 2014, when a woman reported that he had assaulted and threatened her (Schrotenboer, 2015). Hardy played the first game of the 2014 season, but he was added to the exempt list beginning September 17, reportedly until the domestic violence case was legally resolved. Being on the Commissioner's exempt list allowed him to still receive his $13.1 million salary, but he could not play or practice with his team. No actual game suspension happened for Hardy. Hardy instead remained on the NFL exempt list throughout the season. His ex-girlfriend, whom he reportedly struck and threatened, made a deal with prosecutors in exchange for a payout from Hardy and a restraint order. Charges were dropped against Hardy on February 9, 2015. Hardy was reinstated with the NFL thereafter and soon after recruited by the Dallas Cowboys ("Cowboys sign," 2015).

The most controversial incident of domestic violence over the course of the 2014/2015 season was the case involving Ray Rice, a running back who played for the Baltimore Ravens. Rice reportedly punched his then-fiancée, Janay Palmer, in the face, knocking her unconscious, and dragged her from an elevator at an Atlantic City casino ("Ray Rice suspended," 2014). When the incident was first reported in February 2014, Rice was ordered to partake in the diversion program offered by the NFL, fined, and he received a two-game suspension that was slated for the first two games of the regular season to begin in September 2014. He also publicly apologized for his actions. Goodell had set Rice's two-game suspension under the existing 2007 PCP. He also defended his charging Rice with a two-game suspension and was quoted by *Time Magazine* on August 1, 2014 as stating that he stood by the decision (Worland, 2014).

The first week of the 2014/2015 regular season kicked off with video footage released publicly by *TMZ* of the actual act of Rice punching his fiancée ("Ray Rice elevator," 2014). The video enraged the public. Although the act and details of Rice punching his fiancée was already known, actually seeing the brutality of the event on video, and seeing Janay lying on the floor unconscious, brought on a whole new level of reputational challenge. This veracity of evidence resulted in increased public outrage and subsequent pushback. Immediately following the video release, Goodell announced Rice's suspension had been indefinitely extended and the Ravens dropped Rice from the team. No circumstances had changed in the case, however, except for the release of the actual video footage.

The one child abuse incident that occurred during the 2014/2015 season involved Adrian Peterson, a Minnesota Vikings running back. He was indicted on

September 11, 2014, for felony child abuse after repeatedly striking his 4-year-old son with a tree branch ("Adrian Peterson suspended," 2014). He pled no contest to a lesser charge of misdemeanor reckless assault and was fined $4,000 and required to complete 80 hours of community service (Schrotenboer, 2015; "United States District Court," 2015). Peterson was later suspended by the NFL for the rest of the 2014/2015 season, without pay, under the rules of the newly updated PCP ("Adrian Peterson suspended," 2014). The release announcing the season-long suspension noted that Peterson originally was suspended for six games, but that "aggravating circumstances would warrant higher levels of discipline" ("Adrian Peterson suspended," 2014, para. 4). This was in reference to his case involving a "particularly vulnerable person such as a child."

Corrective Action

As noted above, SCCT prescribes adjusting information for physical or psychological coping in response to crises. Corrective action is one form of adjusting information and, due to the nature of the crises during the 2014/2015 season, corrective action was prescriptive and necessary for the NFL to employ. For example, the Rice video offered the public and stakeholders a veracity of evidence for NFL-connected domestic violence, which thus increased crisis responsibility. Such a veracity of evidence coupled with the repeated occurrences of similar reports throughout the season, or increased crisis history, resulted in higher attributions of blame. Arguably, the blame attribution and reputational challenges from this troubled season eventually transferred from the players who allegedly committed the violent acts onto the NFL organization instead. In other words, as the number of occurrences grew, the league endured less favorable reputational reviews (Schrotenboer, 2015).

Negative affective and behavioral reactions from stakeholders increased in tandem with the less favorable reputational perceptions. Domestic violence groups, governmental oversight committees, and other advocates against such physically aggressive acts challenged the NFL to institute harsher discipline for players who are physically abusive off the field. Throughout the season, a highly noted and cited hashtag campaign spread throughout social media outlets, where people shared their individual domestic violence stories about #WhyIStayed or #WhyILeft while challenging the NFL to take a stand. The pressure was building on the league to protect "particularly vulnerable groups" and to stop the violent off-field behavior from recurring. Even the government got involved. Additional outcry from U.S. Senator John Thune (R-South Dakota), ranking member and then-incoming chairman of the Senate Committee on Commerce, Science, and Transportation, resulted in a Capitol Hill challenge for all sports leagues to develop a more sufficient policy to address the domestic violence prevalence among professional athletes (Patel, 2014; "Senators praise NFL conduct," 2014; "Statement of Troy Vincent," 2014; Strong, 2014).

The NFL applied corrective action by updating and rereleasing the Personal Conduct Policy. This corrective action was in response to the public outcry that specifically challenged the NFL to institute harsher discipline for players who are physically abusive off the field. The punishment guidelines for a domestic violence charge in the updated policy increased from a two-game suspension to a six-game suspension as a direct response to that accountability and discursive pushback.

Commissioner Goodell officially announced the newly updated NFL PCP on December 10, 2014, at a league meeting held in Dallas, Texas ("NFL Commissioner," 2014; "Personal Conduct Policy," 2014). The newly updated PCP included few changes from the PCP Goodell released in 2007, which was a re-formation of the original 1997 Violent Crime Policy. This latest updated PCP was eight pages in length. The PCP included the following statements:

> In order to uphold our high standards, when violations of this Personal Conduct Policy do occur, appropriate disciplinary action must follow. With regard to violations of the Personal Conduct Policy that involve assault, battery, domestic violence, dating violence, child abuse and other forms of family violence, or sexual assault involving physical force or committed against someone incapable of giving consent, a first offense will subject the offender to a baseline suspension without pay of six games, with consideration given to any aggravating or mitigating factors. The presence of possible aggravating factors may warrant a longer suspension. Possible aggravating factors include, but are not limited to, a prior violation of the Personal Conduct Policy, similar misconduct before joining the NFL, violence involving a weapon, choking, repeated striking, or when an act is committed against a particularly vulnerable person, such as a child, a pregnant woman, or an elderly person, or where the act is committed in the presence of a child. A second offense will result in permanent banishment from the NFL.
>
> *"Personal Conduct Policy," 2014, p. 6*

The language used above was deliberative. Parts of the PCP's additions are an overuse of the key words that brought on the organization's reputational challenges.

Furthermore, the PCP clearly reads, "Initial decisions regarding discipline will be made by a disciplinary officer, a member of the league office staff who will be a highly-qualified individual with a criminal justice background" ("Personal Conduct Policy," 2014, p. 5), but Goodell did not await such a process when he suspended Rice and Peterson. In so doing, his actions allowed for the players to appeal their respective suspensions ("Former U.S. District Judge," 2014).

The league's new PCP additionally stated legal proceedings surrounding the deviant behavior should first be settled before taking a definitive stance on discipline. "If you are convicted of a crime or subject to a disposition for a criminal proceeding (as defined in this Policy), you are subject to discipline" ("Personal Conduct Policy," 2014, p. 2). In the Rice case, Goodell did not announce the two-game suspension until after the court accepted Rice's plea to participate in a diversion program to expunge the act from his record after one year. Such passive language in the policy offers the NFL numerous excuses and possibility for delays when pressured to discipline for such acts.

The PCP featured other loose, noncommittal language concerning the specifics of discipline. For example, the following excerpt shows no definitive NFL approach on discipline. "Depending on the nature of the violation and the record of the employee, discipline may be a fine, a suspension for a fixed or an indefinite period of time, a requirement of community service, a combination of the three, or banishment from the league" ("Personal Conduct Policy," 2014, p. 6). Such loosely defined language enabled the league to make excuses case-by-case in its disciplinary actions, which is exactly what happened in the Hardy case.

The lack of streamlined discipline was placed on the loose verbiage of the PCP, which states that the league can await law proceedings before a definitive punishment. In cases in which a violation relating to a crime of violence is suspected but further investigation is required, the Commissioner may determine to place a player on leave with pay to permit the league to conduct an investigation ("Key elements," 2014). Based on the results of the investigation, the player or employee may return to duty, be placed on leave with pay for a longer period, or be subject to discipline ("Personal conduct," 2014, p. 5). Three players were exonerated from their respective domestic violence charges because the victim in each of those cases declined to testify, refused to press charges, or cut a deal. The league did not discipline McDonald or Enunwa, but Hardy was put on the exempt list (Newton, 2014).

The inconsistencies that accompanied the NFL's corrective action made it difficult for the public and stakeholders to be accepting of the attempted adjusting information. Recall that adjusting information aids in the stakeholders' ability to psychologically cope with the crisis. The veracity of evidence concerning the series of player transgressions off the field caused both negative affective and behavioral reactions, thus increasing the reputational threats for the league overall. The attempted corrective action, while prescriptive, was carried out with many inconsistencies. More on this follows in the sections below, but first a review of the NFL's secondary strategy of ingratiation is discussed.

Ingratiation Strategies

The PCP, and the accompanying package of releases, also offered ample ingratiation strategies. The league, on NFLCommunications.com, posted a packaged group of media releases and other documents with the release of the updated PCP. Among the releases was an announcement that Goodell had named a "conduct committee" ("Conduct committee," 2014). The release noted that "nine representatives of NFL ownership" make up the inaugural committee membership ("Conduct committee," 2014; "New NFL Personal," 2014). Another press release included in that package announced that the players "unanimously endorsed" the PCP ("NFL teams unanimously," 2014). In the player endorsement release, the conduct committee members are named. The Commissioner's chosen committee was not free from representing teams that had players who have been arrested for past deviant behaviors. In fact, all of the represented teams had many prior player arrests since 2000, all but one had at least one player arrested in the 2014/2015 season, and one player from the team of the chairman of the conduct committee was arrested for domestic violence during the 2014/2015 season, just prior to the December construction of the committee.

The NFL highlighted that governmental leaders applauded its efforts with the updated PCP ("Senators praise NFL conduct," 2014). Another release focused on the "benefits" offered to NFL-related personnel who violate the PCP ("NFL teams unanimously," 2014). This positive spin on the punishment for bad behavior states the "privilege" working under the NFL shield brings, because even when in trouble the NFL will increase education and expand services to all NFL employees, survivors, children, and families ("NFL's response," 2014).

The league also announced its collaboration with several special interest groups that voiced concern over the repetitive domestic violence incidents ("NFL consults," 2014). This particular release included a list of experts and organizations with which the NFL consulted in updating its PCP from a two-game suspension to a six-game suspension for acts of domestic violence, specifically. Most of the entities listed are domestic violence and sexual abuse nonprofit organizations, and included the NFLPA, the National Football Players Fathers Association (NFPFA), the Professional Football Players Mothers Association (PFPMA), and the NFL Wives Organization. This particular ingratiation strategy shows stakeholders that the league is including external groups and highlights that individuals closest to its players are both responsible for and in agreement with the updated PCP.

The league's ingratiation efforts also highlighted the NFL's updated "Mission and Values." The release included subheadings that highlight "leadership," "respect," "integrity," "responsibility to team," and "resiliency" ("Mission and Values," 2014). These ideographs were an attempt to symbolically address the ongoing reputational crisis and apply positive descriptors the league wishes to akin to its reputation (McGee, 1980). For example, the "integrity" section read:

"We do the right thing when no one is looking, and even if it's unpopular when they are looking. We demand accountability and we expect fair play" ("Mission and Values," 2014, para. 4).

The truthfulness of the release and its claims come into question, however, because a search of the NFL Communications microsite, the NFL website, and a general Google.com search turned up no other NFL mission statement, or mission and values statement or policy, at that time.

Additional ingratiation attempts by the NFL included personnel changes ("NFL names Capitol Hill," 2015; "NFL names Dawn Hudson," 2014; "NFL names former White House," 2014), sponsorship and advertising deals, and announcements on record-breaking viewership ("NFL opener," 2014). The PCP-packaged releases touted plentiful donations offered to entities that serve the overarching social disparities for which the NFL was under fire, such as domestic violence, child abuse, and brain trauma organizations. Several financial donations were given to nonprofit entities located in Phoenix, Arizona, which was that season's Super Bowl city (Graff, 2015, January 29; Graff, Gordon, & McCollum, 2015; "Katy Perry," 2015). Also, the league donated a $4.5 million 30-second commercial spot during the Super Bowl to the No More Campaign, complete with access to the league's internal advertising agency to help the domestic violence prevention organization create the public service announcement (Hess, 2015).

The ingratiation strategies were mostly successful for reputational remediation with external stakeholders. The combination of bolstering the updated policies, announcing donations, and the highlighting and promotion of the support and collaboration of a variety of social organizations aided in the psychological coping of the public and thus increased the public's positive reputational assessment of the league. Unfortunately, these many ingratiation strategies were not enough to overcome the inconsistent corrective action strategies, which is discussed in more detail in the next section.

Effectiveness of the NFL's Policy

Crisis history and the veracity of evidence influenced crisis responsibility and increased blame placement. The combination of these matters resulted in negative affective and behavioral outcomes due to negative assessments of the league's reputation (Coombs, 2004, 2007). These crisis perceptions combine to make the NFL's knee-jerk policymaking ineffective in response to the reputational challenges of the 2014/2015 season. Inconsistencies in carrying out the prescriptive corrective actions are where the league went wrong in remediating the ongoing crises. This resulted in increased instead of decreased attribution of blame. To explain, the league could have effectively scapegoated any attribution of blame had the league been consistent across disciplinary actions. That consistency would have been effective in leaving the blame placement on the players guilty of the wrong-doing (Coombs, 1995). The problems increased during the 2014/2015 season, however, because so many instances occurred in such a short amount of time and each case was disciplined differently. Attribution of blame was resultantly placed on the league instead of the perpetrating individual. Again, this reaches back to the three factors of crisis perceptions in SCCT: crisis responsibility, crisis history, and past reputation and relationship. Each of those three factors included negative affective perceptions, and the inconsistencies in corrective action only increased those negative perceptions.

As crisis responsibility shifted onto the league, some players were even sympathized with as victims themselves, instead of the perpetrators of the social and moral wrong-doings that spurred the crises throughout the season. For example, stakeholder groups such as the NFLPA were key in this resultant shift, because the NFLPA challenged the NFL's inconsistent corrective action strategies. The NFLPA filed appeals on behalf of Rice and Peterson for the disciplinary actions and extended suspensions that were outside of what the PCP and the players' CBAs defined. The most vehement argument between the NFL and the NFLPA that season was spurred by Peterson's child abuse case and lengthy suspension. The NFLPA argued in its appeal that Peterson was only reprimanded by the NFL because of the timing of his incident. Peterson's case was publicized during the throes of when Commissioner Goodell was in America's hot seat over the Ray Rice elevator incident and the rampant publicity over "the NFL's historically lenient treatment of acts of domestic violence" (NFLPA v. National Football League, 2015, p. 3). The NFLPA argued that Goodell only revised the PCP in response to the public and media outcries encircling the Rice incident because the most substantial update to the PCP was the change from the two-game maximum suspension for first-time offenders of domestic violence to a six-game suspension.

Peterson was suspended for six games under the new domestic violence rule but Goodell also requested that Peterson seek counseling, and only upon the results reported at the end of the therapeutic program might Peterson be reinstated to play again in the NFL. The NFLPA felt that Peterson's CBA, signed August 4, 2011, should be the determining policy for his discipline and the NFLPA challenged Goodell and the NFL for the lengthy suspension and the order to seek therapy (NFLPA, 2015). The NFLPA argued that Peterson's incident of corporal punishment of his 4-year-old son in May 2014 preceded the newly updated PCP, which was released the following December ("Petition filed," 2014). The NFLPA asked Goodell to step down from leading the proceedings concerning Peterson's punishment. Goodell consented and appointed Harold Henderson, a longtime employee of the NFL organization. Henderson upheld the original NFL mandated disciplinary actions. The NFLPA subsequently appealed.

The dust had not yet settled in the Peterson case appeals when the Goodell-appointed conduct committee chairman, Michael Bidwill (Arizona Cardinals), began actively recruiting Peterson from the Vikings team. Meanwhile, Rice won his appeal and was awarded half of his salary, or $1.588 million, in a wrongful termination case he won against the Baltimore Ravens (Fredericks, 2014; Verderame, 2015). He was also offered a $1 million contract from ProDraftLeague. com ("TMZ: Ray Rice," 2015), and Mark Tadros, CEO of the fantasy football league website, was quoted as saying, "Mr. Rice has shown deep remorse for his act of domestic violence and I feel he deserves a second chance" ("TMZ: Ray Rice," 2015, para, 3).

The NFLPA's costly appeals to disciplinary action mandated by the NFL have since become commonplace. Several seasons later, the league still faces continued reputational challenges stemming from the PCP and the inconsistencies in disciplinary action. Each time the costly process is lengthened by months and in some cases years, and the reputational challenges are also stretched along that timeline. Such cases serve as prime examples for the importance of consistent corrective action strategies. Similar responsive legal appeals include the Tom Brady and Deflategate case in 2016 and the Ezekiel Elliot domestic violence case in 2017. These legal cases extend the crisis storyline and increase negative reputation perceptions of the NFL, instead of increasing the negative reputation perceptions of the players who carried out the wrong-doings.

Crisis history, one of the three factors in assessing organizational crisis, was proven key in crisis assessment of the 2014/2015 season. Repeated acts by the players throughout the season resultantly transferred blame onto the league due to the onslaught of cases, which coupled with the incidences from past seasons even decades prior. Second, crisis responsibility shifted from the individuals who allegedly committed domestic violence onto the league that was not stopping its players from committing these harmful acts. These matters were further complicated by the inconsistencies in discipline, which was at the epicenter of the league's corrective action, and the lack of dissociation between the league and the players who carried out the wrong-doings. This resultantly increased the negative reputational challenges for the NFL. Third, prior reputation and relationship came into question due to prior similar wrong-doings. All three factors were further enhanced by the ongoing legal appeals following inconsistent disciplinary actions, which coupled with increased media coverage concerning each appeal and the subsequent rulings. The NFLPA won both the Rice and Peterson cases, for example. As a result, each reputational challenge carried out by NFL players increased the reputational threat for the next one to come, thus eventually transferring blame to the league for allowing such behaviors to continue.

Conclusion

The NFL's reactivity to crises has long been evident, as historical instances have proven. The 1997 Violent Crime Policy, the 2007 Personal Conduct Policy, and the updated 2014 Personal Conduct Policy each exhibit similar reactiveness to player deviance of those time periods in NFL history. The reputational threats during the 2014/2015 season necessitated corrective action for stakeholder psychological coping; however, the inconsistencies in that corrective action resulted in even more negative affective and behavioral outcomes for the league.

Overall, the NFL's inconsistent remediation strategies resulted in harsher crisis assessment and the shift of attribution of blame placed on the league instead of the individual players who committed the wrong-doings. Had the league preemptively had a comprehensive policy and stuck with consistent disciplinary actions, the league could have scapegoated blame attribution because the reputational challenges would have remained with the players.

This case study highlights the importance of strategic, proactive, and consistent policymaking when tackling controversial or ongoing topics. Consistency is key in sticking to the policy in every instance, no matter the star quality of each player. Unfortunately, the knee-jerk policymaking during the 2014/2015 season created insurmountable divisiveness among the NFL's stakeholders, and the league resultantly endured repeated reputational challenges as a result.

References

Adrian Peterson suspended without pay for at least the remainder of 2014 season. (2014, November 18). *NFL*. Retrieved from http://nflcommunications.com/2014/11/18/adrian-peterson-suspended-without-pay-for-at-least-the-remainder-of-2014-season/

Aleaziz, H., & Sernoffsky, E. (2014, November 10). 49ers' Ray McDonald not charged in domestic violence case. *SFGate.com*. Retrieved from www.sfgate.com/bayarea/article/49ers-Ray-McDonald-not-charged-in-domestic-5883191.php

Barrabi, T. (2014, September 17). NFL domestic violence timeline: A look at major incidents and arrests since 1994. *International Business Times*. Retrieved February 27, 2015, from www.ibtimes.com/nfl-domestic-violence-timeline-look-major-incidents-arrests-1994-1690807

Benedict, J., & Yaeger, D. (1998). *Pros and cons: The criminals who play in the NFL*. New York: Warner Books.

Berry, B., & Smith, E. (2000). Race, sport, and crime: The misrepresentation of African Americans in team sports and crime. *Sociology of Sport Journal*, *17*(2), 171–197.

Conduct committee. (2014, December 10). *NFL*. Available at https://nfllabor.files.wordpress.com/2014/12/12-10-14-conduct-committee.pdf

Coombs, W. T. (1995). Choosing the right words: The development of guidelines for the selection of the "appropriate" crisis-response strategies. *Mass Communication Quarterly*, *8*, 447–474.

Coombs, W. T. (2004). Impact of past crises on current crisis communication: Insights from situational crisis communication theory. *Journal of Business Communication*, *41*(3), 265–289.

Coombs, W. T. (2007). Protecting organization reputations during a crisis: The development and application of Situational Crisis Communication Theory. *Corporate Reputation Review*, *10*(3), 163–176. doi:10.1057/palgrave.crr.1550049

Coombs, W. T., & Holladay, S. J. (2008). Comparing apology to equivalent crisis response strategies: Clarifying apology's role and value in crisis communication. *Public Relations Review*, *34*(3), 252–257. doi:10.1016/j.pubrev.2008.04.001

Cowboys sign DE Greg Hardy. (2015, March 19). *ESPN Dallas*. Available at www.espn.com/dallas/nfl/story/_/id/12508402/dallas-cowboys-greg-hardy-agree-one-year-deal

Fainaru-Wada, M., & Fainaru, S. (2014, November 2). OTL: NFL didn't enforce own policies. *ESPN.com*. Retrieved from http://espn.go.com/espn/otl/story/_/id/11849798/outside-lines-most-nfl-players-domestic-violence-cases-never-missed-down

Former U.S. District Judge Barbara Jones to serve as hearing officer in Ray Rice appeal. (2014, October 2). *NFL*. Retrieved from http://nflcommunications.com/2014/10/02/former-u-s-district-judge-barbara-jones-to-serve-as-hearing-officer-in-ray-rice-appeal/

Fredericks, B. (2014, November 28). Ray Rice cleared to play. *New York Post*. Retrieved from nypost.com/2014/11/28/ray-rice-reinstated-to-nfl-becomes-free-agent/

Goodell suspends Pacman, Henry for multiple arrests. (May 17, 2007.) *ESPN*. Retrieved from http://www.espn.com/nfl/news/story?id=2832015.

Graff, C. (2015, January 29). NFL announces $2 million Super Bowl legacy grant, benefitting more than 25 community projects throughout super bowl host community. *NFL*. Available at https://nfllabor.files.wordpress.com/2015/01/legacygrantrelease15.pdf

Graff, C., Gordon, D., & McCollum, E. (2015, January 16). NFL national and local organizations host more than 30 Super Bowl XLIX community outreach events in Arizona. *NFL*. Available at https://nfllabor.files.wordpress.com/2015/01/super-bowl-xlix-community-release-final.pdf

Hess, A. (2015, January 27). Watch the first anti-domestic violence Super Bowl commercial. *Slate*. Retrieved from www.slate.com/blogs/xx_factor/2015/01/27/anti_domestic_violence_super_bowl_ad_the_nfl_and_no_more_team_up_on_a_commercial.html

Joint NFL-NFLPA statement on changes to steroids policy. (2014, September 17). *NFL*. Retrieved from http://nflcommunications.com/2014/09/17/joint-nfl-nflpa-statement-on-changes-to-steroids-policy/

Joint NFL-NFLPA statement on wide-ranging changes to drug programs. (2014, September 19). *NFL*. Retrieved from http://nflcommunications.com/2014/09/19/joint-nfl-nflpa-statement-on-wide-ranging-changes-to-drug-programs/

Katy Perry to auction off guitars from Pepsi Super Bowl XLIX halftime show to benefit break the cycle. (2015, February 1). *NFL*. Retrieved from http://nflcommunications.com/2015/02/01/katy-perry-to-auction-off-guitars-from-pepsi-super-bowl-xlix-halftime-show-to-benefit-break-the-cycle/

Key elements of new Personal Conduct Policy. (2014, December 10). *NFL*. Retrieved from http://nflcommunications.com/2014/12/10/information-on-the-new-personal-conduct-policy/

McGee, M. C. (1980). The "ideograph": A link between rhetoric and ideology. *Quarterly Journal of Speech*, *66*(1), 1–16.

Mission and Values. (2014, December 10). *NFL*. Available at http://static.nfl.com/static/content/public/photo/2014/12/19/0ap3000000445869.pdf

Murray-Garrigan, L. (2000, January 13). How police bent the rules for a Titans player who assaulted his girlfriend. *Nashville Scene*. Retrieved from www.nashvillescene.com/nashville/personal-foul/Content?oid=1183896

New NFL Personal Conduct Policy. (2014, December 10). *NFL*. Retrieved from http://nflcommunications.com/2014/12/10/information-on-the-new-personal-conduct-policy/

Newton, D. (2014, September 18). Greg Hardy placed on exempt list. *ESPN.com*. Retrieved from http://espn.go.com/nfl/story/_/id/11543641/greg-hardy-carolina-panthers-expected-placed-exempt-list

NFL Commissioner Roger Goodell & EVP Jeff Pash League meeting press conference. (2014, December 10). *NFL*. Retrieved from http://nflcommunications.com/2014/12/10/nfl-commissioner-roger-goodell-evp-jeff-pash-league-meeting-press-conference-december-10-2014/

NFL consults with experts, organizations, former player, and NFL wives organization. (2014, December 10). *NFL*. Retrieved from http://nflcommunications.com/2014/12/10/information-on-the-new-personal-conduct-policy/

NFL names Capitol Hill veteran Nicole Gustafson Vice President for Public Policy and Government Affairs. (2015, February 27). *NFL*. Retrieved from http://nflcommunications.com/2015/02/27/nfl-names-capitol-hill-veteran-nicole-gustafson-vice-president-for-public-policy-and-government-affairs/

NFL names Dawn Hudson Chief Marketing Officer. (2014, September 22). *NFL*. Retrieved from http://nflcommunications.com/2014/09/22/nfl-names-dawn-hudson-chief-marketing-officer/

NFL names former White House official Cynthia C. Hogan Senior Vice President of Public Policy and Government Affairs. (2014, September 16). *NFL*. Retrieved from http://nflcommunications.com/2014/09/16/nfl-names-former-white-house-official-cynthia-c-hogan-senior-vice-president-of-public-policy-and-government-affairs/

NFL opener watched by 26.9 million. (2014, September 5). *ESPN*. Retrieved from http://m.espn.go.com/nfl/story?storyId=11472029&src=desktop

NFL record & fact book (2013). *Chronology of professional football*. Retrieved from http://static.nfl.com/static/content/public/image/history/pdfs/History/2013/353-372-Chronology.pdf

NFL teams unanimously endorse comprehensive new conduct policy; ownership committee named, new disciplinary officer to be hired. (2014, December 10). *NFL*. Retrieved from http://nflcommunications.com/2014/12/10/information-on-the-new-personal-conduct-policy/

NFLPA v. National Football League, 88 F. Supp. 3d 1084 (D. Minn. 2015).

NFL'sresponse to domestic violence, child abuse, and sexual assault. (2014, December 10). *NFL*. Retrieved from http://nflcommunications.com/2014/12/10/information-on-the-new-personal-conduct-policy/

Patel, N. A. (2014, December 10). Heller reaction to revised NFL conduct policy. *NFL*. Retrieved from http://nflcommunications.com/2014/12/11/senators-praise-nfl-conduct-policy/

Patel, N. A. (2014, December 11). Senators praise NFL conduct policy. Available at https://nfllabor.files.wordpress.com/2014/12/senators-praise-conduct-policy1.pdf.

Personal Conduct Policy. (2014, December 10). *NFL*. Retrieved from http://nflcommunications.com/2014/12/10/information-on-the-new-personal-conduct-policy/

Petition filed against NFL on behalf of Adrian Peterson. (2014, December 15). *NFLPA.com*. Retrieved from www.nflpa.com/news/all-news/petition-filed-against-nfl-on-behalf-of-adrian-peterson

Ray Rice elevator knockout: Fiancee takes crushing punch [video]. (2014, September 8). *TMZSports.com*. Retrieved from www.tmz.com/2014/09/08/ray-rice-elevator-knockout-fiancee-takes-crushing-punch-video/

Ray Rice suspended without pay for two games and fined an additional game check for violating NFL Personal Conduct Policy. (2014, July 24). *NFL*. Retrieved from http://nflcommunications.com/2014/07/24/ray-rice-suspended-without-pay-for-two-games-and-fined-an-additional-game-check-for-violating-nfl-personal-conduct-policy/

Schrotenboer, B. (2014, October 2). History of leniency: NFL domestic cases under Goodell. *USA Today*. Retrieved from www.usatoday.com/story/sports/nfl/2014/10/01/nfl-domestic-abuse-history-under-roger-goodell/16566615/

Schrotenboer, B. (2015). NFL player arrests: Arrest database. *USA Today*. Retrieved from www.usatoday.com/sports/nfl/arrests/

Slater, D. (2014, October 15) Jets receiver Quincy Enunwa has domestic violence charge dismissed; NFL says discipline unlikely. *NJ.com*. Retrieved from www.nj.com/jets/index.ssf/2014/10/jets_receiver_quincy_enunwa_has_domestic_violence_charge_dismissed.html

Statement of Troy Vincent: Hearing on domestic violence in professional sports. Committee on Commerce, Science, and Transportation; U.S. Senate. (2014, December 2). *NFL*. Retrieved from http://nflcommunications.com/2014/12/02/troy-vincent-to-senate-committee-we-will-set-the-highest-goal-for-personal-behavior-with-clear-rules-fair-process/

Strong, A. (2014, December 10). Following commerce committee hearing on domestic assault in pro sports, NFL issues new personal conduct policy. *NFL*. Retrieved from http://nflcommunications.com/2014/12/11/senators-praise-nfl-conduct-policy/

Titan Sidney to start for Walker. (2000, September 1). *UT Daily Beacon*. Retrieved from http://utdailybeacon.com/sports/2000/sep/1/titan-sidney-to-start-for-walker/

TMZ: Ray Rice offered $1 million from fantasy football league. (2015, February 13). *MyFoxNewsDC*. Retrieved from www.myfoxdc.com/story/28101232/tmz-ray-rice-offered-1-million-from-fantasy-football-league

United States District Court, District of Minnesota (2015). NFLPA statement on 7th Circuit decision to vacate NFL's arbitration decision on Adrian Peterson. *NFLPA.com*. Retrieved February 27, 2015, from www.nflpa.com/news/all-news/nflpa-statement-on-overturning-of-adrian-peterson-s-suspension

Verderame, M. (2015, March 3). Ray Rice awarded $1.588 million in wrongful termination settlement. *SBNation.com*. Retrieved from www.sbnation.com/nfl/2015/3/3/8142765/ray-rice-wrongful-termination-settlement

Walker probation began in August. (2000, January, 11). *ESPN.com*. Retrieved from http://static.espn.go.com/nfl/playoffs99/div/s/2000/0111/285601.html

Worland, J. (2014, August 1). Roger Goodell defends Ray Rice suspension. *Time*. Retrieved from http://time.com/3072840/roger-goodell-ray-rice-suspension-nfl/

7

REPUTATIONAL CHALLENGES IN THE OLYMPICS

The LGBTQ Paracrisis in Sochi

Ryan S. Rigda

In June of 2013, Russian lawmakers passed a unanimous piece of legislation that banned the propaganda of nontraditional lifestyles and imposed fines for any information given to minors about the gay community (Crary, 2013). While this appeared to be directed at Russian citizens, just one month after the bill was signed the first arrests of foreign citizens visiting Russia for a human rights seminar and filming of a gay lifestyle documentary were made. Although these were not athletes, the impending 2014 Olympic Games became an immediate issue; especially after American runner Nick Symmonds publicly denounced the law following his silver medal victory at an event in Moscow (Luhn, 2013). Therefore, leading up to the Olympics in Sochi, many feared that the strict Russian laws could result in the arrest or imprisonment of athletes representing other countries. This would be a clear crisis for any country involved, particularly with the United States, who has historically experienced high tensions with Russia that date back to the Cold War. Therefore, the potential for Russia to cause an international crisis was very high, especially if a participant of the Olympic Games were to be arrested or detained during competition (for more on media frames, see Billings, Moscowitz, & Yang, 2016).

As the 2014 Sochi Olympic Games drew closer, the United States Olympics Committee faced a critical organizational threat: how could they protect American LGBTQ athletes from anti-propaganda laws targeting "nontraditional lifestyles" in Russia while still allowing athletes to represent the United States in the Olympic Games? Because of Russia's anti-propaganda laws regarding the spread of homosexuality and their overall controversial LGBTQ policies, these Olympic Games became extremely significant for LGBTQ athletes as they attempted to show Russia, and the world, that they deserve the same rights and protections as everyone else. Many individuals and groups called on the

International Olympic Committee (IOC) to take the Olympic bid away from Russia because of their unethical treatment of LGBTQ individuals, the poor working conditions, and the high cost associated with creating a Winter Olympic venue in a traditionally rainy area (Whiteside, 2013). Unfortunately, the IOC did little to manage the issue and stood by Russia's assurance that this law would not impact athletes unless they were to openly disobey the law while outside of the Olympic Village (Longman, 2013). With little response coming from the IOC, American attention turned to the United States Olympic Committee (USOC), generating a number of paracrises, or crisis risks, that must be managed publicly (Coombs & Holladay, 2012). The uncertainty of how LGBTQ athletes would be treated in Russia was a major concern for athletes, coaches, fans, and even public sponsors, making it a prominent paracrisis. Consequently, President Obama and the USOC were forced to manage the paracrisis in response to this escalating situation and appease as many groups as possible, including the host country. The threat of a potential crisis for USOC grew exponentially as the public outcry over Russian policies gained traction. Therefore, this event serves as a case study to further understand the role of paracrisis at an institutional level.

In this chapter, I examine the way in which the multiple voices of the rhetorical arena responded to and managed the LGBTQ paracrisis surrounding the 2014 Winter Olympics. Frandsen and Johansen (2016) define the rhetorical arena as a multivocal approach to crisis communication that accounts for every stage of a crisis: before, during, and after. This case study allows for further examination of the largely unstudied "before" period of a crisis, by paying special attention to the prominent LGBTQ paracrisis.

Coombs and Holladay define paracrisis as "a publicly visible crisis threat that charges an organization with irresponsible or unethical behavior" (2012, p. 409). Because of the various groups that exist as stakeholders for the Olympic Games, organizational leaders had to respond in a way that appeased all groups equally to prevent the crisis threat. The LGBTQ paracrisis affords an opportunity to examine how an organization attempts to mitigate a potential crisis and how those efforts are affected by other, powerful crisis communications efforts. Although the rhetorical arena model was developed around the assumptions of crisis communication, I contend that the extension to paracrisis offers a better understanding of dynamic risk management and crisis mitigation. By examining responses from USOC, President Obama, and Russia, we can better understand how the paracrisis involving LGBTQ rights was managed prior to the 2014 Winter Olympics.

In this analysis, I argue that each major voice approached the paracrisis from a different perspective, relying on various paracrisis management strategies (Coombs & Holladay, 2012). The chapter begins by examining the paracrisis of LGBTQ athletes in Sochi and extending the rhetorical arena to paracrisis research. Next, it analyzes the public responses by three prominent voices of the rhetorical arena: The United States Olympic Committee, President Obama, and the host country, Russia. Finally, it offers concluding remarks about the way this paracrisis was managed by simply rearticulating Cold War rhetoric through refutation.

Paracrisis and the Rhetorical Arena

In their 2016 book, Finn Frandsen and Winni Johansen argue that current crisis communication theories, such as Benoit's Image Repair Theory (1997) and Coombs's (1999; Coombs & Holladay, 2004) Situational Crisis Communication Theory (SCCT), failed to account for the multiple voices that exist within an issue or crisis. Following this logic, Frandsen and Johansen (2016) proposed the rhetorical arena as a solution to previous crisis communication theories that were lacking the complexity necessary to examine dynamic crisis threats. Thus, the rhetorical arena served as a multi-vocal approach, recognizing that the concept of crisis communication does not only pertain to the organization in crisis. Instead, Frandsen and Johansen (2016) argued that crisis communication includes the communication activities of all relevant stakeholders playing a role before, during, and after the crisis. This includes various voices, such as media, political constituents, consumers, and public citizens. Whereas previous models were focused on the organization in crisis and crisis response strategies, the rhetorical arena accounts for the many senders and receivers of messages that start communicating when a crisis occurs. Additionally, the rhetorical arena model operates under the assumption that communication is mediated through the context, media, genre, and text, allowing for a more detailed understanding of both text and context of a situation. As a model, the rhetorical arena provides a means of capturing the complex and dynamic configuration of communication processes—before, during, and after a crisis—where various actors, contexts, and discourses (manifested in texts) are related to each other (2016). Furthermore, Frandsen and Johansen (2016) argue that a rhetorical arena begins to open before a crisis is fully recognized. In other words, the rhetorical arena can be applied to paracrises and efforts to mitigate a potential crisis in order to better understand how organizations publicly manage crisis threats. Unfortunately, the current articulation of this model does not develop its application prior to the emergence of a crisis because it is focused primarily on responses to a crisis and not pre-crisis management. However, the ability of an organization to mitigate a crisis prior to its emergence is important to crisis communication and issues management research, making this a useful extension of the rhetorical arena.

Observing crisis management during the pre-crisis period is important because it signifies the start of the crisis management process. Paracrisis, according to Coombs and Holladay (2012), utilizes risk communication to discuss and manage a crisis that almost happens due to increased public attention to an organizational threat. During this time, there is heightened visibility as stakeholders begin to challenge a decision by the organization and express their dissent. This challenge

has the potential to become a crisis because of the heightened visibility, particularly because of the large role played by social media. Following a crisis threat,
an organization has three potential ways of responding: refute, refuse, or reform
(Coombs & Holladay, 2012, 2015). These strategies are defined in Table 7.1.
Whatever strategy the organization chooses to manage the paracrisis, the result
can have lasting impacts on the stakeholder-organization relationship.

The Olympics are an ideal place to study paracrisis management because of
the large public following and potential for reputational threats. For example, in
2008 the Olympic torch was attacked in France on the way to the 2008 Olympics
in Beijing. Coombs (2012) utilized Situational Crisis Communication Theory
(SCCT) and corporate apologia to analyze the resulting organizational crisis. In
his analysis, Coombs (2012) argues that supplementing the rhetorical arena with
other theories provides a more detailed way of deciding what to analyze. In this
case, the Olympic Torch Relay Crisis highlights the importance of both macro-
and micro-level analysis for understanding an international crisis. According to
Coombs (2012),

> SCCT follows the advice from Sturges (1994) by specifying that crisis com-
> municators must provide instructing information (tell stakeholders how to
> protect themselves physically from the crisis) and adjusting information
> (help stakeholders cope psychologically during the crisis) before engaging
> in any efforts to repair reputational damage inflicted by a crisis.
>
> *p. 6*

I argue that this same logic applies when the rhetorical arena and SCCT is used
to examine a paracrisis rather than a crisis and thus is important to the analysis of
the paracrisis at hand in this chapter. By managing the paracrisis strategically, a
potential crisis threat can be successfully mitigated and managed.

The Rhetorical Arena of LGBTQ Rights

The nature of sport and the international stage of the Olympics make it an ideal
place to raise concerns about political issues. Consequently, this presents clear

TABLE 7.1 Paracrisis Response Strategies

Strategy	Definition
Refute	Organization defends current practices; relies on core values shared with stakeholders
Refuse	1. No public response made by organization
	2. Draw attention from challenge by focusing on positive aspects of organization
Reform	Change organizational practices to match stakeholder desires

reputational challenges for iational and international Olympic organizations when these political issues create organizational and reputational threats. The way in which an organization responds to a potential crisis threat has major implications for its future reputation. While the Olympic Charter prevents athletes from making political statements, implicitly or explicitly, athletes are still ideal candidates to be political, because of their ethos. For example, during the 1968 Olympics in Mexico City, sprinters Tommie Smith and John Carlos raised their black-gloved fists during the medal ceremony for the 200-meter dash This became one of the most political statements in the history of the Olympic Games (Hartmann, 2004). The months leading up to the 2014 Winter Olympics in Sochi represent a modern political crisis of the Olympic Games, particularly because of the increased public nature of the event and the lucrative sponsorship money associated with them. In this section, I analyze the rhetorical arena of the 2014 Olympic Games and the ways the LGBTQ paracrisis was managed. I begin this section by contextualizing the Olympic Games and the events leading up to the crisis threat before offering an analysis of responses from three prominent voices of the rhetorical arena, highlighting paracrisis response strategies for each.

The Olympic Games

The Olympic Games are a lucrative international business, with many different stakeholder groups and a large public following. First of all are the athletes who compete in the Games. With a recent rise in professional athletes coming out as gay and the acceptance of homosexuality in professional sport (see Buzinski & Ziegler, 2007), the potential to be prevented from competing in the Olympic Games is a major setback for international LGBTQ rights. Next, NBC, which has broadcasting rights for the Olympics, makes large profits from selling advertisements during Olympic coverage. In the 2014 Olympics, NBC broadcast 539 hours of televised Olympic coverage, with another 1,000 hours streaming online (Chemi, 2014). Because of this, NBC in particular would be drastically impacted by any decision to boycott the Sochi Olympics. Likewise, any sponsors who have paid for advertisements or drafted endorsement deals hold a stake in the profitability of the Olympics. On the other hand, the athletes must be appeased as well, because without athletes the USOC has no product to offer stakeholders like NBC. Finally, the consumer is largely impacted by any decisions made by the USOC to protest or respond in any way. Because sport plays a large role in American culture, any decision that impacts their beloved athletes or hinders American performance in the Games would cause public outrage. Not only would this be detrimental to the IOC and its sponsors, but it could have serious political ramifications for countries like Russia and the United States as well.

The issue of LGBTQ athletes and international LGBTQ rights, therefore, can cause problems for the success of the Games and their future as an international event. Should a country boycott the Olympic Games, serious organizational consequences could arise from sponsors and the international community. Therefore, how an organization like the USOC manages a potential crisis threat is important for their organizational reputation. However, the USOC is not the only voice within the current crisis threat. The macro-level analysis of this rhetorical arena features three main voices. The first is USOC, serving as the leader of the American Olympic organization and the advocate for American athletes. As an organization, the USOC faces the most to lose from a public crisis threat and, therefore, is the primary voice in the paracrisis. The second major voice of the rhetorical arena is that of the American people, led by President Barack Obama. President Obama and the American people are responsible for bringing attention to the paracrisis, and therefore must be managed by both the USOC and the third major voice, Vladimir Putin and the host country of Russia. Using these three prominent voices of the rhetorical arena, I analyze the paracrisis management strategies from both the USOC and Russia during the 2014 Olympic Games.

Changing Strategy: The US Olympic Committee

Leading up the 2014 Olympics, the USOC faced pressure from multiple groups to boycott the Olympics due to Russia's drastic anti-LGBTQ legislation. Many feared this would be placing athletes, especially American athletes, in danger. In an open letter to the USOC, member of the United States Congress expressed that they were "concerned about the treatment of athletes and spectators traveling to Sochi for the 2014 Winter Olympics who disagree with Russia's violation of the human rights of LGBT people" (Lavers, 2013). The letter was drafted by openly gay California Congressman Mark Takano and US Representative Ileana Ros-Lehtinen, but was signed by dozens of members of Congress. The letter goes on to state:

> We call on the United States Olympic Committee to ensure that any American athlete, or someone associated with an American team, is afforded the right to show solidarity with, and support of, LGBT people around the globe to be free from discrimination and harm. Wearing a pin or another outward manifestation of solidarity with LGBT athletes should not be defined as "political" if it is not intended to support any clear political party or position but is intended, instead, to highlight the spirit of the Olympic games, which celebrates the unique humanity of all athletes from every country and culture.
>
> *Lavers, 2013*

Public statements like this signified the opening of the rhetorical arena and the emerging paracrisis for the USOC. Although other paracrises regarding the

2014 Olympics emerged (poor worker conditions for instance), the LGBTQ paracrisis drew large public attention because of social media. Given the large public presence and the potential for damaged stakeholder-organization relationships, the USOC needed to choose a management strategy for the paracrisis. Following the lead of the IOC, the USOC chose a strategy of refutation, challenging the public petitions regarding the LGBTQ paracrisis. The USOC assured the public that American athletes would be protected, turning to statements from the IOC regarding adherence to Russian law (Zaccardi, 2013) USOC Chairman Scott Blackmun told Russian news agency, R-Sport, that he would like to United States athletes comply with all laws in place, adding that

> Our job, first and foremost, is to make sure that our athletes are prepared to compete and aren't distracted while they're here. We're a sports organization, and we'll leave the diplomacy on the legal issues to the diplomats, and we're not going to get involved.
>
> *Zaccardi, 2013*

In other words, as long as athletes did not use their time at the Olympics to be political, they would be free from harm and from the law. These statements are consistent with the initial strategy of refutation and reflects the stance that the Olympics are about athleticism and competition, not about politics. In this way, the USOC faced the challenge directly, escalating the conflict with stakeholders, but falling back on core values of the organization.

Predictably, simply refuting the public petition did not last long for the USOC. Eventually, more prominent organizations began to speak out against the issue, pushing the paracrisis closer to a full crisis for the organization. The Human Rights Campaign (HRC), a prominent supporter of LGBTQ rights, drafted a letter urging prominent leaders from Dow Chemical, Coca-Cola, General Electric, McDonald's, Procter & Gamble, Panasonic, Samsung, Omega, Visa, and Atos to support LGBTQ rights and denounce Russia's actions. The letter detailed six steps these companies could take:

1. Adopt a clear and unequivocal public position in opposition to anti-LGBT laws like the one adopted by the Russian government.
2. Denounce targeted violence against LGBT people in Russia and demand investigation and accountability from Russian authorities.
3. Ask the IOC to obtain concrete, written commitments from the Russian government about the safety of international Olympic athletes and attendees—and urge the IOC to reject future Olympic bids from countries with laws that outlaw support for LGBT equality.
4. Affirm unequivocal support for non-discrimination and equality, and ensure that policies and practices reflect this commitment.

5. Put marketing and creative advertising resources to use—helping to build awareness and demonstrate support for LGBT equality in Russia and globally.
6. Support the local LGBT community in Russia.

Guequierre, 2013

This letter, because it was directed at major sponsors of the Olympic Games, holds critical implications for the success of the Olympics as a profitable organization. If these organizations did not respond to the call from the HRC, then the American people could view them as supports of LGBTQ discrimination, causing a loss in profit. However, if they openly speak out against Russian policy, there could be potential backlash in their ability to continue as Olympic sponsors. As it is, the American public hijacked numerous social media campaigns put forth by these organizations to show their anger over the problems that existed in Russia. For example, McDonald's' #CheerstoSochi campaign was taken over by activists in order to show support for a Russian man who was tackled and detained after waving a rainbow flag when the Olympic torch went through this hometown. Again, groups were calling for action from the USOC, but they did little to respond, except to support what was being said by the IOC. The USOC even clarified their earlier statements, noting that Russian polices are "inconsistent with the Olympic and Paralympic movements" (Geidner, 2013). Again, however, Blackmun and the USOC refuted claims LGBTQ athletes would face problems, and focused attention on getting athletes ready for competition.

When it became apparent that simply refuting public petitions would not successfully manage the paracrisis, the USOC switched tactics, choosing instead to reform their message. In October of 2013, the USOC revised its non-discrimination policy to include sexual orientation (Murray, 2013). This was a large shift in policy for the USOC, but a necessary one to successfully manage the crisis threat. Recognizing that current practices were inconsistent with stakeholder desires, the USOC implicitly took action to reform their policies in order to save their reputation. At the same time, this decision to reform the message creates impacts for other voices in the rhetorical arena. Drawing on historical tensions between the United States and Russia, dating back to the Cold War, the decision by the USOC to reform their message ultimately positioned Russia as the villain, impacting their paracrisis strategy. Like the 1980 and 1984 Olympics, which were boycotted by the United States and the Soviet Union when the opposing country hosted, these Olympic Games were highly politicized. This rearticulation of Cold War rhetoric perpetuated by the USOC positioned Putin and Russia as symbolic villains that needed to be defeated and became a key piece of information in public coverage of the period leading up to the 2014 Olympics. In this case, those who opposed this legislation, like the United States, became the symbolic heroes, serving as the protectors of LGBTQ rights.

Consequently, when Russia threatens to take away or prevent American success, in this case Olympic medals, they are preventing American progress. In this way, the USOC successfully reformed their message, turning attention away from the LGBTQ paracrisis and towards a common enemy: Russia.

President Obama

Perhaps the most prominent public voice leading up the 2014 Sochi Winter Olympics was that of the American people, who felt these laws were endangering their beloved athletes and the potential fans that were traveling to Russia. To be sure, sports play a major role in American culture, which means that any threat to an American athlete is a threat to American culture. As the leader of the American people, then, President Obama had to help the American people through the issue being presented in Russia. Ultimately, the American people turned to Obama for reassurance that the issue would be taken care of.

Obama's answer to the issue was to create an Olympic delegation that expressed the diversity of America's athletes, while simultaneously sending a message to Russia. This meant that Obama created a clear problem for the initial strategy of refutation coming from the United States Olympic Committee. From the start, Obama's response to the paracrisis was one of refutation. However, unlike the USOC's decision to focus on core values of athleticism and competition, Obama refuted public petitions by bolstering support for LGBTQ athletes. Obama's delegation to the Olympic Games consisted of multiple LGBTQ athletes, instead of the President himself or an immediate member of his family. Obama's decision not to participate in the delegation shows solidarity with the American people and positions him (and America) as the hero. The most notable delegate, former tennis star Billie Jean King, stated,

> I am equally proud to stand with the members of the LGBT community in support of all athletes who will be competing in Sochi and I hope these Olympic games will indeed be a watershed moment for the universal acceptance of all people.
>
> *"Gay athletes," 2013*

King, who is a potential victim of this legislation should she travel to Russia, expressed optimism for the presence of the delegation in Russia and on an international stage. Not only did this send a message to Russia, but also simultaneously reinforced the United States' position on LGBTQ rights around the world. Ironically, the United States has its own problems with LGBTQ rights; however, Obama used this moment to deal with both issues at once by setting a precedent for inclusion and acceptance.

Putin's Russia

Russia's passing of the anti-propaganda law is probably unsurprising to those familiar with the recent surge in lack of acceptance for LGBTQ lifestyles. The conflation of homosexuality with pedophilia has also furthered the issue, resulting in numerous hate crimes within Russia. Still, after the initial outcry, Putin assured the international community that Russia did not ban non-traditional lifestyles, but simply banned propaganda that encourages homosexuality and pedophilia.

Putin made numerous attempts to reassure the IOC that this legislation would not impact the athletes in any way, also consistent with a strategy of refutation. When asked about the impact of the legislation, the Sports Minister of Russia claimed, "An athlete of nontraditional sexual orientation isn't banned from coming to Sochi. But if he goes out into the streets and starts to propagandize, then of course he will be held accountable" (Whiteside, 2013). Furthermore, according to the mayor of Sochi, Anatoly Pakhomov, no gay individuals lived in Sochi and were not the norm in the city. He went on to explain that anyone is welcome in Sochi, as long as they do not push their views or habits on others. These statements are reflective of the values that Russia believes supports their decision to pass this legislation. The framing of homosexuality as pedophilia and "an alternative lifestyle" suggests that it is something that needs to be controlled. However, at the same, the Mayor of Sochi expresses recognition that everyone may not believe the same thing. Whether or not the Mayor supports this is not the issue at hand, but in order to successfully manage the issue they may need to accept that stakeholders (anyone coming for the Olympics) will probably disagree with Russian values.

Unlike previous attempts to refute the public challenge, this did not work for Russia. Consequently, Russia had to appease the international community by creating a free speech zone approximately 10 miles from any Olympic venue. This led to an explicit reform message where Russia publicly admitted to values that were inconsistent with the Charter of the Olympics. In line with the Russian anti-propaganda law, any speech that promotes homosexuality is punishable by law. However, the use of the term "propaganda" is vague and unclear, leaving room for many potential crises to arise should an athlete be suspected of perpetuating homosexuality. The vagueness of this legislation, combined with the failed strategy of refutation, left Russia with no choice but to designate a symbolic "safe space" where athletes would be free from discriminatory legislation.

Implications

This chapter has examined the LGBTQ paracrisis during the 2014 Sochi Olympics, and argued for the need to expand the scope of the rhetorical arena model beyond its traditional focus on crisis response. Utilizing the rhetorical arena approach is ideal for scholars interested in paracrisis because it allows for a deeper understanding of both text and context surrounding the issue at hand during the pre-crisis period. On the contextual level, this chapter painted a picture of the many voices impacted by the Olympic Games and the decision by Russia to enforce their anti-LGBTQ legislation at an international event. On the textual level, this chapter highlighted the ways in which the United States Olympic Committee publicly managed the LGBTQ paracrisis by reforming the message to position Russia as the villain, and thus focusing on how progressive LGBTQ rights are in the United States. In other words, this paracrisis gave the United States a prime opportunity to deal with the paracrisis publicly, all while turning focus on Putin and the Russian government. Therefore, this case study exemplifies how an organization can successfully manage a public risk before it ever becomes a full-blown crisis.

Unfortunately, in terms of this specific rhetorical arena, not all sides or voices can win because competing voices will always exist within the arena. The dichotomy between the United States and Russia creates a right versus wrong scenario, reflecting historical sentiments between the two countries. As the supporters of equal rights, the United States Olympic Committee and President Obama would always end up as the hero of the situation; existing as the champions of LGBTQ athletes around the world. Therefore, the International Olympic Committee and the host country Russia would always be fighting an uphill, and losing, battle. This case study gives organizational scholars the opportunity to examine paracrisis strategies that have failed. In no situation would Russia ever be considered the hero, especially if prominent athletes were not allowed to compete because their safety might be compromised. However, in a time when the organization in question, in this case the Russian government, is put in the international spotlight, there must be ways to manage the paracrisis. For Russia, this was relying on the Olympic Charter that prevents athletes from speaking about political issues during the Olympics or using their position as Olympic athletes to protest anything political. However, by creating a "free speech zone," Russia accepted the needs of visiting athletes, while still maintaining their anti-propaganda laws. This strategy protected the interests of Russia and the incoming athletes, which, had any athlete been detained while competing in an organization meant to promote international cooperation, could have resulted in a true international crisis.

Following the closing ceremonies of the Olympic Games, little attention was given to Russia and their anti-LGBTQ legislation. In fact, had Russia not hosted the Olympics that year, the news may have never made international headlines. However, the conflicting values of inclusion and exclusion resulting from an exclusive Russia hosting an inclusive event created a paracrisis that needed to be managed. Some might say that the paracrisis was effectively managed for all the main actors in the rhetorical arena. Russia created a free speech zone for individuals to speak out, while maintaining their values. President Obama used the situation to denounce Russian politics while openly supporting LGBTQ rights in the United States, ultimately painting the United States as a progressive and accepting country. The USOC avoided a potential boycott of a lucrative business that has many powerful stakeholders. From an organizational standpoint, it may be best to say, cheers to Sochi.

References

Benoit, W. L. (1997). Image repair discourse and crisis communication. *Public Relations Review, 23*(2), 177–186.

Billings, A. C., Moscowitz, L. M., & Yang, Y. (2016). Frames of the Olympic host: Media coverage of Russia's anti-gay legislation. In R. Lind (Ed.), *Race and gender in electronic media: Challenges and opportunities* (pp. 38–54). New York: Routledge.

Buzinski, J., & Ziegler, C. (2007). *The Outsports revolution.* New York: Alyson Books.

Chemi, E. (2014, February 7). NBC's own Olympic event: Selling 11,000 ads in two weeks. *Bloomberg.* Retrieved from www.bloomberg.com/bw/articles/2014-02-07/ nbcs-own-olympic-event-selling-11-000-ads-in-two-weeks

Coombs, W. T. (1999). *Ongoing crisis communication. Planning, managing, and responding.* Thousand Oaks, CA: Sage.

Coombs, W. T. (2012). *The Olympic torch relay crisis: Insights from a rhetorical arena approach.* Paper presented at 61st Annual International Communication Association Convention in Phoenix, AZ, May 24–28.

Coombs, W. T., & Holladay, S. J. (2004). Reasoned action in crisis communication: An attribution theory-based approach to crisis management. In D. P. Millar and R. L. Heath (Eds.), *Responding to crisis: A rhetorical approach to crisis communication* (pp. 95–115). New York: Routledge.

Coombs, W. T., & Holladay, J. S. (2012). The paracrisis: The challenges created by publicly managing crisis prevention. *Public Relations Review, 38,* 408–415.

Coombs, T., & Holladay, S. (2015). CSR as crisis risk: expanding how we conceptualize the relationship. *Corporate Communications: An International Journal, 20*(2), 144–162.

Crary, D. (2013, November 7). Foes of Russia's anti-gay law ponder new tactics. *Associated Press.* Retrieved from http://bigstory.ap.org/article/foes-russias-anti-gay-law-ponder-new-tactics

Frandsen, F., & Johansen, W. (2016). *Organizational crisis communication: A multivocal approach.* Thousand Oaks, CA: SAGE Publications.

Gay athletes to represent US. (2013, Dec. 19). *ESPN.* Retrieved from http://espn. go.com/olympics/story/_/id/10154712

Geidner, C. (2013, August 16). U.S. Olympic Committee clarifies: Russian law is "inconsistent with Olympic principles." *Buzzfeed.* Retrieved from www. buzzfeed.com/chrisgeidner/us-olympic-committee-clarifies-russian-law-is-inconsistent-w?utm_term=.rtbrleeOm#.vtggjQQV1

Guequierre, P. (2013, August 29). Anti-LGBT law in Russia. *Human Rights Campaign.* Retrieved from www.hrc.org/blog/hrc-calls-on-olympic-sponsors-to-condemn-anti-lgbt-law-in-russia-advocate-f

Hartmann, D. (2004). Race, culture, and the revolt of the black athlete: The 1968 Olympic protests and their aftermath. Chicago, IL: University of Chicago Press.

Lavers, M. K. (2013, October 7). Lawmakers press U.S. Olympic Committee over Russia LGBT rights record. *Washington Blade.* Retrieved from www.washingtonblade. com/2013/10/07/lawmakers-press-u-s-olympic-committee-russia-lgbt-rights-record/

Longman, J. (2013, August 6). Outrage over antigay law does not spread to Olympic officials. *New York Times*. Retrieved from www.nytimes.com/2013/08/07/sports/games-officials-tiptoeing-around-russias-antigay-law.html

Luhn, A. (2013, August 14). US athlete Nick Symmonds speaks out against Russia's antigay low in Moscow. *Guardian*. Retrieved from www.theguardian.com/world/2013/aug/14/nick-symmonds-speaks-russia-anti-gay-law

Murray, R. (2013, October 11). US Olympic Committee adds "sexual orientation" to non-discrimination policy. *GLAAD*. Retrieved from www.glaad.org/blog/us-olympic-committee-adds-sexual-orientation-non-discrimination-policy

Sturges, D. L. (1994). Communicating through crisis: A strategy for organizational survival. *Management Communication Quarterly, 7*(3), 297–316.

Whiteside, K. (2013, August 1). IOC stands by Russia's reassurance on anti-gay law. *USA Today*. Retrieved from www.usatoday.com/story/sports/olympics/2013/08/01/ioc-russia-anti-gay-law-sochi-olympics/2609765/

Zaccardi, N. (2013, August 14). USOC CEO: "It's our strong desire that our athletes comply with the laws of every nation." *NBC Sports*. Retrieved from http://olympics.nbcsports.com/2013/08/14/russia-anti-gay-law-sochi-2014-winter-olympics-scott-blackmun-usoc/

8

CRISIS COMMUNICATION AND THE NBA LOCKOUT

Exploring Fan Reactions to Crisis Response Strategies in Sport

Melanie J. Formentin

Although major professional sports leagues and teams operate within the framework of collective bargaining agreements (CBA), recent years have seen an increase in collective bargaining *dis*agreements (CNN Library, 2017). Since 1993, each of the four major professional United States sports leagues—Major League Baseball (MLB), National Basketball Association (NBA), National Football League (NFL), and National Hockey League (NHL)—have ridden out at least one lockout or strike. During that time the NBA, NHL, and NFL combined for seven lockouts; five of the CBA disputes resulted in missed games, and the NHL's 2004–05 lockout stands as the only dispute to end with an entirely canceled season. As recently as January 2013, the NHL emerged from a four-month lockout that resulted in 510 canceled games and a shortened schedule (Klein, 2013).

Prior to the NHL's latest dispute, the NBA and NFL faced simultaneous, similar lockouts in 2011. In each case, disagreements between players and owners centered on salary caps and revenue sharing (McMenamin, 2011). Additionally, both sides faced a players' association that dissolved both to file antitrust lawsuits and to speed up the bargaining process. Ultimately, only the NBA lost games—including their full pre-season schedule and six weeks of play—because of their lockout (ESPN.com news service, 2011). Although the league's reputation faced threats at the time, they also had opportunities to learn from other leagues that experienced and successfully emerged from lockouts (Beck, 2011; Klein, 2011).

Arguably, professional sport provides a unique context for studying communication strategies, particularly crisis communication (Bruce & Tini, 2008). And arguably, lockouts provide an opportunity to examine and learn about communication strategies in the context of re-occurring but ever-changing crises. Although crises are normally defined as unexpected events (Coombs, 2014;

Fearn-Banks, 2017), lockouts still present challenges such as lost revenue, reputational damage, and the persistent threat of ceasing operations. Professional sport organizations experience the added threat of being in conflict with their employees, players who happen to be their product. As such, examining lockouts can shed light on the effectiveness of crisis communication strategies while illuminating how theoretical approaches may be received by specialized stakeholder groups such as fans (Brown & White, 2011; Bruce & Tini, 2008). This chapter explores the impact of crisis response strategies using the 2011 NBA lockout for context. Existing empirical research exploring the effectiveness of specific communication strategies is explored before the four-factor pre-test, post-test design is presented. Finally, an analysis of the results highlights how fandom may create a confound when communicating about sports-related crises.

Conceptualizing SCCT

Using attribution theory to underpin his approach, Coombs (1995) synthesized literature about crisis response strategies to provide an early typology that eventually became the Situational Crisis Communication Theory (SCCT). As described in Chapter 2, organizations can use appropriate crisis response strategies to protect their reputation in the wake of crises. Although SCCT has become one of the most widely tested and cited public relations theories (Avery, Lariscy, Kim, & Hocke, 2010), it is not without its gaps. Avery et al. (2010) found that most research testing SCCT was experimental, but the body of research lacked variance in organization and entity types. Answering similar calls to expand the literature beyond case-study analysis (Coombs, 2007), this chapter examines an existing, long-term crisis event—the NBA lockout—as a framework for testing selected SCCT crisis response strategies.

Exploring the Two-Step Process

Crises are envisioned as events that interrupt business, pose financial threats, and potentially harm organizational reputation (Coombs, 2007; Fearn-Banks, 2017). As described in Chapter 2, crises may be unpredictable and threatening to an organization. However, SCCT offers an approach for protecting organizational reputation by ethically addressing stakeholder concerns and suggesting organizational messaging strategies for reducing negative crisis impacts (Coombs 1995, 2007, 2014; Coombs & Holladay, 2002).

Important to this chapter is the two-step process for considering best crisis communication strategies (see Chapter 2). First, organizations must identify and establish the perceived level of crisis responsibility among stakeholders, determining whether crisis attributions fall in the victim, accidental, and intentional clusters. Second, organizations should adjust the potential reputational threat by considering crisis history and prior reputation. Once responsibility attributions have been addressed, organizations can choose crisis response types based on a continuum of potential strategies (Coombs, 2007; Coombs & Holladay, 2002), ranging from accommodative to defensive: the more organizational fault in a crisis, the more accommodative the response can be; the less organizational fault in a crisis, the more defensive the response can be.

Applying SCCT Strategies

The popularity and testability of SCCT has yielded numerous case studies and experiments. In sports, Bruce and Tini (2008) found that poorly and non-trained communicators naturally used SCCT strategies when communicating about a salary cap cheating scandal within a New Zealand rugby organization. Although mismatched strategies resulted in heightened reputational threats, they were mitigated by the unexpected use of *diversion* strategies. Diversion was presented as a sport-specific strategy that allowed organizations to limit a team's reputational damage by divorcing the product—or players—from crisis blame. Here, proper application of SCCT may have further reduced a team's reputational damage. However, when the non-profit organization ACORN (Association of Community Organizations for Reform Now) responded to allegations about tax evasion and child prostitution, prescribed SCCT strategies failed to reduce reputational and organizational damage (Sisco, 2012). ACORN's situation suggested proper execution of SCCT was tied to organizational resources as much as crisis knowledge, which may have helped in the case of the rugby team. For example, after allegedly hitting a photographer, NASCAR's Tony Stewart was supported by his team and engaged in SCCT-prescribed strategies that alleviated the reputational damage both to him and his team (Jerome, 2008). Similar to Stewart, professional sport organizations have advantages that the rugby team and ACORN may not have had—they have financial resources, trained professionals, and loyal stakeholders.

While important, these studies failed to meet calls for theoretical testing. Experiments have shown that crisis history negatively intensifies reputational threat during crises (Coombs, 2004) and that beliefs about performance history can influence negative behaviors and opinions that further increase reputational damage (Jeong, 2009). However, research has yielded mixed results when testing specific communication strategies. Brown and White (2011) examined the impact of organization-public relationships (OPR) and crisis responses, finding that participants with positive organizational relationships were less likely than people in negative organizational relationships to attribute crisis blame to the test organization, a university, regardless of communication strategy. Similarly, Claeys, Cauberghe, and Vyncke (2010) found that "matching crisis types and crisis responses [did] not lead to more positive perception of firm reputation than mismatches" (p. 261). This suggests important implications for sport organizations, which boast historically loyal stakeholders—fans (Bruce & Tini, 2008).

Specifically, a boundary condition may exist wherein the positive relationships created by fandom serve to negate the reputational benefits of using specific crisis attribution or response-matching strategies. That is, the emotional connection that fans feel for sport organizations may shift both how they interpret the ways in which crises unfold and how they will process specific crisis response strategies.

As such, this chapter attempts to address some of the limitations noted in SCCT literature. Although case studies are useful, they serve as anecdotal evidence for the practicality of SCCT (Avery et al., 2010; Coombs, 2007). And, in their study of OPR and SCCT, Brown and White (2011) acknowledged that they failed to address the impact of crisis history and prior reputation. Similarly, Claeys et al. (2010) believed using a fictitious company may have led to attitude formation rather than reputation measurement, and they failed to incorporate a control condition in their experiment. As such, this chapter examines an existing, long-term crisis (the NBA lockout) via experimental methods to explore how the crisis was perceived among participants who were also organizational stakeholders (fans). Knowledge of crisis history and prior reputation were accounted for, and using an actual case and stakeholders meant changes created by different SCCT strategies could help us better understand whether specific strategies might change beliefs about crisis attributions and organizational reputation.

To understand how SCCT strategies might impact fan perceptions of the NBA following a lockout, it is first important to understand how SCCT variables such as crisis history and reputation are perceived by participants. Second, it is important to test how specific strategies might impact fan perceptions about reputation and crisis responsibility. As such, this chapter first explores how a history of lockouts impacted perceptions of the NBA's reputation. Next, to understand the impact of audiences (fans) receiving information about the lockout, the reputations of both the NBA and NBPA (National Basketball Players Association) are explored before determining which of the two groups was more likely to shoulder the blame for the lockout. Finally, attempts are made to test how different SCCT communication strategies impact perceptions of player or owner blame. Specifically, it is posited that the more owners are blamed for the crisis, the more damage it will do to the NBA's reputation. Conversely, the more players are blamed for the crisis, the more positive the impact will be on the NBA's reputation. However, different SCCT communication strategies are likely to yield different perceptions of responsibility; while scapegoat strategies should naturally increase beliefs about player responsibility, excuse and apology strategies will increase beliefs about owner responsibility.

Testing SCCT Strategies

To explore SCCT in the context of the NBA lockout, this study measured the impact of specific strategies on perceived levels of organizational responsibility following the lockout. A pre-test, post-test four-factor (scapegoat, excuse, apology, control) design was implemented using press releases portraying potential NBA communication strategies. Embedded quotes were designed to modify stakeholder perceptions following the lockout. While SCCT suggests organizations should assess perceived crisis responsibility before choosing communication strategies (see Chapter 2), this study envisioned communication strategies shifting attribution following a crisis, particularly among active stakeholders for an existing organization (Avery et al., 2010; Bruce & Tini, 2008; Jerome, 2008).

Experimental materials included quotes embedded in a press release, with strategies chosen for their clarity in expressing major communication response types: deny, diminish, and rebuild. Quotes portrayed the league as apologizing for, excusing, or blaming (scapegoating) players for the lockout. These strategies were chosen because they represent opposing (scapegoat and apology) and central (excuse) strategies on the crisis response spectrum. Although apology is a somewhat controversial approach, particularly because other strategies may generate similar reactions from stakeholders (Coombs & Holladay, 2008; Tyler, 1997), it is still helpful to examine an approach that assumes the most crisis responsibility. Finally, because bolstering is considered a supplemental strategy that builds positive connections, each message included the same ingratiation strategy (Coombs, 2014). To strengthen external validity, experimental quotes were evaluated by outside coders. Table 8.1 presents the experimental quotes used.

Running the Experiment

The experiment was conducted online using Qualtrics to allow more flexibility for participants. Participants received questions related to sport organization lockouts and reputation and a set of articles related to the lockout. All items were measured on scales of 1 (strongly disagree/very unfavorable) to 7 (strongly agree/very favorable), and professional sport league reputation was measured using items that were both modified from existing reputation studies (Fombrun & Gardberg, 2000; Sung & Yang, 2008) and newly designed. The one-item "global evaluation" of "overall, my impressions of X is . . ." (Coombs & Holladay, 2008, p. 254) was also used.

The study's purpose was concealed by first asking participants to provide their overall impression (on a favorability scale) of four major professional sports leagues and their corresponding players' associations. Next, participants evaluated the National Football League's (NFL), National Basketball Association's (NBA), and National Hockey League's (NHL) reputation (see Table 8.3 for a list of items). Three questions designed to gauge *stakeholder activity* were included. Participants were asked whether they enjoyed watching league games, regularly followed the league or one of its teams, or owned league merchandise. Finally, items established how much participants knew about major professional sport lockouts, including whether specific leagues had experienced lockouts or strikes, and whether owners or players can initiate lockouts.

TABLE 8.1 Experimental Conditions, Communication Strategies

Communication Strategy Condition	Quote
Scapegoating	"It is a shame games were canceled, but the NBA players were unwilling to cooperate soon enough to save the early season schedule," Stern continued. "We thank the fans for their continued support, and are glad that the Players Association decided to reorganize so we could move forward with negotiations."
Excusing	"We regret that games were canceled, but the NBA owners believed this was the only way to achieve a deal that would benefit all parties involved," Stern continued. "We thank the fans for their continued support, and hope you understand this was the best way to bring your favorite teams back to the court."
Apologizing	"We regret that games were canceled, and the NBA owners take full responsibility and apologize for having lost games due to a league-imposed lockout," Stern continued. "We want to thank the fans for their continued support, and hope you can forgive us for the disappointing game cancelations during the negotiations."
Control Group	No quote presented.

Next, participants read an article, "The NBA Lockout: Wrap Up," before reading the experimental press release about the lockout. The article provided objective, factual details about the lockout, including an inset "timeline" of important dates. This allowed participants to learn about the lockout without receiving leading or biased information. Next, the randomization feature randomly presented participants a modified version of a press release, "Statement from the NBA." Using a release was appropriate, as NBA fans consume a considerable amount of online, team- and league-based content (Gaille, 2015). This "official release" was based on a league-generated release detailing the league's opinion at the end of the lockout. As such, the release included real and fabricated quotes from the league and ended with a shortened list of the "key agreement points" that originally appeared on the league's official website. Experimental, embedded quotes were attributed to league commissioner David Stern. Participants in the control condition did not receive a press release and were directed to the end of the questionnaire. Data regarding the number of participants assigned to each condition is provided in Table 8.2.

After receiving the stimulus materials, participants completed the questionnaire by re-evaluating their impressions of the NBA and the Players Association

TABLE 8.2 Demographics

		n	*Percent*	*Valid Percent*
Gender	Female	231	68.1	68.1
	Male	108	31.9	31.9
	Total	**339**	**100**	**100**
Race/Ethnicity	African American	21	6.2	6.2
	Asian/Pacific Islander	33	9.7	9.7
	Caucasian	257	75.8	75.8
	Hispanic/Latino	16	4.7	4.7
	Native American	2	0.6	0.6
	Other	10	2.9	2.9
	Total	**339**	**100**	**100**
Academic Standing	Freshman	68	20.1	20.1
	Sophomore	113	33.3	33.4
	Junior	100	29.5	29.6
	Senior	57	16.8	16.9
	Total	**338**	**99.7**	**100**
Conditions	Apology	86	25.4	25.4
	Excusing	87	25.7	25.7
	Scapegoating	85	25.1	25.1
	Control Group	81	23.9	23.9
	Total	**339**	**100**	**100**

(NBPA) and the NBA's reputation. They also identified whether they believed the league or players were at fault for the lockout. Standard demographic questions closed the questionnaire.

Participant Demographics

Participants were recruited from undergraduate courses in a communications-based college at a large Northeastern U.S. university. Participants were primarily young adults, which aligns with NBA viewer demographics. In 2015, more than 60% of fans were between 18 and 54 years old, with 45% of the league's viewership coming from adults 35 or younger (Gaille, 2015). Out of 410 completed questionnaires, $n = 339$ were retained for analysis. Participants were between 18 and 53 years old, with 97.6% indicating they were 22 or younger ($M = 19.98$, $SD = 2.46$). Participants were primarily female ($n = 231$, 68.1%) and Caucasian ($n = 257$, 75.8%). Table 8.2 provides participant demographics.

Participants as Fans

To understand the fan profile of participants, this study gauged knowledge about, perceptions of, and investment in the NBA. Participants strongly agreed they had heard of the NBA (Mean [M] = 6.58, Standard Deviation [SD] = 1.15), but only had a somewhat favorable impression of the league (M = 4.64, SD = 1.46). An "active NBA stakeholder" index was calculated (M = 3.61, SD = 1.91, skewness = .306, kurtosis = −1.076, Cronbach's α = .894), including items that asked whether participants enjoyed watching NBA games (M = 4.35, 1.95), regularly followed the NBA or an NBA team (M = 3.46, SD = 2.10) and owned NBA merchandise (M = 3.09, SD = 2.25). Although participants generally knew about the league, they did not appear actively involved in supporting it or its partner teams.

Examining Gender-Based Differences

Because this and previous experiments have had an uneven balance of females (i.e., Brown & White, 2011), and marketing research suggested 60.2% of NBA fans were men (Sports Business Daily, 2010), attempts were made to account for gender-based differences. Independent samples t-tests, which test whether the mean responses for two separate groups are statistically different, explored whether gender-based differences existed regarding NBA involvement and perceptions. No significant differences existed between female and male respondents in terms of overall impressions of the NBA ($t(366)$ = −.266, p = .791) or whether they had heard of the NBA ($t(265.76)$ = 1.682, p = .094). For the latter item, degrees of freedom were adjusted from 336 to 265.76 because Levene's test indicated unequal variances (F = 5.53, p = .019). However, results suggested male participants (M = 4.06, SD = 2.10) were more likely than female participants (M = 3.40, SD = 1.78) to be active NBA stakeholders, $t(182.14)$ = 2.84, p = .005 (Levene's test (F = 9.37, p = .002)), meeting market research expectations.

TABLE 8.3 Reputation Scales, Time 1 and Time 2

	NBA Reputation Time 1		NBA Reputation Time 2	
	M	SD	M	SD
1. . . . makes fans a top priority.	5.04	1.10	3.88	1.39
2. . . . is an organization with strong prospects for future growth.	5.22	1.19	4.62	1.34
3. . . . is well-managed.	4.75	1.20	3.90	1.40
4. . . . does a lot of good in its communities.	4.88	1.16	4.32	1.41
5. . . . has strong revenues.	5.46	1.19	4.91	1.46
6. I admire the . . .	4.33	1.54	3.91	1.52
7. I respect the . . .	4.80	1.42	4.16	1.53

Although these differences did not necessarily suggest high overall engagement with the NBA through viewing and purchasing behavior, both gender- and stakeholder-based differences were examined to account for potential confounds.

Establishing NBA Reputation

To explore the NBA's reputation, indexes were computed for pre- and post-experimental exposure beliefs about the league. Indexes reflected the NBA's reputation at Time 1, prior to participants receiving literature about the lockout ($M = 4.93$, $SD = .1.00$, Cronbach's $\alpha = .902$), and at Time 2, after participants received literature about the lockout ($M = 4.24$, $SD = 1.12$, Cronbach's $\alpha = .887$). Table 8.3 contains NBA reputation scale items. To explore index consistency across sports, reliability analysis was conducted for NFL (Cronbach's $\alpha = .877$) and NHL (Cronbach's $\alpha = .870$) reputation, showing similar internal reliability.

Measuring Participant Knowledge About Lockouts

Participant knowledge about professional sport labor disputes was evaluated, with participants somewhat agreeing the NBA ($M = 5.12$, $SD = 2.05$), NFL ($M = 5.07$, $SD = 2.03$), and NHL ($M = 5.6$, $SD = 1.96$) had experienced lockouts or strikes. Participants were less familiar with MLB labor disputes ($M = 4.01$, $SD = 2.10$). These findings made sense, because the NHL was missing games when data was collected and the NFL and NBA had overlapping lockouts in 2011. However, because the most recent MLB strike was in 1994, labor dispute knowledge may have been lower due to participant age. Participants somewhat agreed there was a difference between a lockout and a strike ($M = 5.03$, $SD = 1.45$), and paired samples t-tests, which test whether the mean responses for two different items are statistically different, revealed an accurate belief that owners ($M = 5.57$, $SD = 1.42$) rather than players ($M = 4.99$, $SD = 1.87$) could initiate a lockout, $t(337) = 4.99$, $p < .000$. To account for active stakeholder differences, linear regression analysis was used. Linear regression examines relationships between continuous variables to determine the degree to which one variable influences changes in another. The *R-squared* measure then explains variations in the fit of the linear model. Here, regression tests suggested being a stakeholder predicted lockout awareness, $b = .329$, $t(334) = 6.37$, $p < .001$, which explained a low, but significant proportion of variance in overall lockout knowledge, $R^2 = .108$, $F(1, 334) = 40.63$, $p < .001$.

To account for potential differences based on the unequal number of female participants in the study, independent samples t-tests showed men ($M = 5.67$, $SD = 1.99$) were significantly more likely than women ($M = 4.87$, $SD = 2.03$) to be aware of the NBA having lockouts or strikes, $t(336) = 3.41$, $p = .001$. However, paired samples t-tests revealed a non-significant difference between whether men ($M = 4.98$, $SD = 2.15$) and women ($M = 5.00$, $SD = 1.73$)

believed players could initiate lockouts ($t(174.39) = -.060$, $p = .952$, Levene's test ($F = 10.08$, $p = .002$)). However, men ($M = 5.86$, $SD = 1.45$) were more likely than women ($M = 5.43$, $SD = 1.39$) to believe owners initiated lockouts, $t(337) = 2.606$, $p = .010$. Aligning with the notion that female participants in this study were less likely to be active NBA stakeholders, it also seems they were simply less aware of NBA lockout history.

Impact of Lockout History on League Impressions and Reputation

Linear regression analysis suggested knowing about the NBA lockout significantly predicted overall impressions of the NBA, $b = .183$, $t(335) = 3.42$, $p = .001$ and explained a low, but significant proportion of variance in overall league impressions, $R^2 = .034$, $F(1, 335) = 11.66$, $p = .001$. Similarly, knowledge about the NBA lockout significantly predicted perceived NBA reputation, $b = .218$, $t(335) = 4.09$, $p < .001$. Again, however, knowledge of lockout history only explained a low, but significant proportion of variance in reputation, $R^2 = .048$, $F(1, 335) = 16.721$, $p < .001$.

Although being an active stakeholder was significantly predicted by knowledge about the NBA lockout ($b = .329$, $t(334) = 6.37$, $p < .001$), linear regression showed this knowledge explained only a small proportion of variance in reputation, $R^2 = .106$, $F(1, 345) = 40.625$, $p < .001$. One-way analysis of covariance (ANCOVA) examined potential gender differences in perceptions of the NBA, controlling for knowledge of lockout history. ANCOVA is used to evaluate the difference between multiple group means while accounting for moderating variables. In this case, it was important to understand whether gender differences impacted participant impressions about the league and its reputation. ANCOVA showed impressions of the league (F (F (1,334) = .790, $p = .375$) and league reputation (1,334) = .012, $p = .912$) were not different between genders when controlling for knowledge of lockout history.

Exploring Perceptions of the NBA and NBPA

Paired samples t-tests were used to examine the differences between impressions of the NBA and NBPA reputation before (Time 1) and after (Time 2) receiving information about the lockout.

NBA Reputation

In addition to there being a significant difference between overall impressions of the NBA prior to ($M = 4.64$, $SD = 1.47$) and after ($M = 4.24$, $SD = 1.251$) receiving information about the lockout ($t(333) = 4.817$, $p < .001$), there was also a significant difference between NBA reputation prior to ($M = 4.93$,

$SD = 1.00$) and after ($M = 4.24$, $SD = 1.11$) receiving information about the lockout ($t(337) = 13.58$, $p < .001$).

Linear regression analysis determined whether being a stakeholder impacted perceptions of the league after receiving information about the lockout. Results suggested being an active NBA stakeholder strongly predicted NBA Time 1 reputation, $b = .609$, $t(335) = 14.05$, $p < .001$, explaining a significant proportion of Time 1 reputation variance, $R^2 = .371$, $F(1, 335) = 197.472$, $p < .001$. However, while being an active NBA stakeholder predicted NBA Time 2 reputation, $b = .466$, $t(335) = 9.65$, $p < .001$, the explained variance in Time 2 reputation dropped considerably, $R^2 = .210$, $F(1, 335) = 93.137$, $p < .001$. Next, independent samples t-tests revealed that, while there was not a significant gender difference related to Time 1 reputation, $t(166.256) = .733$, $p = .465$ (Levene's test ($F = 9.024$, $p = .003$)), reputation was perceived more positively by men ($M = 4.42$, $SD = 1.20$) than women ($M = 4.16$, $SD = 1.05$) after receiving information about the lockout (Time 2), $t(337) = 2.073$, $p = .039$. However, no significant gender-related differences were noted related to impressions of the NBA prior to ($t(336) = -.266$, $p = .791$) and after ($t(333) = -1.350$, $p = .178$) receiving information about the lockout.

NBPA Reputation

Paired t-tests showed that, prior to receiving information about the lockout, participants had a small, but significantly greater overall impression of the NBA ($M = 4.64$, $SD = 1.47$) than of the NBPA ($M = 4.36$, $SD = 1.26$), $t(336) = 5.27$, $p < .001$. However, after receiving information about the lockout, participant perceptions reversed. Although the difference was small, overall impressions of the NBA were lower ($M = 4.24$, $SD = 1.26$) than overall impressions of the NBPA ($M = 4.36$, $SD = 1.26$), $t(333) = 1.974$, $p = .049$, which stayed the same.

Finally, being an active NBA stakeholder predicted impressions of the NBPA before ($b = .526$, $t(334) = 11.316$, $p < .001$) and after receiving ($b = .351$, $t(332) = 6.84$, $p < .001$) information about the lockout. However, stakeholder activity significantly explained a greater proportion of the variance of overall impressions of the NBPA before receiving information about the lockout ($R^2 = .277$, $F(1, 334) = 128.05$, $p < .001$) than after receiving information about the lockout ($R^2 = .123$, $F(1, 332) = 46.732$, $p < .001$). Additionally, independent samples t-tests showed no significant gender differences existed when examining impressions of the NBPA either before ($t(336) = .668$, $p = .505$) or after ($t(334) = .659$, $p = .510$) receiving information about the lockout.

Understanding Participant Perceptions of Blame

Paired t-tests showed that, after receiving information about the lockout, the NBA ($M = 5.15$, $SD = 1.19$) was significantly more likely than the NBPA ($M = 4.47$, $SD = 1.32$) to be held at fault for the lockout, $t(338) = 7.35$, $p < .001$.

Linear regression analysis showed being an active stakeholder significantly predicted beliefs about the NBA being at fault for the lockout ($b =.128$, $t(335) = 2.36$, $p = .019$), accounting for a small, but significant proportion of variance of perceptions related to NBA fault, ($R^2 = .013$, $F(1, 335) = 5.59$, $p = .019$). However, being an active stakeholder did not significantly predict beliefs about the NBPA being at fault for the lockout ($b = -.025$, $t(335) = -.451$, $p = .652$). Additionally, independent samples t-tests showed men ($M = 5.39$, $SD = 1.30$) were significantly more likely than women ($M = 5.03$, $SD = 1.15$) to believe the league was at fault for the lockout, $t(183.60) = 2.45$, $p = 015$, (Levene's test ($F = 5.708$, $p = .017$)). However, there was no difference between male and female beliefs about player fault for the lockout $t(172.60) = .297$, $p = .767$ (Levene's test ($F = 10.92$, $p = .001$).

Examining the Relationship Between Blame and League Reputation

Overall, NBA reputation was not impacted by either blaming owners ($b = .090$, $t(337) = 1.65$, $p = .100$) or blaming players ($b = .046$, $t(337) = .843$, $p = .400$) for the lockout. Multiple regression analyses examined whether being an active stakeholder and blaming either owners or players could predict league reputation. The linear combination of stakeholder activity and owner blame was significant ($F(2, 334) = 46.66$, $p < .001$); however, only stakeholder activity ($b = .463$, $t(334) = 9.49$, $p < .001$) accounted for the variance in participant beliefs about NBA reputation. Similarly, the linear combination of stakeholder activity and player blame was significant ($F(2, 334) = 47.36$, $p < .001$); again, variance in participant beliefs about NBA reputation was explained only by stakeholder activity ($b = .468$, $t(334) = 9.68$, $p < .001$). ANCOVA also revealed that controlling for owner blame did not impact beliefs about NBA reputation based on gender, $F(1,336) = 3.471$, $p = .063$. However, ANCOVA suggests blaming players did impact beliefs about NBA reputation based on gender ($F(1,336) = 4.233$, $p = .040$). Men ($M = 4.42$, $SD = 1.20$) were slightly but significantly more likely than women ($M = 4.16$, $SD = 1.05$) to have higher evaluations of NBA reputation when controlling for beliefs about player blame.

Exploring How Specific Communication Strategies Impact Crisis Attribution

To analyze perceptions of player responsibility based on communication strategies, one-way ANOVA showed scapegoating communication strategies did not significantly affect overall beliefs about player responsibility for the lockout, $F(3, 335) = .307$, $p = .820$. ANCOVA showed that controlling the active stakeholder variable did not impact perceptions of player responsibility based on communication strategy, $F(3, 332) = .294$, $p = .830$. When communication strategy was analyzed in conjunction with participant gender, gender did not impact beliefs about player responsibility, $F(3, 331) = .741$, $p = .528$.

To analyze perceptions about owner responsibility, one-way ANOVA showed communication strategies failed to significantly effect overall beliefs about owner responsibility for the lockout, $F(3, 335) = .361$, $p = .781$. ANCOVA analysis showed that controlling for active stakeholders slightly but significantly impacted perceptions of league fault, $F(1, 332) = 5.80$, $p = .017$, $\eta^2 = .017$. When controlling the active stakeholder variable, participants in the apology ($M = 5.21$, $SD = 1.21$) and excusing ($M = 5.16$, $SD = 1.27$) conditions were more likely than participants in the scapegoating condition ($M = 5.04$, $SD = 1.21$) to believe the league was at fault for the lockout. Finally, a small but significant gender difference did emerge when examining the effect of communication strategy on beliefs about owner responsibility, $F(1, 331) = 6.82$, $p = .009$, $\eta^2 = .020$. Men who received excusing messages ($M = 5.30$, $SD = 1.32$) were more likely than women ($M = 5.09$, $SD = 1.24$) to believe the owners were at fault for the lockout. Additionally, men who received apology messages ($M = 5.33$, $SD = 1.07$) were more likely than women ($M = 5.15$, $SD = 1.06$) to hold the owners at fault.

Interpreting the Findings

Using an experimental method, select SCCT strategies were tested within the context of an actual crisis—the NBA lockout—to understand the degree to which specific communication strategies can alter crisis responsibility attributions and, subsequently, organizational reputation. Results suggested that boundaries exist depending on the crisis context and strategies used wherein specific communication strategies may impact perceptions of crisis responsibility and organizational reputation differently in specialized industries (Brown & White, 2011; Claeys et al., 2010). Findings primarily suggested that non-stakeholders react to crisis strategies differently than active stakeholders.

Examining Stakeholder Differences When Applying SCCT

Steps for SCCT suggest that organizations and communicators should establish perceived levels of crisis responsibility and adjust the reputational threat depending on organizational crisis history and existing reputation before choosing appropriate crisis communication strategies (see Chapter 2). Participants accurately believed owners initiate lockouts, lending support to the notion that current participants were knowledgeable about sports. However, because some participants still felt that players could initiate lockouts (which is impossible by definition). lockout-based knowledge serves as one way to establish perceptions of crisis responsibility. Arguably, lockouts can only be considered *intentional* because they reflect a purposeful decision by league management to prevent players from working.

Next, crisis history knowledge and beliefs about prior reputation were addressed. Participants were aware of sport lockouts, and being an active stakeholder predicted knowledge of crisis history, suggesting general crisis history awareness. Notably, the league did not enjoy a good reputation among participants. Participants knew about the NBA, but had only a somewhat favorable impression of the league and its reputation. Based on the literature, these findings suggest the NBA would have to carefully consider its communication strategies, potentially leaning toward diminishing or rebuilding strategies during a lockout (Coombs, 2014). However, contrary to previous findings (Coombs, 2004), results suggested that knowledge of lockout history did not impact the NBA's reputation. Although knowing about the lockout significantly predicted overall impressions of the league ($R^2 = .034$) and league reputation ($R^2 = .048$), the explained variance was small in a practical sense. And, while being an active stakeholder increased the explained variance in predicting reputation ($R^2 = .106$), the findings were still negligible. This suggests that active stakeholders—fans—did not necessarily rely on crisis history or prior reputation when evaluating the league. In fact, fans historically continued to support leagues and teams after lockouts; in the NHL, attendance *increased* after the end of the 2012–13 lockout (Hughes, 2013). This highlights the importance of tailoring crisis responses to unique stakeholder knowledge and relationships. For example, although participants were aware of the lockout going into the study, results showed that receiving information about the lockout significantly reduced league reputation and overall participant impressions of the league. Being an active fan significantly predicted league reputation before and after receiving information about the lockout, but the percentage of explained variance dropped from 37% to 21% between Times 1 and 2. A similar trend was noted with NBPA impressions, in which significant explained variance—based on fan activity—dropped from 27% to 12%. And, while NBPA impressions remained the same at Times 1 and 2, league impressions dropped significantly. The practical differences were small, but this implies that simply reading about the lockout harmed the owners instead of the players. Such findings support the argument that sport public relations may be more nuanced than anticipated (Bruce & Tini, 2008). For example, Bruce and Tini (2008) suggested sport organizations may use *diversion* strategies to effectively protect the actual league product—players—from reputational harm. Here, lockout knowledge and prior reputation seemingly did not impact perceptions about the crisis situation, but the situation impacted league perceptions—particularly among active stakeholders.

Finally, findings suggested crisis responsibility attributions were not enough to harm the league's overall reputation. However, stakeholder activity and gender accounted for differences in league reputation, regardless of perceptions of blame. This is not to say that females perceive responsibility or reputation differently than males. Instead, gender differences in this study may be an artifact of men being more active stakeholders, which is reflected in the participant sample and mirrors market research (Sports Business Daily, 2010). As such, active stakeholders may process crisis messages and perceive organizational reputation differently than non-stakeholders. For example, fans in this study were more likely to understand that owners begin lockouts. This is further validated by the fact that, overall, the tested communication strategies did not impact league perceptions. However, when controlling for gender and stakeholder activity, crisis strategies logically impacted perceptions of league fault. As expected, participants in the apology and excuse conditions were significantly more likely than those in the scapegoat condition to believe owners were at fault for the crisis. Further, these impacts only occurred for owners, suggesting active stakeholders may consider the organization-athlete relationship more discreetly. The larger implications for crisis communication suggest that active stakeholders may be impacted by crisis strategies differently than non-stakeholders. When determining best practices for communicating during crises, the strength of stakeholder relationships and how they are formed may impact the success of the chosen strategies.

Conclusion

Heeding calls to explore more diverse organizations (Avery et al., 2010), to explore attitudes related to existing organizations (Claeys et al., 2010), to "consider crisis history and prior reputation as intensifiers of the crisis situations" (Brown & White, 2011, p. 90), and to extend SCCT research beyond case study analysis (Coombs, 2007), this research experimentally explored the impact of crisis communication strategies in the context of an existing organizational crisis. By using the NBA lockout as an example, this study explored how professional sport may provide a unique context for studying reputation (Bruce & Tini, 2008), while finding stakeholder investment may be important when applying SCCT strategies. Because of the nature of sport fandom, it can be presumed that stakeholders may be more knowledgeable about crisis history and more set in their perceptions of the NBA. This may serve to protect the league from reputational damage during a crisis such as a lockout. Notably, overall participant perceptions of the NBA were unaffected by specific communication strategies (scapegoat, excuse, and apology), but those strategies impacted perceptions of reputation among active stakeholders and males. Here, fan activity and gender predicted knowledge about lockouts and lockout history, higher overall league reputation, and an increased likelihood of blaming owners—instead of players—for the crisis. While it should be reiterated that gender discrepancies are interpreted within the context of men being more likely than women to be NBA fans or stakeholders (Sports Business Daily, 2010), gender discrepancies served to validate stakeholder-based findings. Overall, understanding how active stakeholders process communication strategies differently than non-stakeholders may enhance knowledge about SCCT, increasing the usefulness of the approach when communicating during crises.

Building This Research and Looking Ahead

Obvious limitations exist within this study. For example, statistical analysis revealed significant results but the practical differences were often small. This may be due to the experimental materials, the relatively homogenous sample, or the lack of active stakeholders within the sample. First, the communication strategies presented were arbitrarily chosen to reflect different degrees to which an organization might accept responsibility for a crisis. This is a common problem with current SCCT research, because researchers tend to pick and choose which strategies they will test (i.e., Brown & White, 2011; Claeys et al., 2010). Future research should consider testing comparable communication strategies (e.g., only deny strategies) or testing the same strategies across multiple studies. Next, while messages were examined for external validity, no measure of strategy acceptance was used to determine whether participants accepted the strategies or differentiated between them. Without this, it is difficult to know whether the chosen message strategies had the intended consequences. And because a timer was not used to restrict participants from advancing through the study prematurely, it is possible participants did not clearly read the press releases or engage the strategy. Future research should consider using a timer to encourage participant engagement or could present the response strategies alone rather than embedded in a release. Additionally, similar to previous studies (Brown & White, 2011), the sample was predominantly female, meaning all research questions and hypotheses were explored within the context of gender. Although differences existed—for example, females were less likely to be active fans and know about league lockout history—this seems to be an artifact of NBA fandom. Future studies should achieve better representation of participant gender, particular because NBA fans are primarily (60.2%) male (Sports Business Daily, 2010). This then reveals the importance of exploring active stakeholder perceptions related to crisis. A severe limitation of this study is that, overall, participants did not appear to be active NBA fans. Previous studies using fictitious organizations suggest the need to study existing organizations to better gauge actual perceptions of reputation (Claeys et al., 2010). This study attempted to do that—and revealed interesting results when accounting for active stakeholders—but future research should make concerted efforts to survey a larger number of self-identified fans.

Finally, future SCCT research should consider investigating the role of stakeholder investment in the formation of beliefs and perceptions about an organization in crisis. In this case, stakeholders such as fans knew about crisis history and blamed the league, but their perceptions remained relatively unchanged regardless of communication strategy. This makes practical sense, because league fans will know more about league history, but may not form their opinions of the league based on crises such as a lockout. As previously suggested by Brown and White (2011), it may be worth exploring whether positive relationships can override or confound the use of specific strategies during organizational crises.

References

Avery, E. J., Lariscy, R. W., Kim, S., & Hocke, T. (2010). A quantitative review of crisis communication research in public relations from 1991 to 2009. *Public Relations Review, 36*(2), 190–192. doi:10.1016/j.pubrev.2010.01.001

Beck, H. (2011, February 18). After stagnant 12 months, NBA faces its own labor countdown. *New York Times*, p. B11.

Brown, K. A., & White, C. L. (2011). Organization–public relationships and crisis response strategies: Impact on attribution of responsibility. *Journal of Public Relations Research, 23*(1), 75–92. doi:10.1080/1062726X.2010.504792

Bruce, T., & Tini, T. (2008). Unique crisis response strategies in sports public relations: Rugby league and the case for diversion. *Public Relations Review, 34*(2), 108–115. doi:10.1016/j.pubrev.2008.03.015

Claeys, A. S., Cauberghe, V., & Vyncke, P. (2010). Restoring reputations in times of crisis: An experimental study of the Situational Crisis Communication Theory and the moderating effects of locus of control. *Public Relations Review, 36*(3), 256–262. doi:10.1016/j.pubrev.2010.05.004

CNN Library (2017, May 25). Pro sports lockouts and strikes fast facts. *CNN.com.* Retrieved from www.cnn.com/2013/09/03/us/pro-sports-lockouts-and-strikes-fast-facts/index.html

Coombs, W. T. (1995). Choosing the right words: The development of guidelines for the selection of the "appropriate" crisis-response strategies. *Management Communication Quarterly, 8*(4), 447–476.

Coombs, W. T. (2004). Impact of past crises on current crisis communication insights from Situational Crisis Communication Theory. *Journal of Business Communication, 41*(3), 265–289. doi:10.1177/0021943604265607

Coombs, W. T. (2007). Protecting organization reputations during a crisis: The development and application of situational crisis communication theory. *Corporate Reputation Review, 10*(3), 163–176. doi: 10.1057/palgrave.crr.1550049.

Coombs, W. T. (2014). *Ongoing crisis communication: Planning, managing, and responding* (4th ed.). Thousand Oaks, CA: Sage.

Coombs, W. T., & Holladay, S. J. (2002). Helping crisis managers protect reputational assets: Initial tests of the Situational Crisis Communication Theory. *Management Communication Quarterly, 16*(2), 165–186. doi:10.1016/j.pubrev.2008.04.001

Coombs, W. T., & Holladay, S. J. (2008). Comparing apology to equivalent crisis response strategies: Clarifying apology's role and value in crisis communication. *Public Relations Review, 34*(3), 252–257.

ESPN.com news service (2011, November 17). Players file 2 antitrust suits vs. NBA. *ESPN.com.* Retrieved from http://espn.go.com/nba/story/_/id/7239168/source-nba-cancels-games-dec-15

Fearn-Banks, K. (2017). *Crisis communication: A casebook approach* (5th ed.). New York: Routledge.

Fombrun, C. J., & Gardberg, N. (2000). Who's tops in corporate communication? *Corporate Reputation Review, 3*(1), 13–17.

Gaille, B. (2015, October 1). 23 terrific NBA fan demographics. *BrandonGaille.com.* Retrieved from http://brandongaille.com/23-nba-fan-demographics/

Hughes, J. (2013, February 21). *NHL rebounds from the lockout as attendance hits decade-high pace.* Retrieved from http://bleacherreport.com/articles/1538189-nhl-rebounds-from-the-lockout-as-attendance-is-on-track-for-a-decade-high

Jeong, S. H. (2009). Public's responses to an oil spill accident: A test of the attribution theory and situational crisis communication theory. *Public Relations Review, 35*(3), 307–309. doi:10.1016/j.pubrev.2009.03.010

Jerome, A. M. (2008). Toward prescription: Testing the rhetoric of atonement's applicability in the athletic arena. *Public Relations Review, 34*(2), 124–134. doi:10.1016/j.pubrev.2008.03.007

Klein, J. Z. (2011, October 13). Season lost by the NHL could teach the NBA. *New York Times*, p. B13.

Klein, J. Z. (2013, January 12). Sides sign agreement; Training camps to open. *New York Times*, p. SP11.

McMenamin, D. (2011, September 15). Derek Fisher: Rift among owners. *ESPNLosAngeles.com*. Retrieved from http://espn.go.com/los-angeles/nba/story/_/id/6973675/nba-lockout-derek-fisher-los-angeles-lakers-emails-players-says-owners-rift

Sisco, H. F. (2012). The ACORN story: An analysis of crisis response strategies in a nonprofit organization. *Public Relations Review. 38*(1), 89–96. doi:10.1016/j.pubrev.2011.11.001

Sports Business Daily (2010, June 9). *Fan demographics among major North American sports league*. Retrieved from www.sportsbusinessdaily.com/Daily/Issues/2010/06/Issue-185/The-Back-Of-The-Book/Fan-Demographics-Among-Major-North-American-Sports-Leagues.aspx

Sung, M. & Yang, S. (2008). Toward a model of university image: The influence of brand personality, external prestige, and reputation. *Journal of Public Relations Research, 20*(4), 357–376. doi:10.1080/10627260802153207

Tyler, L. (1997). Liability means never being able to say you're sorry: Corporate guilt, legal constraints, and defensiveness in corporate communication. *Management Communication Quarterly, 11*(1), 51–73.

PART III

Applications Using Image Repair Theory (IRT)

9

INVESTIGATING ATHLETES AND THEIR IMAGE REPAIR STRATEGIES DURING CRISES

Marion E. Hambrick

Sports scandals involving athletes occur frequently. TMZ Sports reported a litany of incidents within the U.S. professional sports realm during the first half of 2017. Headline makers spanned multiple sports and received attention for a variety of scandals. Numerous National Football League (NFL) players faced charges, including Buffalo Bills Adolphus Washington—possession of a weapon; Detroit Lions Tavon Wilson—domestic violence; Green Bay Packers Letroy Guion— driving under the influence (DUI); New York Jets Lorenzo Mauldin—assault; Dallas Cowboys Damien Wilson—aggravated assault; and Minnesota Vikings Michael Floyd—house arrest violation. National Basketball Association (NBA) players also involved in scandals included Golden State Warriors Matt Barnes— disorderly conduct; Detroit Pistons Kentavious Caldwell-Pope—DUI; and Minnesota Timberwolves Taj Gibson—driving with a suspended license. While not illegal, New York Knicks Carmelo Anthony was accused of having an affair and impregnating his mistress. Major League Soccer Orlando City Cyle Larin and professional golfer Tiger Woods were charged with DUI. Finally, professional tennis player Venus Williams faced a civil lawsuit for an automobile accident resulting in a fatality.

This chapter provides a review of research examining individual athletes and their image repair strategies employed during scandals and crises. Athlete image repair studies published in academic journals and textbooks from 1984 to June 2017 were investigated. The findings detail the strategies used by athletes when faced with crises and the effectiveness of their strategies. These findings also outline the research approaches used in the exploration of this topic. Insights into how researchers conducted their studies also emerge, including (a) type of media explored, (b) timeframe(s) examined, (c) number of data points used, and

(d) types of analyses completed. Finally, the review identifies opportunities to institute new or different approaches with future studies in this context.

Research Addressing Athlete Image Repair

Osborne, Sherry, and Nicholson (2016) noted the frequency of athletes encountering an array of scandals and crises. The researchers reviewed off-field scandals, and their study focused specifically on Australian professional male athletes and coverage of these scandals within print media. An analysis of 1,868 articles published over six months yielded 26 "socially unacceptable behaviors" (p. 262). The most frequently reported incidents involved recreational drug use (31), assault (31), professional misconduct (22), sexual assault (17), DUI and other incidents with an automobile (13), illegal or problem gambling (10), racism (8), adultery (8), civil disobedience (6), murder (5), and fraud (3). The authors asserted their findings, "while somewhat self-evident, demonstrate empirically the impact of celebrity on media focus in periods of crisis management" (p. 266).

In response to these scandals, athletes utilize image repair strategies to address them. These strategies represent an attempt to shift focus from the crisis, and return the athlete to a more positive position with their respective sports teams and organizations, fans, family, and friends. Benoit (1995) initially identified numerous image repair strategies. These include denial, evading responsibility, reducing offensiveness, corrective action, and mortification. (Chapter 2 includes a more detailed discussion.) Researchers focused on athlete image repair strategies have reported additional ones: (a) stonewalling (Frederick et al., 2014; Schmittel & Hull, 2015; Smith, 2013b), (b) suffering (Bernstein, 2013; Sanderson, 2008; Thomsen & Anderson, 2015) and victimization (Frederick et al., 2014; Schmittel & Hull, 2015), (c) conforming (Hambrick, Frederick, & Sanderson, 2015) and leveling the playing field (Thomsen & Anderson, 2015), (d) exposing critics (Schmittel & Hull, 2015), and (e) retrospective regret (Frederick et al., 2014; Hambrick et al., 2015).

Stonewalling occurs when an athlete assumes a less than helpful stance while addressing a crisis, whether slowing down the delivery of information about the event or refusing to provide information about it. Athletes also can engage in stonewalling by avoiding questions or failing to offer answers to the questions asked. They can provide incomplete responses or only information about minor aspects of the event. Stonewalling also entails changing the conversation or shifting the focus to other areas (Frederick et al., 2014; Hambrick et al., 2015; Schmittel & Hull, 2015; Smith, 2013b).

Suffering and *victimization* represent additional image repair strategies. With suffering, athletes regard themselves as the target of the crisis, harmed by critics such as the media and once adoring fans. Athletes who adopt this stance assert they have faced judgment prematurely, before they have a chance to explain their version of events. They provide specific evidence of their suffering—whether personally (e.g., loss of friends) or professionally (e.g., loss of sponsors)—resulting from these allegations. Victimization is closely related to suffering, as the athletes again portray themselves as a casualty of the crisis. Feeling prematurely disparaged, athletes indicate how much the event has affected them both personally and negatively. This portrayal allows athletes to potentially elicit sympathy from those who accept their version of events and side with them (Bernstein, 2013; Frederick et al., 2014; Hambrick et al., 2015; Sanderson, 2008; Schmittel & Hull, 2015; Thomsen & Anderson, 2015).

Conforming and *leveling the playing field* occur when athletes explain their actions as necessary based upon the environment in which they operate. They argue they did what others within the same or similar contexts have or would have done. Athletes using these image repair strategies make the argument of "everyone was doing it" to explain actions they recognize others view as suspicious or unethical. They assert they are simply complying with the norms of their group. Coupled with conforming, athletes may explain their behaviors as leveling the playing field. Not engaging in these actions would put them at a disadvantage to competitors, and they would be foolish to not take part (Hambrick et al., 2015; Thomsen & Anderson, 2015).

Exposing critics happens when athletes highlight the negative behaviors of those taking a negative stance against them or their actions. Athletes focus on critics who make judgments about the athletes or call their behaviors into question. This allows the athletes to take some of the attention focused on them and redirect it towards others, particularly those whose comments can be perceived as excessively disparaging or inflammatory. The athletes may in turn receive sympathy as the recipients of this negative treatment (Schmittel & Hull, 2015).

Retrospective regret occurs when athletes reflect upon their past actions and express remorse for these events after the fact. This remorse can include expressions of guilt for how certain events evolved and/or their responses to them. With this strategy, athletes might display feelings of remorse and potential offer an apology for their behaviors (Frederick et al., 2014; Hambrick et al., 2015).

Researchers examining individual athletes and their image repair strategies noted that, combined, these studies provide a more comprehensive view of strategies used by athletes and document their varying levels of success in restoring an athlete's image (Brown, 2016; Brown, Murphy, & Maxwell, 2017).

> To be sure, these many case studies illuminated the nature and function of defensive discourse. Throughout the years some of the claims that returned thematically time after time were: (1) mortification and corrective action are effective as partner strategies; (2) some categories (for instance denial and corrective action) ought to be mutually exclusive; (3) multi-wave campaigns that re-tool after initial failure are less effective; (4) legal considerations may limit rhetorical options; and (5) channels for distributing the reparative message matter because of questions of audience reach and interaction with message platform (text, video, audio, etc.).
>
> *Blaney, 2016, p. 4*

Previous sports-related image repair studies frequently focused on a single athlete and used rhetorical analysis to assess athlete image repair strategies with different communication channels (Brown, 2016). Looking at this research, Blaney (2016) and Brown (2016) suggested the potential for different methodological tools in examining image repair strategies, particularly those leveraging quantitative data collection and analysis. Likewise, Glantz and Benoit (2017) expressed a need for greater creativity in this research area, stating that "typically, these studies analyze messages from speeches, press releases, press conferences, and various other media appearances. Few scholarly articles focus on individuals or organizations that have used social media in their image-repair efforts" (p. 169). These authors argued image repair activities conducted via social media reflect current trends with this communication channel, allowing athletes, organizations, and others to control their image repair and information dissemination process and speak directly to their followers.

Review Approaches

In response to these criticisms, this chapter reviews the existing athlete image repair studies in order to quantify these claims (Blaney, 2016; Brown, 2016; Glantz & Benoit, 2017). Questions for examination include how frequently do athletes use certain image repair strategies and what is the relative effectiveness of these strategies? Also, how often do researchers focus on qualitative rhetorical analysis versus other methodological tactics? An approach similar to the Arendt, LaFleche, and Limperopulos (2017) study was used. Their meta-analysis reviewed 110 image repair, apologia, and crisis studies published in 51 academic journals over a 30-year period from 1986 to 2017. Their study focused on image repair and crisis communication in multiple contexts, rather than one context or industry such as sports. They did note, however, that "apologia in sports is [an] area that has been extensively researched" (p. 520). In their meta-analysis, they also discussed how numerous studies focused on athletes and sports organizations and how communications and public relations journals helped disseminate these works.

The Arendt et al. study (2017) produced several findings. First, the results revealed balance in the image repair strategies in their sample, split among denial (46 percent), reducing offensiveness (42 percent), corrective action (38 percent), and shifting blame (18 percent). Corrective action and evading responsibility were two of the more successful image repair strategies. The authors also noted the use of corrective action with either reducing offensiveness or bolstering as effective. Conversely, denial used alone or in combination with reducing offensiveness or evasion of responsibility resulted in the least successful outcomes. Finally, their study indicated factors such as perceived guilt or innocence, litigation possibilities, crisis scope, and timeliness in responding to the crisis also influenced the relative successes or failures of the chosen image repair strategies.

The current review adopted a similar approach by concentrating on athlete image repair research published from January 1984 to June 2017. These studies were identified by (a) using academic search engines and the search terms "sport" and "image repair" to find related studies, and (b) reviewing the references from these studies to identify additional research. This two-part process led to a total of 38 studies in 10 academic journals and 2 books. Three studies each examined multiple athletes, which led to a total of 43 instances where individual athletes and their image repair strategies were documented. Academic journals included in the investigation were *Communication & Sport, International Journal of Sport Communication*, and *Journal of Sports Media*. The sample also included studies from two texts, Blaney's (2016) *Putting Image Repair to the Test* and Blaney et al.'s (2013) *Repairing the Athlete's Image: Studies in Sports Image Restoration*.

Longitudinal Trends

This review of the 38 published image repair studies indicated researchers examined athlete image repair strategies from 1984 to 2017, starting with Nelson's (1984) study of Billie Jean King. The bulk of this research was published in 2013, with a high of 20 cases included within 16 studies that year. 2015 and 2016 were the next highest years, with five studies both years. Three cases were each published in 2008 and 2010. Two cases also were published in 2014. One case was published in each of 1984, 1994, 2011, 2012, and 2017 (through June 2017). The biggest driver of the 2013 number of studies was Blaney et al.'s (2013) *Repairing the Athlete's Image: Studies in Sports Image Restoration*, published that year. This text included 13 cases, the most of any publication. Blaney's (2016) *Putting Image Repair to the Test* contained two additional studies. Researchers also published athlete image repair studies in the following academic journals: *Journal of Sports Media* (7), *Public Relations Review* (6), *International Journal of Sport Communication* (4), *Communication & Sport* (3), *Elon Journal of Undergraduate Research in Communications* (3), *Journalism & Mass Communication Quarterly* (1), *Qualitative Research in Sport, Exercise, and Health* (1), and *Western Journal of Sport Communication* (1).

Athlete Image Repair

The most popular athletes examined during this timeframe were Lance Armstrong (3), Barry Bonds (3), Kobe Bryant (3), and Tiger Woods (3). The most frequently examined sports were football (11), baseball (8), basketball (5), and cycling (4). Football included athletes such as Plaxico Burress, Maurice Clarett, Frank Gore, Richie Incognito, Rashard Mendenhall, Terrell Owens, Ben Roethlisberger, Aqib Talib (2), Manti Te'o, and Michael Vick (2). Baseball athletes included Barry Bonds (3), Roger Clemens (2), Mark McGwire (2), and Alex Rodriguez. Athletes from basketball included Gilbert Arenas, Kobe Bryant (3), and LeBron James. Cycling athletes were Lance Armstrong (3) and

Floyd Landis. The following athletes also were examined during the sample time period: swimmer Michael Phelps (2), soccer players Elizabeth Lambert and John Terry, tennis players Billie Jean King and Serena Williams, automobile racer Tony Stewart, figure skater Tonya Harding, hockey player Jordan Weal, and track and field athlete Marion Jones.

The athletes used multiple communications channels, which researchers in turn studied in their respective analyses, as illuminated in Table 9.1.

TABLE 9.1 The Sample Media, Timeframes, and Methods

Researcher(s) (Year)	Communication Channel(s)	Timeframe	Method
Benoit (2013)	Personal statements	Longitudinal	Qualitative
Benoit and Hanczor (1994)	TV interview	One-time	Qualitative
Bernstein (2013)	Personal statements	Longitudinal	Qualitative
Brazeal (2008)	Press conference	One-time	Qualitative
Brazeal (2013)	Press conference, personal statements	Longitudinal	Qualitative
Brown (2016)	Personal statement	One-time	Experimental
Brown, Anderson, and Dickhaus (2016)	Online article	One-time	Experimental
Brown, Billings, and Devlin (2016)	Online article	One-time	Experimental
Brown, Billings, Mastro, and Brown-Devlin (2015)	Personal statement	One-time	Experimental
Brown and Brown (2016)	Online article	One-time	Experimental
Brown, Dickhaus, and Long (2012)	Online article	One-time	Experimental
Brown et al. (2017)	Online article	One-time	Experimental
Compton (2013)	Personal statement, print interview	Longitudinal	Qualitative
Frederick et al. (2014)	TV interview	One-time	Qualitative
Glantz (2010)	TV interviews, press conference	Longitudinal	Qualitative
Glantz (2013)	TV interview	One-time	Qualitative
Griffin (2013)	Personal statement	One-time	Qualitative
Haigh and Alwine (2016)	News articles	Longitudinal	Mixed

Hambrick et al. (2015)	Tweets	Longitudinal	Qualitative
Holdener and Kauffman (2014)	Press conference	One-time	Qualitative
Huxford (2013)	Print interview	One-time	Qualitative
Jerome (2008)	Interviews, personal statements	Longitudinal	Qualitative
Kennedy (2010)	Personal statement, government testimony	Longitudinal	Qualitative
Kramer (2013)	TV interview	One-time	Qualitative
McGuire and McKinnon (2013)	Government testimony	One-time	Qualitative
Meng and Pan (2013)	Personal statement	One-time	Qualitative
Nelson (1984)	Press conference, TV interview, print interview	Longitudinal	Qualitative
Pfahl (2015)	Online article	Longitudinal	Qualitative
Sanderson (2008)	Press conference	One-time	Qualitative
Schmittel and Hull (2015)	TV interview, tweets	Longitudinal	Qualitative
Sheckels (2013)	Personal statements, tweets, newspaper op-ed, sentencing	Longitudinal	Qualitative
Smith (2013a)	Interviews	Longitudinal	Qualitative
Smith (2013b)	Press conference	One-time	Qualitative
Smith (2013c)	Press conferences, personal statement	Longitudinal	Qualitative
Thomsen and Anderson (2015)	TV interview	One-time	Qualitative
Troester and Johns (2013)	Personal statement	One-time	Qualitative
Utsler and Epp (2013)	TV interview, press conference	One-time	Qualitative
Walsh and McAllister-Spooner (2011)	Personal statement	One-time	Qualitative

Personal statements (14) represented the most common communication channel for image repair, followed by press conferences (9), television interviews (8), online articles (6), print interviews (3), tweets (3), other interviews (2), government testimony (2), newspaper op-ed (1), and criminal sentencing (1).

Image Repair Strategy	Effective	Mixed Effectiveness	Not Effective
Denial	Burress, Lambert	Arenas, Armstrong, Rodriguez, Vick, Woods	Bonds, Clemens, Harding, Incognito, Landis, McGwire, Te'o, Williams
Evading Responsibility	Bryant, Burress, Lambert, Phelps	Arenas, Armstrong, Rodriguez, Vick	Clemens, Harding, Incognito, Landis, McGwire, Te'o, Williams
Reducing Offensiveness	Bryant, Burress, King, Lambert, Phelps, Roethlisberger	Arenas, Armstrong, Clarett, Rodriguez, Terry, Vick, Woods	Bonds, Clemens, Harding, Incognito, Jones, Landis, McGwire, Owens, Te'o, Williams
Corrective Action	Bryant, Lambert, Phelps, Roethlisberger, Stewart	Arenas, Armstrong, Clarett, Vick, Woods	McGwire, Williams
Mortification	Bryant, Burress, Lambert, Phelps, Roethlisberger, Stewart	Arenas, Armstrong, Rodriguez, Vick, Woods	Clemens, Incognito, McGwire, Owens, Te'o, Williams

FIGURE 9.1   Image Repair Strategies and Their Effectiveness

This number exceeds the sample size of 43, as athletes used multiple methods to disseminate their respective stories and stances.

The athletes also used a combination of image repair strategies—denial, evading responsibility, reducing offensiveness, corrective action, mortification—with varying levels of success, from effective to mixed effectiveness, to not effective. Athletes who used denial, evading responsibility, and reducing offensiveness received less effective results. Conversely, using corrective action led to image repair ratings from effective to mixed effectiveness. For athletes who used mortification, their image repair efforts spanned from effective to mixed effectiveness to ineffective.

Many athletes used a variety of image repair strategies rather than focusing on a single approach, and some combinations proved more effective than others. Burress effectively used denial, evade responsibility, reduce offensiveness, and mortification. Glantz (2013) suggested this approach was deemed effective because Burress went to prison for his actions. This in combination with his image repair efforts demonstrated evidence of his willingness to accept his punishment and make amends. Lambert used every strategy as part of her image repair.

Compton (2013) concluded this approach led to a positive response, because Lambert apologized for her actions and actively took steps to correct them. Conversely, Williams's image repair included every strategy, and these efforts were deemed largely ineffective. Brazeal (2013) noted Williams did not start with an apology, but rather offered a series of other explanations for her behaviors. In doing so, critics viewed her delayed apology as insincere and inadequate. McGwire likewise used all of the image repair strategies. McGuire and McKinnon (2013) concluded McGwire should have offered an apologetic message from the outset to generate a more effective response.

The athletes frequently used mortification as an image repair strategy as evidenced above. In no instance did they use mortification alone, but instead they coupled this strategy with others. Those who used denial with mortification often received less than effective outcomes. Their apologies appeared as part of an inconsistent message, did not feel sincere, or came at the end rather than the beginning of their image repair campaign. As such, they saw few positive results from this approach. Others derived benefits from apologizing and taking responsibility for their actions. Those athletes who used mortification with evading responsibility, reducing the offensiveness of their actions, and corrective action frequently benefited from their actions. Researchers concluded athletes can gain from using mortification, but they should apologize and take ownership for their actions early in order to receive the full advantages of this image repair strategy (Blaney, 2016; Brazeal, 2013; McGuire & McKinnon, 2013).

Most of the sport image repair research focused on actual athletes and events. Fewer measured the potential effectiveness of using one or more image repair strategies in a controlled environment (Brown, 2016; Brown, Anderson, & Dickhaus, 2016; Brown, Billings, & Devlin, 2016; Brown et al., 2012, 2015, 2017). Those studies using experimental designs, however, drew similar conclusions. Mortification again proved the most effective strategy in most instances. Making an apology generated the most positive responses for these athletes (Brown, 2016; Brown, Billings, & Devlin, 2016; Brown et al., 2012, 2015). In one case, coupling mortification with corrective action or mortification with bolstering proved more effective than using mortification or bolstering in isolation (Brown et al., 2017). Brown, Anderson, and Dickhaus (2016) found in another case that using mortification, defeasibility, or provocation led to similar results. The researchers concluded athletes do not always have to apologize for their actions, if they can provide an adequate explanation for them. However, overall, mortification consistently appeared as one of the most effective image repair strategies utilized by the athletes.

Athlete Image Repair Studies

Moving from the individual athletes to the published studies, the vast majority of cases adopted a qualitative approach (35). The researchers primarily employed rhetorical analysis, as they examined text stemming from personal statements, press conferences, interviews, and other documents. In some instances, multiple text sources were used. For example, Benoit (2013) and Bernstein (2013) reviewed several personal statements issued by Woods, and Pfahl (2015) used multiple blog posts from Clarett to examine their different image repair strategies. Other studies explored information stemming from a combination of sources. For example, Nelson (1984) reviewed details disseminated through a news conference, TV interview, and magazine interview in the examination of King. Two studies reviewed social media usage of athletes. Hambrick et al. (2015) looked at tweets generated by Armstrong, while Schmittel and Hull (2015) combined tweets with a TV interview in their study of Incognito.

Most researchers relied heavily upon qualitative analysis as evidenced above. A smaller number, however, used experimental design (7) to study the efficacy of the various image repair strategies. These studies most frequently used a real athlete (Brown, 2016; Brown & Brown, 2016; Brown, Anderson, & Dickhaus, 2016; Brown et al., 2012, 2017). Two studies used fictitious athletes, in both cases hypothetical professional tennis players (Brown, Billings, & Devlin, 2016; Brown et al., 2015). These researchers examined the potential successes of various image repair strategies, through most commonly an investigation of bolstering, provocation, and mortification (Brown, Anderson, & Dickhaus, 2016; Brown et al., 2015, 2017). They developed scenarios whereby the athletes used one or a combination of these strategies, and online news outlets similar to *Bleacher Report* and *Deadspin* published the stories. With these scenarios, the researchers collected data from sports consumers and assessed which strategies the respondents deemed most effective. They also examined the effects of other variables such as crises type (criminal versus non-criminal), gender, and race on the image repair strategy outcomes.

Only one of the 38 studies employed a mixed method approach. Haigh and Alwine (2016) examined Armstrong's image repair strategies via qualitative and quantitative methods. Their qualitative analysis proved similar to the previous studies conducting rhetorical analysis, where they examined Armstrong's image repair strategies reported in news articles published from 1999 to 2013. They followed this investigation with a second one using experimental design. Research participants were asked to review either a video or print document about Armstrong, and offer their personal assessments regarding his credibility. This mixed method strategy allowed the researchers to review Armstrong's approach and more accurately evaluate its effectiveness from a sport consumer's perspective.

Most of the studies examined one moment in time (28) versus taking a longitudinal perspective (15). Examples of one-time analysis included Brazeal's (2008) study of Owens and Kramer's (2013) study of Jones. In the first study, Brazeal focused on a press conference held by Owens and his agent, while Kramer examined the TV interview between Oprah Winfrey and Jones. Longitudinal studies took advantage of multiple appearances by the athletes or documents from multiple sources. These studies spanned days, or in some cases years, surrounding a single scandal. For example, Jerome (2008) investigated the multiple interviews conducted with personal statements issued by Stewart. Smith (2013a) used Vick's personal statements and press conferences to study his image repair. Haigh and Alwine (2016) adopted a longer perspective in their 1999–2013 study of Armstrong and how his image repair strategies changed over time.

The results of these studies revealed researchers investigating athlete image repair strategies examined a variety of athletes and their respective scandals. This research took advantage of different communication channels employed by athletes, whether during a single instance or over a longer timespan. The results documented the myriad image repair strategies used by the athletes, highlighting the relative effectiveness of mortification when used early and in combination with other strategies. The findings also indicated researchers adopted a more limited approach in their data analyses. Most studies focused on qualitative data analysis and a single point in time, while fewer studies used a longitudinal or quantitative/mixed methods data collection and analysis.

Image Repair Implications

A number of implications arose from these investigations. Arendt et al. (2017) in their meta-analysis of image repair studies highlighted the numerous studies focused on sports contexts, whether with individual athletes or sports organizations. Their study also documented the dissemination of information regarding these strategies within communications and public relations journals. The current analysis of athlete image repair noted similar findings. A total of 38 studies containing 43 cases emerged on this topic, published from January 1984 to June 2017. Researchers reported their findings in communications and public relations journals and texts. Given the number of athletes facing scandals, an opportunity seemingly exists in perpetuity to continue addressing these scandals. Arendt et al. (2017) highlighted the practical implication of their work—to provide public relations organizations with guidance on how to address crises. The resulting research from this chapter can provide athletes with insights on the different image repair strategies used by their peers. Athletes would benefit from apologizing for their actions, but could couple this strategy with others such as bolstering and corrective action. Regardless of which complementary strategies they choose, they should apologize early. They also should forgo using denial to avoid offering a less than adequate image repair presentation.

The results of this investigation also reflected the conclusions drawn by Blaney (2016) and Glantz and Benoit (2017), who studied and summarized previously published sport image repair research. Blaney (2016) reported corrective action and mortification represented the most effective strategies used by athletes. These strategies differ somewhat from the rankings reported by Arendt et al. (2017), who found more evidence of denial in their meta-analysis. Their study did reveal that reducing offensiveness (which includes bolstering) and corrective action were the second and third most used image repair strategies, respectively. Athletes in this study also used denial, but not as frequently or as effectively as the other strategies. Future research could address why some strategies are used more often or more effectively than others within specific sport contexts involving athletes. This could be accomplished by specifically speaking with the athletes and other individuals involved with an athlete's public relations and image repair efforts.

Next, the results showed the athletes used different communication channels to address their crises. Most of the studies in this sample focused on channels such as print and TV stories and interviews, press conferences, and personal statements, as also noted by Glantz and Benoit (2017). Researchers gravitated towards these channels, presumably following the preferred delivery methods chosen by the athletes. Fewer athletes and studies centered their efforts on social media usage. Of course, the studies spanned 1984 to 2017, where some emerged before social media's existence. In other cases, athletes—and their PR representatives—may not have felt as comfortable using social media as part of their image repair tactics. This could change if future athletes believe a benefit exists from speaking directly to fans and other stakeholders via this communication channel.

Only three of the 38 studies investigated athletes' usage of social media—and more specifically Twitter. These studies included Scheckels (2013), Hambrick et al. (2015), and Schmittel and Hull (2015). Glantz and Benoit (2017) advocated for further examination of image repair via social media, as athletes as well as sports teams, leagues, and other organizations and entities use these platforms to communicate with their followers. Janicki and Miller (2017) most recently examined the social media pages—Twitter and Instagram—of Duke University men's basketball player Grayson Allen, who tripped opposing players during multiple games. Their blog post documented how he used both platforms to present a more favorable image, quoting Bible verses and posting photographs of him engaged in community service. More athletes will likely turn to social media platforms as part of their image repair, as they can reach their fans and other followers more readily. An opportunity exists to study these efforts on one or more social media platforms and to combine this with image repair strategies used in more traditional media formats to assess consistency and effectiveness across communication channels.

Most of the studies in this sample focused on a singular event or moment in time. Using one data point for analysis (e.g., a press conference or TV interview) creates limitations in terms of the analysis conducted and generalizability of the resulting findings (Blaney, 2016; Coombs, 2006; Jerome, 2008). Researchers, however, are limited by the content provided. An athlete may only conduct a single interview or issue one personal statement. In contrast, some athletes made multiple statements and used several outlets selected a variety of strategies (e.g., Landis: Glantz, 2010) or their personal tribulations lasted for an extended period of time (e.g., Armstrong: Haigh & Alwine, 2016; Hambrick et al., 2015).

In these instances, researchers have a better opportunity to understand the potential effectiveness of combined image repair strategies in concert with how these strategies could change over time.

Finally, most of the studies adopted a qualitative approach through rhetorical analysis, while fewer branched into quantitative or mixed methods. Blaney (2016) stressed the importance of venturing into these methodological areas in order to move beyond conventional image repair analysis and to build upon existing research in this area. "We look forward to the contribution of this empirical [quantitative] turn and hope it will prompt more such research in the field" (p. 4). Sport communication researchers led by Kenon Brown have produced seven studies to date using experimental design. Some of these studies investigate real athletes, while others focus on fictitious athletes and scandals with their analysis. Adopting this experimental approach gives researchers an opportunity to assess specific image repair strategies in isolation or in conjunction with other factors, including types of crises faced and demographic variables such as the age and gender of athletes. This line of work aligns with the Arendt et al. (2017) meta-analysis, which identified important factors such as crises scope and timeliness of response to determine the most efficacious usage of image repair strategies. Researchers can continue this exploration with different athletes, image strategies, and other variables as suggested in the experimental design research. They also can combine experimental designs with rhetorical analysis, similar to the work of Haigh and Alwine (2016), to provide a richer and more comprehensive examination of image repair strategies. Collecting details about what strategies athletes use with stakeholder responses to these strategies can provide more insights about their relative effectiveness. This also can allow researchers to provide specific recommendations for athletes and others seeking to improve their public relations campaigns.

Conclusion

This chapter reviewed 43 cases investigating individual athletes and their selected image repair strategies employed during various crises. Findings from the 38 studies, which ranged from 1984 to June 2017, indicated athletes' most frequently used image repair strategies such as bolstering, corrective action, and mortification to address scandals and crises. They commonly relied upon communication mechanisms such as personal statements, press conferences, and interviews with their chosen strategies. Likewise, researchers focused on these outlets in their investigations of athlete image repair. Fewer studies documented this usage within social media platforms, such as Twitter. Additionally, most of the studies examined one moment in time and used rhetorical analysis. Fewer employed a longitudinal approach or quantitative (experimental) and mixed method designs. Opportunities continue to exist for building upon the existing studies in this area, adopting different approaches, and moving this research agenda forward.

References

Arendt, C., LaFleche, M., & Limperopulos, M. A. (2017). A qualitative meta-analysis of apologia, image repair, and crisis communication: Implications for theory and practice. *Public Relations Review, 43*, 517–526.

Benoit, W. L. (1995). *Accounts, excuses, and apologies: A theory of image restoration discourse.* Albany, NY: State University of New York Press.

Benoit, W. L. (2013). Tiger Woods's image repair: Could he hit one out of the rough? In J. R. Blaney, L. R. Lippert, & J. S. Smith (Eds.), *Repairing the athlete's image: Studies in sports image restoration* (pp. 89–96). Lanham, MD: Lexington Books.

Benoit, W. L., & Hanczor, R. S. (1994). The Tonya Harding controversy: An analysis of image restoration strategies. *Communication Quarterly, 42*, 416–433.

Bernstein, B. (2013). Crisis management and sports in the age of social media: A case study analysis of the Tiger Woods scandal. *Elon Journal of Undergraduate Research in Communications, 3*, 1–16.

Blaney, J. R. (2016). Image restoration theory: Time for the quantitative turn. In J. R. Blaney (Ed.), *Putting image repair to the test: Quantitative applications of image repair restoration theory* (pp. 3–6). Lanham, MD: Lexington Books.

Brazeal, L. M. (2008). The image repair strategies of Terrell Owens. *Public Relations Review, 34*, 145–150.

Brazeal, L. M. (2013). Belated remorse: Serena Williams's image repair rhetoric at the 2009 U.S. Open. In J. R. Blaney, L. R. Lippert, & J. S. Smith (Eds.), *Repairing the athlete's image: Studies in sports image restoration* (pp. 239–252). Lanham, MD: Lexington Books.

Brown, K. A. (2016). Is apology the best policy? An experimental examination of the effectiveness of image repair strategies during criminal and noncriminal athlete transgressions. *Communication & Sport, 4*, 23–42.

Brown, K. A., Anderson, M. L., & Dickhaus, J. (2016). The impact of the image repair process on athlete-endorsement effectiveness. *Journal of Sports Media, 11*, 25–48.

Brown, K. A., Billings, A., & Devlin, M. (2016). Image repair across the racial spectrum: Experimentally exploring athlete transgression responses. *Communication Research Reports, 33*, 47–53.

Brown, K. A., Billings, A. C., Mastro, D., & Brown-Devlin, N. (2015). Changing the image repair equation: Impact of race and gender on sport-related transgressions. *Journalism & Mass Communication Quarterly, 92*, 487–506.

Brown, K. A., & Brown, N. A. (2016). Responding to criminal accusations: An experimental examination of Aqib Talib's 2011 aggravated assault case. In J. R. Blaney (Ed.), *Putting image repair to the test: Quantitative applications of image repair restoration theory* (pp. 113–129). Lanham, MD: Lexington Books.

Brown, K. A., Dickhaus, J., & Long, M. C. (2012). LeBron James and "The Decision": An empirical examination of image repair in sports. *Journal of Sports Media, 7*, 149–175.

Brown, K. A., Murphy, B., & Maxwell, L. C. (2017). Tried in the court of public opinion: Effects of involvement in criminal transgressions on athlete image. *Communication & Sport.* doi:10.1177/2167479517697426

Compton, J. L. (2013). Unsports(wo)manlike conduct: An image repair analysis of Elizabeth Lambert, the University of New Mexico, and the NCAA. In J. R. Blaney, L. R. Lippert, & J. S. Smith (Eds.), *Repairing the athlete's image: Studies in sports image restoration* (pp. 253–264). Lanham, MD: Lexington Books.

Coombs, W. T. (2006). Crisis management: A communicative approach. In C. H. Botan & V. Hazleton (Eds.), *Public relations theory II* (pp. 171–197). Mahwah, NJ: Lawrence Erlbaum Associates.

Frederick, E. L., Burch, L. M., Sanderson, J., & Hambrick, M. E. (2014). To invest in the invisible: A case study of Manti Te'o's image repair strategies during the Katie Couric interview. *Public Relations Review, 40,* 780–788.

Glantz, M. (2010). The Floyd Landis doping scandal: Implications for image repair discourse. *Public Relations Review, 36,* 157–163.

Glantz, M. (2013). Plaxico Burress takes his best shot. In J. R. Blaney, L. R. Lippert, & J. S. Smith (Eds.), *Repairing the athlete's image: Studies in sports image restoration* (pp. 187–202). Lanham, MD: Lexington Books.

Glantz, M., & Benoit, W. L. (2017). The world's all atwitter: Image repair discourse on social media. In L. L. Austin & Y. Jin (Eds.), *Social media and crisis communication* (pp. 168–179). New York: Routledge.

Griffin, R. A. (2013). Power, privilege, and the surprising absence of repair: Kobe Bryant and interest convergence. In J. R. Blaney, L. R. Lippert, & J. S. Smith (Eds.), *Repairing the athlete's image: Studies in sports image restoration* (pp. 97–122). Lanham, MD: Lexington Books.

Haigh, M. M., & Alwine, L. (2016). "I'm sorry" is hard to say for Lance Armstrong: Examining how this impacts public perception. In J. R. Blaney (Ed.), *Putting image repair to the test: Quantitative applications of image repair restoration theory* (pp. 99–111). Lanham, MD: Lexington Books.

Hambrick, M. E., Frederick, E. L., & Sanderson, J. (2015). From yellow to blue: Exploring Lance Armstrong's image repair strategies across traditional and social media. *Communication & Sport, 3,* 196–218.

Holdener, M., & Kauffman, J. (2014). Getting out of the doghouse: The image repair strategies of Michael Vick. *Public Relations Review, 40,* 92–99.

Huxford, J. (2013). Strategies of silence: The John Terry affair and the British press. In J. R. Blaney, L. R. Lippert, & J. S. Smith (Eds.), *Repairing the athlete's image: Studies in sports image restoration* (pp. 123–148). Lanham, MD: Lexington Books.

Janicki, J., & Miller, G. (2017, April 24). *A tripped up image: Grayson Allen and his image repair tactics.* Retrieved from https://jenjanickiblog.wordpress.com/2017/04/24/grayson-allen-paper/

Jerome, A. M. (2008). Toward prescription: Testing the rhetoric of atonement's applicability in the athletic arena. *Public Relations Review, 34,* 124–134.

Kennedy, J. (2010). Image reparation strategies in sports: Media analysis of Kobe Bryant and Barry Bonds. *Elon Journal of Undergraduate Research in Communications, 1,* 95–103.

Kramer, M. R. (2013). The image repair media interview as *apologia* and *antapologia*: Marion Jones on the *Oprah Winfrey Show*. In J. R. Blaney, L. R. Lippert, & J. S. Smith (Eds.), *Repairing the athlete's image: Studies in sports image restoration* (pp. 59–70). Lanham, MD: Lexington Books.

McGuire, J., & McKinnon, L. M. (2013). "Big Mac" with a side of steroids: The image repair strategies of Mark McGuire. In J. R. Blaney, L. R. Lippert, & J. S. Smith (Eds.), *Repairing the athlete's image: Studies in sports image restoration* (pp. 27–40). Lanham, MD: Lexington Books.

Meng, J., & Pan, P. L. (2013). Revisiting image-restoration strategies: An integrated case study of three athlete sex scandals in sports news. *International Journal of Sport Communication, 6,* 87–100.

Nelson, J. (1984). The defense of Billie Jean King. *Western Journal of Speech Communication, 48*, 92–102.

Osborne, A., Sherry, E., & Nicholson, M. (2016). Celebrity, scandal, and the male athlete: A sport media analysis. *European Sport Management Quarterly, 16*, 255–273.

Pfahl, M. (2015). The prison blogs: The mind of Maurice Clarett and image repair on the Internet. *Qualitative Research in Sport, Exercise, and Health, 7*, 125–147.

Sanderson, J. (2008). "How do you prove a negative?": Roger Clemens's image-repair strategies in response to the Mitchell Report. *International Journal of Sport Communication, 1*, 246–262.

Schmittel, A., & Hull, K. (2015). "Shit got cray cray #MYBAD": An examination of the image-repair discourse of Richie Incognito during the Miami Dolphins' bullying scandal. *Journal of Sports Media, 10*, 115–137.

Sheckels, T. F. (2013). The failed comedy of the NBA's Gilbert Arenas: Image restoration in context. In J. R. Blaney, L. R. Lippert, & J. S. Smith (Eds.), *Repairing the athlete's image: Studies in sports image restoration* (pp. 169–186). Lanham, MD: Lexington Books.

Smith, J. S. (2013a). Bad Newz Kennels: Michael Vick and dogfighting. In J. R. Blaney, L. R. Lippert, & J. S. Smith (Eds.), *Repairing the athlete's image: Studies in sports image restoration* (pp. 151–168). Lanham, MD: Lexington Books.

Smith, J. S. (2013b). Defense of an anti-hero: Barry Bonds's "State of the Great Address." In J. R. Blaney, L. R. Lippert, & J. S. Smith (Eds.), *Repairing the athlete's image: Studies in sports image restoration* (pp. 41–58). Lanham, MD: Lexington Books.

Smith, J. S. (2013c). From the Mitchell Report to Brian McNamee: Roger Clemens's image repair discourse. In J. R. Blaney, L. R. Lippert, & J. S. Smith (Eds.), *Repairing the athlete's image: Studies in sports image restoration* (pp. 9–26). Lanham, MD: Lexington Books.

Thomsen, S. R., & Anderson, H. (2015). Using the rhetoric of atonement to analyze Lance Armstrong's failed attempt at redeeming his public image. *Journal of Sports Media, 10*, 79–99.

Troester, R. L., & Johns, L. (2013). The Michael Phelps saga: From successful Olympian, to pot smoker caught on camera, to renewed role model and brand. In J. R. Blaney, L. R. Lippert, & J. S. Smith (Eds.), *Repairing the athlete's image: Studies in sports image restoration* (pp. 71–85). Lanham, MD: Lexington Books.

Utsler, M., & Epp, S. (2013). Image repair through TV: The strategies of McGwire, Rodriguez, and Bonds. *Journal of Sports Media, 8*, 139–161.

Walsh, J., & McAllister-Spooner, S. M. (2011). Analysis of the image repair discourse in the Michael Phelps controversy. *Public Relations Review, 37*, 157–162.

10

#14FOREVER

Nostalgia, Pete Rose, and the Cincinnati Reds

Todd F. McDorman

The raucous Cincinnati crowd greeted their favorite son with a hero's welcome. First, for the anniversary of the returning 1976 World Championship team. Then for the retirement of his uniform number, 14. Finally, for his induction into the team's Hall of Fame. It might have been 1991, shortly preceding a nearly unanimous National Baseball Hall of Fame election. The central character would have been Pete Rose, the hometown hero, a 50-year-old manager, coming off a 1990 World Series title, with shaggy salt-and-pepper hair, a slightly expanding waistline, and a cocky, self-assured intensity. It would have been a different ceremony, there would have been a different energy, and it would have reflected a different era—one without smartphones or social media, and before labor strife wiped out a World Series, eight-figure annual contracts had become the norm, or the sport was engulfed by rampant speculation over performance-enhancing drugs.[1]

This idealized vision of the celebration reflects a seducing nostalgia that is a longing not "for the past the way it was, but for the past the way it could have been" (Boym, 2001, p. 351). Instead, it was June 2016. There was not a World Series championship as a manager, or an induction in Cooperstown.[2] Pete Rose was 75 years old with thinning, unnaturally dark hair and had been out of a major league uniform since 1989. It has been a difficult second act for the "Hit King," one that has played out over talk radio and cable news, the Internet, and social media. What a different story it has been.

For Cincinnati Reds fans, and for Pete Rose in particular, the June 24–26, 2016 celebration of Reds Hall of Fame induction weekend (identified across social media as #14Forever) was a long-awaited and nostalgic return to a time when the Cincinnati Reds were the center of the baseball universe. It was an opportunity to display reverence to the greatest era in the franchise's history, and it was an opportunity to improve the reputation of both Rose and the Reds.

In this chapter I argue that #14Forever weekend was an exercise in nostalgia designed to encourage fans to focus on the past as a way to control—and obscure—the present. This is how nostalgia, a sentimental longing for the past, works. It creates a sense of comfort and security that can soothe uncertainties of the present, a motive shared by the Cincinnati Reds, mired in rebuilding, and Pete Rose, a disgraced icon whose efforts to gain formal re-entry to the sport have failed. In this chapter I, first, introduce Pete Rose, explain his downfall and unsuccessful efforts at gaining baseball re-entry, and offer nostalgia as an alternative image repair strategy. Second, I provide a three-part analysis of #14Forever weekend, focusing on the Reds' promotion of restorative nostalgia to create a place of comfort and shared identity during a painful period of team rebuilding; the Reds' deft use of reflective nostalgia in acknowledging Pete Rose's justifiably compromised status out of baseball while still paying homage to him; and Rose's induction speech as marking a surrender of traditional image repair in exchange for post-apologetic rhetoric that appeals to home and uses the cultural intimacy of nostalgic communication to by-pass his troubled past.

The Success and Tragedy of Pete Rose

Pete Rose (b. 1941) is one of the most iconic—and tragic—athletes of his generation. Recognized for his aggressive play and charismatic persona, Rose has been in the public eye for more than 50 years. For the first half of his public life (1963–1989) he embodied the American Dream and was revered for his hustle, drive, and determination (McDorman, 2011). By the time his playing career ended, in 1986 at age 45, Rose had won a Most Valuable Player award (1973), three batting titles (1968, 1969, 1973), and three World Series rings (1975, 1976, 1980), in addition to holding baseball's all-time mark for hits with 4,256. As of 2018, Rose remains prominent in baseball record books, ranking first in hits, games played, at bats, plate appearances, singles, and times on base (as well as most outs made). He is also second in doubles, sixth in runs scored, and eighth in total bases ("Pete Rose," 2017).

In February 1989, while Rose was managing the Cincinnati Reds, his hometown team and the franchise with which he spent most of his career, Major League Baseball (MLB) began an investigation over allegations that Rose was betting on baseball. It was a startling charge against one of baseball's most recognized players. The sport's gambling prohibition is its most sacred rule of conduct, made necessary by early concerns over the legitimacy of the sport, the pinnacle of which was the 1919 "Black Sox" scandal, when several members of the Chicago White Sox accepted bribes to throw the World Series against, coincidentally, the Cincinnati Reds. Major League Rule 21, which is posted in every major league clubhouse, holds that any player who bets on a game in which the player is a participant "shall be declared permanently ineligible" ("The Pete Rose case," 1989).

As the investigation proceeded, the outlook for Rose was bleak. Despite that, Rose refused to offer any admission of guilt. As one Cincinnati writer following the story put it, Rose "never cracked," despite intense daily scrutiny. He "had the will of a steel door. It was amazing" (Daugherty, 1999). Amazing perhaps, but the strategy also set in motion the chain of events that would place Rose outside baseball.

Conducted by John Dowd, the investigation resulted in a 225-page report (Dowd, 1989), supported with seven volumes of evidence and testimony, that included the contention that Rose bet at least $10,000 on 52 different Reds' games in 1987. On August 24, 1989, just eight days before he would die of a heart attack, Baseball Commissioner A. Bartlett Giamatti closed the investigation by banning Rose. Said Giamatti (1989), "The banishment for life of Pete Rose from baseball is the sad end of a sorry episode." While it was, as Giamatti indicated, "sad," it was by no means the "end." For 15 years Rose steadfastly refused to admit his baseball gambling, before finally relenting in 2004. Rose has spent the second half of his public life seeking to regain his standing in sport and society, to repair his image and restore his reputation. It is only because Pete Rose was so important to baseball that his fall and efforts at redemption have maintained public attention.

Image Repair

As addressed earlier in this volume, image repair refers to the use of rhetorical strategies to rebuild one's image after accusations of moral failure or public transgressions (Benoit, 2014). An expansive body of scholarship exploring image repair in a variety of political, corporate, and sports contexts demonstrates the genre's breadth (e.g., Benoit, 1995; Benoit & Brinson, 1994; Benoit & Hanczor, 1994; Blaney, Lippert, & Smith, 2012; Brazeal, 2008; Kruse, 1981; McDorman, 2003; Nelson, 1984). Building from four modes of defense initially offered by Ware and Linkugel (1973)—denial, bolstering, differentiation, and transcendence—more recently scholars, most notably Benoit and a series of co-authors, have used the term "image repair" to identify a broader array of discourse strategies available for rhetors in their efforts to regain public favor while responding to accusations. Benoit and Brinson (1994), for example, offer a more complex typology that, in addition to denial, also suggests the discourse strategies of evasion, reducing offensiveness, mortification, and correction, each comprised of additional specific tactics.

Pete Rose is a unique image repair subject given his baseball stature, the duration of his efforts, and the range of strategies he has employed. In fact, one might identify five image repair phases in Rose's public rhetoric since 1989. He began by denying his gambling, while also attacking his accusers, a strategy developed most comprehensively in his autobiography *Pete Rose: My Story*, adamantly declaring, "I never bet baseball. I swear I never bet baseball" (Rose & Kahn,

1989, p. 251). Then, using baseball's 1999 All-Century team celebration and sympathy garnered by an on-field interview in which Jim Gray infamously badgered Rose for a gambling admission, Rose pursued a second-chance apologia that relied upon renewed public interest, fading memories that created questions about his guilt, and the emerging feeling that the passage of time was punishment enough (McDorman, 2003). Rose continued to deny his baseball gambling, but also offered vague expressions of mortification and attempted to reduce his offensiveness by appeals to transcendence and bolstering.

By maintaining consistency in his denials while also portraying himself as both repentant and a victim, Rose seemed to be gaining traction and may have been on the precipice of reinstatement (Blum, 2002; Erardi, 2003; Stark, 2003). Then, in January 2004, the third phase of his image repair launched with a new autobiography, *My Prison Without Bars* (Rose with Hill, 2004). The book offered Rose's gambling confession inside an explanatory framework that sought to minimize and evade responsibility while again attacking his accusers. Rose's image repair effort was unsuccessful due to failing to take responsibility for his actions or to adequately convey remorse and contrition. In addition, the loss of consistency suffered by finally admitting to gambling cost Rose public support and reinforced negative perceptions of his character. Ultimately it was a public relations disaster and Rose's reinstatement prospects were more remote than at any point since his original 1989 banishment.

A fourth phase of image repair was signaled by Rose's first on-field appearance in Cincinnati since 1989, with the 2010 celebration of the 25th anniversary of Rose setting the all-time hits record. In this phase Rose built upon his gambling admission by offering more visible contrition and shifted to transcendent rhetoric to move past his misdeeds in favor of broader promotion of baseball. Although MLB Commissioner Rob Manfred formally rejected Rose's reinstatement application in December 2015, while doing so he also made a distinction between Rose's ban and participation in honorific events. To that end, Manfred explained that his "concern has to be the protection of the integrity" of baseball, which involves MLB participation and employment, as opposed to "ceremonial activities that present no threat to the integrity of the game," and which Manfred said he would "continue to allow" Rose to participate in so long as approved in advance (Manfred, 2015, pp. 3, 5). The Reds immediately seized on the distinction, announcing the following month that Rose would be inducted into the team's Hall of Fame (Sheldon, 2016). The event was a three-day celebration featuring a reunion of the 1976 World Championship team, Rose's Hall of Fame induction, and a ceremony retiring his uniform number. With his induction speech, Rose entered a fifth phase of his public presentation—which will be analyzed here—one that utilizes nostalgic commemoration as a means of reputation enhancement.

Nostalgia as Image Repair

In the traditional framework of image repair, the rhetorical symbols examined here might be understood as efforts to reduce offensiveness. More particularly, they resemble bolstering, in which the accused responds with "positive characteristics they possess or positive actions they have taken in the past," and transcendence, which puts an event in a larger, "more favorable context" (Benoit & Hanczor, 1994, p. 420). However, unlike in traditional image repair, neither Rose nor the Reds were faced with responding to an active crisis or accusation. Instead, bolstering and transcendence were offered indirectly through nostalgic appeals which, interestingly, Boym (2001) describes in part as a "defense mechanism" (p. xiii). I contend this variant tactic had the effect of temporarily casting Rose and the Reds in a more positive light, aiding their reputations.

Nostalgia, as Hasian (2001) notes, has a "lengthy, but checkered past" (p. 341). Communication scholars have often approached the concept as a corollary of public memory and, in its lesser form, a contaminant to history. At the same time, as Von Burg and Johnson (2009) observe, "while other discursive communities eschew nostalgia as regressive, baseball embraces rhetorics of nostalgia as essential to its character. Nostalgia in baseball is not dismissed as irrational or emotionally immature; rather the game functions" to celebrate "lasting American ideals" (p. 354).

In one of the most comprehensive scholarly explorations of nostalgia, Svetlana Boym (2001) identifies two forms—restorative and reflective—which function in intertwining fashion across #14Forever weekend. Restorative nostalgia emphasizes *nostos*, a desire to return home and, potentially, rebuild what was lost in recreating an idealized past (p. 41). On the other hand, reflective nostalgia emphasizes remembrances of "longing and loss" in ways that can be ironic and fragmentary (pp. 41, 50). Either form, as Aden (1995) argues, might indicate a "desire to regain some control . . . in an uncertain time" (p. 21). Quoting Davis (1979), Aden (1995) offers that "nostalgia is one of the . . . more readily accessible" means "we employ in the never ending work of constructing, maintaining, and reconstructing our identities" (p. 22). The relationship of such efforts to image repair is obvious in that maintaining and reconstructing one's identity is a process of reputation management and presentation of face.

In summarizing the concept, Aden (1995) concludes that "Overall nostalgic communication can be conceptualized as a process of inviting escape from contemporary conditions that are perceived to be inhospitable in order to provide individuals with a secure place of resistance" (p. 22). In what follows, I examine how appeals to nostalgia across #14Forever weekend provided Rose and the Reds an escape from inhospitable contemporary conditions in favor of a more secure place of past success and higher standing, in the process illustrating how appeals to nostalgia can serve as a tactic for reputation enhancement.

Nostalgic Celebration of a Winning Past

Just as Pete Rose was one of baseball's biggest stars, the Cincinnati Reds were arguably baseball's most successful team in the 1970s. They won two World Series titles (1975, 1976) while winning more games, appearing in more World Series (4), and making more playoff appearances (6) than any other team. The Big Red Machine, as they were known, was a talented team with all of the Great Eight (their everyday lineup) selected to all-star teams, players capturing six National League Most Valuable Player awards in the decade, and three players elected to the National Baseball Hall of Fame (Johnny Bench, Joe Morgan, and Tony Perez). Although the years that followed were not as successful, the Reds won another World Series (1990), earned multiple playoff appearances, and were led by recognizable stars like Barry Larkin, Ken Griffey, Jr., and, more recently, Joey Votto. After reaching the playoffs three times in four years between 2010 and 2013, the Reds, a "small market" team (based on local television market and economic resources), were unable to retain many core players when they became eligible for the big money contracts that come with free agency. As a result, in 2015 they started trading established players for "prospects," young, inexpensive players who are attractive for their future potential. These moves resulted in a 2015 record of 64 wins and 98 losses, second worst in franchise history, and 66 wins and 96 losses in 2016, with both years netting the second pick in the amateur draft.

This process of tearing down a team, called rebuilding, is a modern phenomenon brought about by contemporary sports economics. The 2016 World Champion Chicago Cubs had the worst record in the National League Central for five straight seasons before emerging as a rebuilt powerhouse. Similarly, the 2017 World Series champion Houston Astros lost over 100 games three consecutive seasons, and the team's rebuild reached such depths that local Nielsen television ratings dipped to literally zero (Tayler, 2014). Likewise, Astros' game attendance plummeted from over 3 million fans annually to last in the league in 2012, averaging about half what they drew at their peak ("Houston Astros attendance," 2017). This is because, while a rebuild is premised on future success, it gives fans in the present little for which to root. Appeals for patience only work so long, and eventually fans are bound to ask, as *Cincinnati Enquirer* columnist Paul Daugherty (2017) puts it, "At what point does 'rebuilding' become a conname for misguided optimism?" Thus, for sports franchises "rebuilding" can be a perilous proposition.

The 2016 Reds were squarely in a rebuild. Team payroll was slashed to 70 percent of its 2015 level, and attendance was down more than a half-million fans, putting the team second to last in the National League ("Cincinnati Reds attendance," 2017). Local beat writer C. Trent Rosecrans constantly reminded fans, "It's not about 2016," and he and fellow writer Zach Buchanan (2016) outlined "the plan" of Reds management to build a winner. When "the big-league product" proves "hard to watch" and even the team's general manager addresses constant losing by saying, "we're trying everything we can to pull out of it, but we know this is one of the challenges of rebuilding," a team is faced with a fundamental challenge to its reputation (Buchanan & Rosecrans, 2017; Daugherty, 2017). While winning is the ultimate goal, in the interim how does a team continue to appeal to fans and reassure them of both the team's prospects and its community value?

For the Cincinnati Reds, #14Forever weekend was an effort to produce what Aden would term a "temporal escape" to "a secure place . . . of community and identity" (1995, p. 20). The escape was a nostalgic transportation of fans to 1976, and a respite from 2016. In this regard the weekend was designed to encourage fans to think about past success, using it as a way to control—and obscure—the more depressing present. To accomplish this task, the weekend included a series of symbolic acts that praised and promoted the 1976 team and other members of the Reds Hall of Fame. The centerpiece was Rose's Hall of Fame induction, a ceremony in which Rose spoke on the field for the first time since 1989, flanked by his teammates and members of the Reds Hall of Fame. However, there also were other symbolic elements that sought to aid the Reds' reputation as a qual-ity franchise and re-validate Rose as deserving to stand with the team's icons. In this way, the nostalgic appeals might be seen as offering a form of bolstering, a traditional image repair tactic, for both team and individual, doing so through "a means of symbolically escaping the cultural conditions that" fans found "depressing and disorienting" (Aden, 1995, p. 35).

The weekend kicked off with the 20 returning members of the 1976 team introduced one by one prior to the start of the Friday game. Each retired player emerged from the dugout wearing his uniform top and took his place along the first base line next to a star with his name and uniform number on it: the young men of 1976 now with gray hair—if they had hair at all—with the notable excep-tion of the last player introduced, Pete Rose, whose hair was unnaturally dark, if also certainly thinner, as he took his position near home plate (another sym-bolic return home). Other weekend events that brought the past into the present included multiple "meet and greet" opportunities with former Reds players; the use of pixelated monochromatic graphics on the scoreboard and in-game features that were from the 1970s; contemporary players wearing 1976 "throw-back" jerseys; a 1976 team picture for attending fans; a Pete Rose bobble head and souvenir pin; the Rose uniform number retirement ceremony; and a post-game fireworks display with a 1976-themed soundtrack. Collectively the symbols underscored how restorative nostalgia reconstructs "emblems and rituals of home and homeland in an attempt to conquer and spatialize time" (Boym, 2001, p. 49).

Beyond the festivities there were still games to play, with some of those playing envisioned as important to the team's future. Prospect Cody Reed, making his first home start, captured the unfinished state of the team, striking out the first batter on Friday before giving up a home run to the second. No doubt, the hope of the Reds is that glory days, nostalgically celebrated by bringing the 1976 World Championship team back "home," are closer to returning than a last place team would lead fans to believe. Remembering Pete Rose and his fellow legends was a salute to what happened, and a promise of what could happen again, thus providing a way and a reason to not dwell on a depressing present. As Boym (2001) contends, "nostalgia is not always about the past; it can be retrospective but also prospective. Fantasies of the past determined by needs of the present have a direct impact on realities of the future" (p. xvi). Thus, the events of #14Forever used nostalgia as a way to deflect the reputational challenges faced by the team in 2016.

Judging by fan attendance it was a successful—or at least appealing—effort, with each game a sellout featuring more than 40,000 tickets sold, almost double the season average. The three games, along with opening day, combined to account for almost 9 percent of the team's home attendance for the season.

Nostalgic Remembrances and Contemporary Understandings

Select choices across the festivities suggested the Reds kept the weekend—and Pete Rose—in perspective, understanding nostalgia cannot fully erase tensions and transgressions, and avoiding the sort of nostalgia that scholars identify as a defect in character or social illness (Hasian, 2001). More specifically, the celebration included elements of reflective nostalgia, a form of remembrance that "can be ironic and humorous" and demonstrate "that longing and critical thinking are not opposed to one another, as affective memories do not absolve one from compassion, judgment or critical reflection" (Boym, 2001, pp. 49–50). Such an orientation allowed the Reds to improve their reputation while simultaneously celebrating Rose's accomplishments and keeping him at a reasonable distance.

The windows on the Reds' Hall of Fame provided a telling symbol that the organization approached Rose's situation with critical reflection. Outside the wall of 4,256 baseballs representing each of Rose's career hits, and overlooking the rose garden that marks the location of his record setting hit, an insightful piece of poetry was displayed across the building's three-story facade. The lines, from the crowd-sourced poem "Seven Hills and a Queen to Name Them," spoke of Pete Rose, though using only his "Hit King" nickname (Faherty, 2015).

> You taught me to avoid the tag,
> to sing the knotted history of the hit king
> with a stubborn tongue.
> To slide head-first into home.[3]

"To sing the knotted history of the hit king with a stubborn tongue" is a fantastic phrase that recognizes Pete Rose's significance, but also his ownership of his problems. It is an homage to the familial, generational nature of baseball, with its use of the second person "you" to reference lessons provided by a parent or perhaps by Rose himself ("*you* taught me") and also an acknowledgment of Rose's responsibility for his situation due to his obstinate and headstrong nature ("stubborn tongue"). The poetry allows a fan-centric celebration of Rose as the "Hit King" and validates his style of play with reference to his trademark head-first slide, but also demonstrates the reflective posture of the Reds as understanding Rose's misdeeds ("knotted history"). The longing for the past is not without critical reflection.

This nimble use of nostalgia was reinforced in an unexpected location: the 1976-themed soundtrack for a postgame fireworks show after the celebration of the World Championship team. It might seem unlikely that the playlist was significant, but several selections from the eight-song, 15-minute display were intriguing for their celebration of the past while also putting the plight of the team's exiled icon in perspective. The music and the reactions it evoked—reaching back 40 years—reflects the ability of nostalgia to capture "a yearning for a different time—the time of our childhood, the slower rhythms of our dreams" (Boym, 2001, p. xv).

The fireworks started with the "Boys are Back in Town" by Thin Lizzy. Regardless of its full message, the title and refrain were applicable enough and the lyrics heralded the return of the boys—the 1976 Reds. It was a fitting and catchy start underscoring the homecoming of the mythical heroes of 1976. Selections that followed included "December, 1963 (Oh, What a Night)" by the Four Seasons (#4 on the Billboard Hot 100 for 1976) and "Don't Go Breaking My Heart" by Elton John and Kiki Dee (#2 in 1976). "Oh What a Night" captured the nostalgic feeling of a crowd able to celebrate a special night on the rare occasion of the 1976 team reunion and having Pete Rose back on his hometown field. It was an event, consistent with the song, that was likely "mesmerizing" and "hypnotizing," producing a "rush" for attending fans. On the other hand, "Don't Go Breaking My Heart" was a playful selection, more aligned with reflective nostalgia for how its back-and-forth lyrics might parallel the relationship of Rose and the city of Cincinnati, with its heart not broken even if Rose tried through his many foibles, from leaving via free agency to his baseball banishment. The song stands in for Rose's enduring place in the hearts of many Cincinnati fans, despite—and even while recognizing—his misdeeds.

The most interesting selection was the closing song, "Dream On" by Aerosmith, which also was representative of reflective nostalgia. Presenting a dramatic shift from the energy and noise of the preceding number, Kiss's "Shout it Out Loud," the wistful song's title might capture the mood of the evening—it could be a dream, one that fans would like to see continue—while the lyrics offer a melancholy reflection on the past and a challenging life that followed. The idea that everybody has amends to make for past mistakes might hit close to home for Rose and his baseball exile, and the song's advice that one must learn to lose in order to grow might suggest a lesson Rose never quite grasped. Finally, the song's chorus and its reflection on the passage of years that evokes both laughter and tears indirectly captures the tribulations related to Rose and the weekend reprieve granted for him and fans to commune with the past. The deeper nostalgic sentiment might reflect a refusal "to surrender to the irreversibility of time" (Boym, 2001, p. xv), despite the passage of 40 years, and offered a particularly contemplative ending following the more upbeat and disco-infused selections that preceded it.

Collectively, the display underscored Boym's (2001) conclusion that "the study of nostalgia inevitably slows us down. There is, after all, something pleasantly outmoded about the very idea of longing. We long to prolong our time, to make it free, to daydream, against all odds resisting external pressures" (p. xix). In this case that consists of largely shutting out the reality of Rose's baseball exile and, to a lesser extent, the Reds own contemporary struggles in favor of promoting a happier, more stable era for both. However, although the fireworks display recalls a time when the reputations of Rose and the Reds were not questioned, it also contains signs that the Reds retained critical judgment on Rose and his situation.

Post-Apologetic Rhetoric, Nostalgia, and a Return Home

It is useful to consider Pete Rose's Reds Hall of Fame induction ceremony in the larger context of Rose's post-ban rhetoric. Unsurprisingly, Rose's best public moments since his ban have been on the field. It has been his off-field actions and comments, some of which were identified earlier in this chapter, that have caused him the most difficulties: the gambling denials in *Pete Rose: My Story* (Rose & Kahn, 1989); the partial and defiant confession of *My Prison Without Bars* (Rose with Hill, 2004); small steps toward potential reinstatement undermined by anger and impatience while pleading for a second chance he seemed to feel entitled to; and decisions that have prioritized money, such as the autobiographies and a Las Vegas autograph residency (Granger, 2015; Greenberg, 2011).

Coming a dozen years after his confession, six years after his on-field appearance for the 25th anniversary of his hits record, and six months after Commissioner Manfred denied his reinstatement bid, #14Forever weekend occurred at an ideal moment and in an ideal environment for Rose. Not only has "guilty Pete" become the accepted norm, increasingly on display at the Reds' Great American Ballpark (GABP) through appearances like the 2015 All-Star game ("Pete Rose, other Reds," 2015) and nationally as a MLB analyst for FOX and FS1 broadcasts (Rosenthal, 2015), but with his faint hope of reinstatement decisively dashed, Rose could dispense with the admissions, apologies, and pleas in his first on-field comments in Cincinnati since his ban. To his credit, in his induction speech,

Rose—a man known for speaking his mind and who seemingly defies being handled (or just has poor handlers)—delivered a post-apologetic address that wasn't dedicated to traditional image repair but was directed at nostalgic celebration of Reds fans and Cincinnati, his teammates, and the Reds franchise. Most of all, Rose's speech celebrated his return home, reflecting Boym's (2001) description of a "return to the imagined community" that serves as "a way of patching up the gap of alienation, turning intimate longing into belonging" (p. 255). In his remarks, Rose was funny, humble, and even grateful, rather than being the vulgar, defiant populist he has been known to be.[4]

Rose's remarks were accompanied by subtle bolstering from the Reds, while direct discussion of his gambling was absent. In leading off the induction ceremony, long-time Reds broadcaster Marty Brennaman praised Rose as a "hometown hero"—a geographic characteristic emphasized twice more in video tributes—who left an "indelible mark" on the franchise while embodying "many of the qualities that have defined Reds baseball."[5] The differentiating use of "many" was a perhaps intentional reference to Rose's troubles. Similarly, while principal owner Bob Castellini's citation said the occasion provided "testimony to our collective belief that you, Peter Edward Rose, are a Hall of Fame player," his only comment hinting at Rose's ban was when he said Rose never lost "hope that this day would finally come." The absence of direct reference to Rose's gambling allowed the induction to take place in a context that accepts what Rose did as known history rather than trying to explain it.

Likewise, Rose's speech let fans supply the reason his Hall of Fame induction took so long to occur. Although Rose might be criticized for not offering another apology or moral lesson, I argue that after his multiple on-field appearances and Commissioner Manfred's reinstatement denial, no such statement was necessary, particularly at the risk of appearing to lack proper contrition or striking a tone of defiance, both of which have been challenges for Rose. Instead, Rose appealed to humor in offering a few allusions to his situation, for instance encouraging the crowd's cheers when he said, "Go ahead. I've waited for 30 years." And Rose offered the sort of candor that might be as close to introspection as he is capable of: "Did I ever think I'd make it" (into the Reds Hall of Fame)? Nope, but I did." In speaking for 11 minutes, Rose exceeded the five minutes allotted to him despite the increasingly frantic signals of a Reds staffer and the music intended to usher him off stage. Once Rose noticed the efforts he offered his most popular line: "The hell with it, I've waited 30 years."

As for Rose's message, by making his speech about the people of Cincinnati, his teammates, and the Reds—rather than about himself—Rose was able to offer a post-apologetic rhetoric that prioritized cultural intimacy and a celebration of home over self-aggrandizement. The effort extended from his early statement that he could spend "five days thanking the people of Cincinnati," to his closing, which emphasized the shared identity of Rose and his fans as Cincinnatians: "And in closing, We've all been raised the same.

We love chili. We love pizza. We love ice cream. We love ribs. And we all love the Cincinnati Reds." This inclusive conclusion made allusion to beloved Cincinnati institutions—Cincinnati-style chili from Skyline and Gold Star, LaRosa's pizza, Graeter's ice cream, and, most of all, the Reds—in illustrating that Rose is one of them and enabling a shared cultural intimacy that validated Rose as an exile returning home.

This connection to the city reaches back across time to an era preceding Rose's baseball downfall, and hence an era in which his reputation is intact. Home and cultural intimacy were further underscored with Rose's praising of Cincinnati knothole (Little League) baseball for instilling deeply held community values (exemplified by major league players from Cincinnati that he named) and by celebrating the city as the "baseball capital of the world" and producing "the greatest fans ever." Most of all, Rose connected himself to the city by crediting the fans as providing his deepest motivations:

> You motivated me to play the way I did. I don't know if it is being brought up in Cincinnati or what it was, but . . . I wasn't diving for me, I was diving for you. I was hitting for you. I was trying to score runs for you.

This reminiscence is not only nostalgic in its appeal to home but improves Rose's reputation due to the use of identification. To reject Rose, who professes to belong to the city, would be a rejection of their very home and identity. By establishing his qualifications of belonging, he enhances his reputation.

In addition to his nostalgic appeals to the city and fans as supplying a welcoming home with whom he identifies and belongs, Rose also enhanced his reputation through the praise he offered his teammates and baseball more universally. The speech did not talk about his own greatness, but associated Rose with others who are recognized and respected as great: Reds Hall of Famers—some of whom he identified by name while noting that he either played with or against all of the assembled players—and the 10 National Baseball Hall of Fame players, recited one by one, that he counted as teammates. He further paid homage to his coaches from Little League to the majors and even thanked Commissioner Manfred "for allowing me to be on the field." Again, by associating himself with the greats of baseball, in Cincinnati and across the sport, Rose is able to enhance his reputation.

Finally, Rose aided in the reputation enhancement of the Cincinnati Reds. He did this through the traditional image repair tactic of bolstering. For example, Rose praised the quality of the Reds' team Hall of Fame while saying others aren't "even close . . . Our Hall of Fame is the best." Further, he praised the history of the franchise, as the first in professional baseball, as the first to play night games, and as producing exciting teams. And, importantly, he endorsed the Reds in their time of rebuilding, saying to fans: "You've got to support the Reds. They're trying. They're playing better. You've got to get behind them." In this way #14Forever was image repair benefiting both Rose, given a forum by the Reds, and the Reds themselves, endorsed by Rose—and in both cases it was an opportunity to nostalgically celebrate a more successful and happier past.

Appearances across the weekend showed a Rose who has been liberated in a way that makes nostalgic communication—not traditional image repair—a natural and better-suited form of rhetoric for him. Rose knows where he stands and it is ground that is difficult to imagine shifting while he is still alive. At the same time, Rose's official banishment is increasingly irrelevant given his advancing age and his presence at ceremonial events—events that, again, are designed to evoke nostalgia and celebrate the past. There may be more ballpark days for Rose, such as the June 17, 2017 unveiling of a statue of him at GABP that again featured an elaborate ceremony and on-field comments (and reflected the same themes as his 2016 induction speech), but the opportunities will become fewer in number. It may well have been, just as Rose said, that his Reds Hall of Fame induction, is the "biggest thing ever to happen" to him in baseball.

Closing Thoughts: Pete Rose and Nostalgic Communication

Using the events of #14Forever as a case study, this chapter has suggested that, in certain circumstances, nostalgia has the potential to function as an image repair tactic that addresses reputational challenges. In the present case, appeals to restorative nostalgia that emphasized past success and winning allowed the Reds franchise to address present deficiencies; the Reds use of techniques of reflective nostalgia allowed the Reds to both celebrate Pete Rose and acknowledge his shortcomings; and nostalgic appeals to home and cultural intimacy allowed Rose to bypass his troubled present by recalling a triumphant past in his Reds Hall of Fame induction speech. Much like Hasian (2014) claimed the James Bond film *Skyfall* nostalgically celebrated British identity and power, #14Forever allowed fans to celebrate the continued relevance of Rose and the Reds, providing evidence that they still mattered (p. 570). In their immediate context, and when considered in regards to their immediate audience, the weekend events successfully defended the reputations of Rose and the Reds by employing nostalgia as a tactic of image repair that reduces offensiveness of individual and team shortcomings in a manner similar to that of the traditional tactics of bolstering and transcendence.

Additional scholarship examining appeals to nostalgia in sports can further explore its benefits and risks as well as its broader potential for reputational improvements. While contextual elements are important in assessing if particular nostalgic appeals have image repair functions, appeals to nostalgia itself are plentiful in sports, including "old-timers" games, Hall of Fame inductions and statue dedications, throwback jersey days, commemorative uniform patches, team and league celebrations of past eras, and museums and museum exhibits. Subsequent analyses might explore further the potential of such nostalgic appeals to improve the reputations of individuals, teams, and sports organizations.

Scholarship on nostalgia appropriately cautions against its prolonged or naive embrace because it "is ultimately insufficient since the reconstructed identity that comes from escape to a new or old place is temporary" (Aden, 1995, p. 23). In this case the escape cannot permanently eliminate Rose's own responsibility for his banishment or the contemporary struggles of the Cincinnati Reds. This caution is useful in the event that nostalgia is used as a prolonged antidote to failed team rebuilding or as a way to ignore and overlook Rose's transgressions.

In the present case, despite the feelgood vibes it is difficult to suggest that Pete Rose has changed and that he suddenly "gets it." Previously Rose has shown what might pass for common sense only to return to more damaging form. And the fragile hold of nostalgia appeals as reputation enhancement were demonstrated by the summer 2017 revelation of Rose's sexual relationship with an underage female in the 1970s. The significance of the issue as a moral failure is such that it might make Rose's gambling appear inconsequential, and it resulted in the Philadelphia Phillies canceling installation of Rose on their Wall of Fame ("Phillies Cancel," 2017; Woo, 2017) and FOX Sports removed Rose from their baseball coverage.[6] Moreover, as the relationship began in 1975 (when Rose was 34 and married with two children), it taints the nostalgic appeal of Rose's playing days. A celebration of his career bypasses his gambling by temporally preceding it. However, #14Forever seeks to remember the very era of this relationship, making it a less pure time and more difficult to celebrate.

The new revelations bring tumult back to Rose and cast the events of #14Forever, a weekend where Rose and the Reds seemingly got it right, in a different light. Although the comfort of nostalgia stirred by the events should not be allowed to erase the past or cause baseball fans to forget the "knotted history of the hit king with the stubborn tongue," to this point Rose also has been recognized and largely accepted as a baseball icon belonging to Cincinnati and the Reds, and Rose's speech was about that, given to the one city and the one fan base that is mostly accepting of him—many enthusiastically so, some more grudgingly.

Notes

1 Portions of this project were previously presented at the 43rd Annual National Undergraduate Honors Conference at DePauw University on April 21, 2017 and the 29th Cooperstown Symposium on Baseball and American Culture on May 31, 2017. I thank those audiences for their feedback.
2 The season following Rose being banned from baseball, the Cincinnati Reds won the 1990 World Series. Then, in 1991, a year before he was to appear on the writer's ballot for the Baseball Hall of Fame, the Hall's Board of Directors passed a rule forbidding anyone on the ineligible list from being considered for the Hall. The Board reaffirmed their stance in December 2015 after Commissioner Manfred ruled on Rose's reinstatement application (Clark, 2017).
3 *Seven Hills and a Queen to Name Them* © 2015 ArtWorks written by Chase Public for the Cincy Ink Project. Used with permission.

4 In attending the ceremony, I also noticed, with a tinge of irony, that as Rose spoke he was framed by a Draft Kings billboard with an MLB logo in left-center field and a billboard for a Cincinnati casino in right field. Although Rose remains banned, baseball's association with gambling is more in the open in 2016 than it was in 1989.

5 All remarks from the ceremony are drawn from a recording posted on MLB.com (Footer, 2016).

6 Rose and his attorney's response is familiar, resorting to unsatisfying use of differentiation: Rose thought the girl was 16 (as if that would be a palatable explanation); attacking his accuser by calling the revelations a distraction from a suit he brought against John Dowd; and vowing to continue with the suit, reflecting Rose's insistence on trying to "win" at any cost while failing to see greater, negative long-term consequences. The situation's public airing is another example of Rose's own hubris, as if he had simply dismissed Dowd's comments about his purported activities, rather than suing for defamation, the issue would have passed without further investigation.

References

Aden, R. C. (1995). Nostalgic communication as temporal escape: *When it was a Game's* re-construction of a baseball/work community. *Western Journal of Communication, 59,* 20–38.

Benoit, W. L. (1995). Sears' repair of its auto service image: Image restoration discourse in the corporate sector. *Communication Studies, 46,* 89–105.

Benoit, W. L. (2014). *Accounts, excuses, and apologies: Image repair theory and research* (2nd ed.). Albany, NY: State University of New York Press.

Benoit, W. L., & Brinson, S. L. (1994). AT&T: "Apologies are not enough." *Communication Quarterly, 42,* 75–88.

Benoit, W. L., & Hanczor, R. S. (1994). The Tonya Harding controversy: An analysis of image restoration strategies. *Communication Quarterly, 42,* 416–433.

Blaney, J. R., Lippert, L. R., & Smith, J. S. (Eds.) (2012). *Repairing the athlete's image: Studies in sports image restoration.* Lanham, NJ: Lexington Books.

Blum, R. (2002, December 12). "Passage of time" changed Selig's mind. *Cincinnati.com.* Retrieved from http://reds.enquirer.com/2002/12/12/wwwroseap.html

Boym, S. (2001). *The future of nostalgia.* New York: Basic Books.

Brazeal, L. M. (2008). The image repair strategies of Terrell Owens. *Public Relations Review, 34,* 145–150.

Buchanan, Z., & Rosecrans, C. T. (2017, July 22). Looking back on the Reds rebuild's most important year. *Cincinnati.com.* Retrieved from www.cincinnati.com/story/sports/mlb/reds/2017/07/22/looking-back-cincinnati-reds-rebuilds-most-important-year/502208001/

Cincinnati Reds attendance, stadiums, and park factors. (2017). *Baseball Reference.com.* Retrieved from www.baseball-reference.com/teams/CIN/attend.shtml

Clark, D. (2017, June 15). Baseball Hall of Fame upholds Pete Rose's ban. *Cincinnati.com.* Retrieved from www.cincinnati.com/story/sports/mlb/reds/2017/06/15/baseball-hall-fame-upholds-pete-roses-ban/399734001/

Daugherty, P. (1999, August 22). Giamatti's death sealed Rose's fate. *Enquirer.com.* Retrieved from enquirer.com/columns/daugherty/1999/08/22/pd_pete_cant_hustle.html

Daugherty, P. (2017, June 25). Doc: Patience, faith will get us through Reds' rebuild. *Cincinnati.com.* Retrieved from www.cincinnati.com/story/sports/mlb/reds/2017/06/25/doc-patience-faith-get-us-through-reds-rebuild/103183620/

Davis, F. (1979). *Yearning for yesterday: A sociology of nostalgia*. New York: The Free Press.

Dowd, J. (1989, May 9). In the Matter of: Peter Edward Rose, manager, Cincinnati Reds Baseball Club. *Dowd Report.com*. Retrieved from www.thedowdreport.com/report.pdf

Erardi, J. (2003, November 23). Rose saga probably will drag into 2004. *Cincinnati.com*. Retrieved from reds.enquirer.com/2003/11/23/red1arose.html

Faherty, J. (2015, February 17). Love for Cincinnati revealed line by line. *Cincinnati.com* Retrieved from www.cincinnati.com/story/news/2015/02/13/love-city-revealed-line-line-cincyink-oh-baby/23364581/

Footer, A. (2016, June 25). Hit King Rose inducted into Reds Hall of Fame. *MLB.com*. Retrieved from m.mlb.com/news/article/186195796/pete-rose-inducted-into-reds-hall-of-fame/

Giamatti, A. B. (1989, August 25). Giamatti: Sad end of sorry story. *USA Today*, p. 10C.

Granger, J. (2015, June 30). Pete Rose still a hit on Las Vegas autograph circuit despite latest revelations. *Las Vegas Sun*. Retrieved from lasvegassun.com/news/2015/jun/30/pete-rose-vegas-mandalay-autographs/

Greenberg, S. (2011, June 3). Pete Rose signs multi-million dollar extension to sign autographs in Las Vegas. *Sporting News*. Retrieved from www.sportingnews.com/mlb/news/188095-pete-rose-signs-multi-million-dollar-extension-to-sign-autographs-in-las-vegas

Hasian, M. (2001). Nostalgic longings, memories of the "good war," and cinematic representations in *Saving Private Ryan*. *Critical Studies in Media Communication*, *18*, 338–358.

Hasian, M. (2014). *Skyfall*, James Bond's resurrection, and 21st-century Anglo-American imperial nostalgia. *Communication Quarterly*, *62*, 569–588.

Houston Astros attendance, stadiums, and park factors. (2017). *Baseball Reference.com*. Retrieved from www.baseball-reference.com/teams/HOU/attend.shtml

Kruse, N. W. (1981). Apologia in team sports. *Quarterly Journal of Speech*, *67*, 270–283.

McDorman, T. F. (2003). The rhetorical resurgence of Pete Rose: A second-chance apologia. In R. S. Brown & D. O'Rourke (Eds.), *Case studies in sport communication* (pp. 1–25). Westport, CT: Praeger.

McDorman, T. F. (2011). The making of Charlie Hustle: Pete Rose and the American dream, 1963–1985. In W. M. Simons (Ed.), *The Cooperstown Symposium on Baseball and American Culture, 2009-2010* (pp. 140–154). Jefferson, NC: McFarland.

Manfred, R. (2015, December 14). Decision of Commissioner Robert D. Manfred, Jr. concerning the application of Rose for removal from the permanently ineligible list. *Office of the Commissioner of Major League Baseball*. Retrieved from http://mlb.mlb.com/documents/8/4/6/159619846/Commissioner_s_Decision_on_Pete_Rose_Reinstatement_u35dqem0.pdf

Nelson, J. (1984). The defense of Billie Jean King. *Western Journal of Speech Communication*, *48*, 92–102.

Pete Rose. (2017). *Baseball Reference.com*. Retrieved from www.baseball-reference.com/players/r/rosepe01.shtml

The Pete Rose case; The 2 rules in the Rose case. (1989, August 25). *New York Times*. Retrieved from www.nytimes.com/1989/08/25/sports/the-pete-rose-case-the-2-rules-in-the-rose-case.html

Pete Rose, other Reds greats honored before All-Star game. (2015, July 14). *ESPN.com*. Retrieved from www.espn.com/mlb/story/_/id/13258082/pete-rose-greeted-cheers-all-star-game

Phillies cancel Pete Rose wall of fame ceremony amid statutory rape allegations. (2017, August 2). *CSNPhilly*. Retrieved from www.csnphilly.com/philadelphia-phillies/phillies-cancel-pete-rose-wall-fame-ceremony-amid-statutory-rape-allegations

Rose, P., with Hill, R. (2004). *My prison without bars*. Rodale.

Rose, P., & Kahn, R. (1989). *Pete Rose: My story*. New York: Macmillan.

Rosecrans, C. T., & Buchanan, Z. (2016, April 4). The plan: How the Reds build for a World Series title. *Cincinnati.com*. Retrieved from www.cincinnati.com/story/sports/mlb/reds/2016/04/01/reds-win-another-world-series/82506716/

Rosenthal, K. (2015, April 16). Pete Rose, baseball's Hit King, to join FOX, FS1 as MLB analyst. *FOXSports.com*. Retrieved from www.foxsports.com/mlb/story/pete-rose-mlb-on-fox-to-join-baseball-analyst-pregame-show-fox-sports-one-ken-rosenthal-041815

Sheldon, M. (2016, January 19). Rose elated over election to Reds Hall of Fame. *MLB.com*. Retrieved from m.mlb.com/news/article/162253924/pete-rose-joining-reds-hall-of-fame-in-2016/

Stark, J. (2003, March 13). Rose's reinstatement remains one big mystery. *ESPN.com*. Retrieved from a.espncdn.com/mlb/columns/stark_jayson/1494267.html

Tayler, J. (2014, April 9). Houston Astros get a 0.0 television rating for game against Los Angeles Angels. *Sports Illustrated*. Retrieved from www.si.com/mlb/strike-zone/2014/04/09/houston-astros-get-0-0-television-rating

Von Burg, R., & Johnson, P. E. (2009). Yearning for a past that never was: Baseball, steroids, and the anxiety of the American dream. *Critical Studies in Media Communication*, *26*, 351–371.

Ware, B. L., & Linkugel, W. A. (1973). They spoke in defense of themselves: On the generic criticism of apologia. *Quarterly Journal of Speech*, *59*, 273–283.

Woo, Jeremy. (2017, August 2). Phillies cancel Pete Rose events following statutory rape allegation. *Sports Illustrated*. Retrieved from www.si.com/mlb/2017/08/02/pete-rose-statutory-rape-allegation-phillies-cancel-giveaway-0

11

LOVE ME OR HATE ME

Predictors of Perceived Athlete Image

Kenon A. Brown, Ziyuan Zhou, and Qingru Xu

In Kruse's "Apologia in Team Sport," published in 1981, she argued that the image repair of athletes or sports organizations was not an issue of importance, because—in the context of sports—"winning isn't everything; it's the only thing" (p. 273). However, the globalization of sports and the expansion of mass media greatly increase the media attention athletes and teams received, in which even a most private conflict could lead to a destructive damage of an athlete's public image (Meyer, 2008). For instance, carrying a burden of a sex scandal, Tiger Woods not only cost his stakeholders up to $12 billion (Knittel & Stango, 2013), his public image as the world's number one golfer was also severely damaged. Even seven years after the accusation, Tiger Woods was still rated as one of the most disliked athletes in the United States (Forbes' list, 2016). In this sense, athletic figures or teams' image repair has become indispensable, in which many public relations researchers have explored the application of image repair strategies during sports crises (e.g., Brown, 2016; Fortunato, 2008).

Researchers have employed two approaches to evaluate image repair attempts in sports communication based on Benoit's (2015) image repair theory (IRT): the case study approach and the experimental approach. Established from a source-oriented perspective, the case study approach, which is typically driven by rhetorical analysis or content analysis, evaluates image repair strategies utilized by accused parties by analyzing mediated content, such as public statements from athletes or teams (e.g., Compton & Compton, 2015), sports news coverage (e.g., Meng & Pan, 2013), or fans' responses on social media (e.g., Brown, Brown, & Billings, 2015). Based on the evaluations, researchers often offer critiques or suggestions to maximize the effectiveness of the image repair (Hambrick, Frederick, & Sanderson, 2015). However, causation relationships based on audience reaction are hard to be attributed through these methodological procedures, leading to difficulties in assessing the effectiveness of a specific image repair strategy (Benoit, 2000).

Moving beyond the case study approach, researchers have applied experimental design to examine the effectiveness of Benoit's image repair strategies from an audience-oriented perspective (e.g., Brown, Dickhaus, & Long, 2012). By manipulating the image repair strategies presented to participants, a causal relationship can be assessed, lending to more grounded recommendations based on empirical evidence (Brown, 2016). Applying this approach, researchers have also been able to evaluate the moderating impact of other contextual variables on the image repair process, such as race (Brown, Billings, & Devlin, 2016) and gender (Brown, Billings, Mastro, & Brown-Devlin, 2015). The experimental approach allows researchers to evaluate the effect of a specific image repair strategy with scientific evidence, providing generalizable findings to guide future studies.

Typically, experimental image repair studies in sports have treated the perceived image as a single variable (e.g. Brown, 2016; Brown et al., 2012). However, Benoit (2016) suggested that current empirical image repair research suffers from a lack of consistency and diversity in its examination of different dependent variables. To address these issues, Benoit (2016) explicated six dependent variables that were most frequently examined in empirical image research: (a) account acceptability, (b) likability of the accused, (c) blame and responsibility, (d) perceived offensiveness of the act, (e) likelihood to commit the act again, and (f) deserved punishment. While previous research (Benoit, 2016; Brown, Murphy, & Maxwell, 2017) has tested the impact of image repair strategies on these variables, the relationship between these six variables and the overall perceived image has not been tested. Therefore, the purpose of this study is to examine the relationship between Benoit's (2016) common dependent variables in empirical image repair studies and the common measurement of the perceived image.

Defining Image

Benoit and Hanczor (1994) defined image as "the perception(s) of a person, group or organization held by the audience, shaped by the words and actions of that person, as well as by the discourse and behavior of other relevant actors" (p. 40). The image of an entity is a representation that is more lasting than an impression, but is still subject to change when audiences are faced with new information (Scott & Jhen, 2003). Public relations and marketing scholars have expressed separate views of the term "image" in comparison to the term "reputation," with "image" having a more negative connotation in public relations and a more neutral one in marketing.

From a public relations perspective, Botan (1993) and Grunig (1993) defined image as the manipulated—often times fabricated—representation of an entity, which expressed the creation of image as more of a publicity tactic rather than an integral function of public relations. In short, an entity's image was seen more as a cover-up of its true identity, particularly when public relation firms representing organizations with subpar images attempt to cover up transgressions by manipulating positive news coverage (Manheim & Albritton, 1983). Because of this connotation, public relations researchers and practitioners have used the term "reputation" to describe the true perception of an entity.

From a marketing perspective, the term has a more neutral connotation. Marketing scholars discuss the maintenance of a positive image as an important aspect of brand marketing. In addition, Nguyen and Leblanc (2001) argued that an entity does not have a single image, but rather differing images based on the perceptions of a specific stakeholder group based on their experiences with the entity—for example, employees may have a different image of a firm than customers. Kennedy (1977) explicated two components to corporate image: a functional component and an emotional component. The functional component addresses the impact a stakeholder group's perception of a firm can have on tangible outcomes, such as willingness to purchase goods and services (for a for-profit) or to donate money and volunteer (for a nonprofit). The emotional component addresses the impact a stakeholder group's perception can have on the attitudes and feelings toward the organization.

The majority of public relations literature defines reputation as a more positive connotation of "image," which assumes that the two terms are synonymous (Coombs, 2005; Grunig, 1993). Until the early 1990s, scholars in marketing also treated image and reputation as synonymous (e.g., Abratt, 1989; Dichter, 1985; Dowling, 1993; Dutton, Dukerich, & Harquail, 1994; Kennedy, 1977). Recently, however, there has been a push in marketing literature for the differentiation of the terms "image" and "reputation." These scholars define reputation as the aggregate perception of an entity and approach reputation as a collection of images over time (e.g., Chun, 2005; Gotzi & Wilson, 2001; Gray & Balmer, 1998; Nguyen & Leblanc, 2001). Gray and Balmer (1998) specifically argued that reputation is historically constructed through consistent performances, while image is usually constructed more quickly through strategic communication messages. In other words, while communication materials, such as press releases and advertisements, can be instrumental in forming and changing an image, reputation requires more time and effort to create and maintain. Based on this more recent comparison of image and reputation, the approach to empirically measuring image is grounded on the premise that it is more theoretically accurate to measure an entity's image in an empirical study rather than their reputation because of the ability to change the image in the public eye more quickly, while measuring reputation would require a longitudinal study to create an aggregate of the entity's images over time.

As stated previously, Benoit (2016) made a call for more consistency in the empirical study of image repair, stressing that previous research suffers from a lack of consistency in its examination of different dependent variables. To remedy this issue, Benoit (2016) explicated six dependent variables that were most frequently examined in empirical image repair research.

Acceptability of the accused's account denotes people's feelings about the accused party's response to a transgression (Coombs & Holladay, 2008). As account acceptance increases, respondents believe the response from the accused is more appropriate. Liu, Austin, and Jin (2011) reveal people's acceptance of the accused's response to transgressions is influenced by information form (e.g. social media, mass media) and source (e.g. third party, organization, spokesperson). *Likability of the accused* represents "the attraction and ability to let others have a positive attitude benefiting both emotion and body" (Park, 2015, p. 2). Dunn and Cody (2000) argued that the accused's selection of a response strategy can influence his/her likability. *Blame and responsibility placed on the accused* is the core variable of Coombs's (1998, 2007) Situational Crisis Communication Theory. The amount of blame stakeholders place on the accused determines the amount of responsibility for his/her actions. During an attack, greater attribution of responsibility can cause a worse evaluation of one's image (Coombs, 1998, 2007).

An attack on one's image can often elicit stakeholders' *perceived offensiveness of the act in question.* Thus, the wrongdoer should attempt to reduce stakeholders' feelings of offensiveness using image repair strategies. In fact, reducing offensiveness is a strategy an accused party could use according to image repair theory's response typology (Benoit, 2015). This strategy does not deny the act; instead, it attempts to reduce people's negative feelings toward the wrong-doer and increase people's esteem (Benoit, 2015).

Benoit (2016) argues that an accuser who frequently uses excuses is believed to more *likely commit the act again* in the future. Finally, the accused's *deserved punishment* is of particular interest, derived from criminal and law studies. Pillsbury (1992) argued the accused's punishment depends on the wrong-doer's intentions rather than the consequences. People believe that somebody deserves punishment because they believe he/she intentionally engaged in a wrong conduct.

The Relationship Between Word-of-Mouth and Image

Consumers often share opinions with their friends and families about celebrity personalities, politicians, products, services, companies, etc. The marketing discipline describes this behavior as "word of mouth" (WOM). According to McKinsey, a management consulting firm, WOM is the primary factor behind 20–50 percent of all purchasing decisions (Bughin, Doogan, & Vetvik, 2010). Marketing literature gives multiple definitions of WOM. Westbrook (1987) defined WOM as "informational communications directed at other consumers about the ownership, usage, or characteristics of particular goods and services or their sellers" (p. 261). Harrison-Walker (2001) explained WOM as "informal, person-to-person communication between a perceived noncommercial communicator and a receiver regarding a brand, a product, an organization, or a service" (p. 63). Theoretically, WOM is a kind of interpersonal communication that includes several forms, such as literal WOM, face-to-face discussion, and online mentions and reviews, which is conceptualized as electronic WOM (eWOM) (Berger, 2014). Generally, WOM information is considered to be more persuasive than messages from other channels such as advertisements or editorial recommendation, because the information is perceived to be more credible (Chatterjee, 2001; Mayzlin, 2006).

Two types of WOM are commonly within discussion: positive WOM (pWOM) and negative WOM (nWOM). Studies finds both pWOM and nWOM can influence the probability of making a purchase (East, Hammond, & Lomax, 2008), attitudes towards a product (Charlett, Garland, & Marr, 1995), service provider switching (v. Wangenheim & Bayon, 2003), and brand equity (Bambauer-Sachse & Mangold, 2011). Arndt (1967) argues nWOM is twice as powerful in affecting purchase intention as pWOM. In addition, Coombs and Holladay (2007) found that nWOM is more effective than pWOM in shaping consumers' and stakeholders' opinions. The amount of nWOM can exacerbate a brand as people receive more negative information (Keller, 2003). Reza Jalilvand and Samier (2012) demonstrated that people who read more negative online reviews about a certain brand show more negative attitude towards the brand image.

Evaluating Predictors of Perceived Athlete Image

Benoit (2016) found that all six proposed variables have moderate to high correlations among each other; however, the relationship of each of these variables to the accused party's perceived image and to a behavioral outcome (like nWOM) was not tested. Thus, using a common measure from previous studies to measure perceived image or perceived reputation—McCroskey's credibility scale (McCroskey, 1966)—this chapter seeks to answer two questions?

1. *Which of the six variables predict a person's overall perception of an athlete's image?*
2. *Which of the six variables predict a person's willingness to share negative information about an athlete?*

In order to empirically evaluate which of Benoit's (2016) proposed variables predicts perceived image, data were collected from 490 participants using Amazon Mechanical Turk (MTurk), which the website describes as "a marketplace for work that requires human intelligence" (Amazon.com, 2017). MTurk provides a labor force (called "workers") that can complete tasks (called "HITs" or "Human Intelligence Tasks") in exchange for a wage (called a "reward") (Paolacci, Chandler, & Ipeirotis, 2010). The sample collected from MTurk consisted of 277 males (56.5 percent) and 204 females (41.6 percent). The mean age of participants was 34.36 years (SD = 10.87 years), and the largest racial groups were Caucasians (361 participants, 73.7 percent), Asian and Asian-Americans (47 participants, 9.8 percent), and Africans and African-Americans (39 participants, 8 percent).

Participants were assigned a blog post that resembled a post from *Deadspin*, the second-most-visited sports blog website, behind *Bleacher Report* (Alexa.com, 2016). The blog post featured Jordan Weal, a backup center for the Los Angeles Kings of the National Hockey League (NHL) at the time of this data collection. A real athlete was chosen to achieve more realistic responses, as fictitious athletes tend to cause responses to skew more positively compared to actual athletes in surveys and experiments (K. Brown et al., 2015). Participants were assigned one of three blog posts that detail a specific offense: a simple assault incident with another patron outside a bar, a domestic violence incident with his girlfriend, and a cocaine possession incident where Weal did not attack another party. These three were chosen during a pretest content analysis from a previous study because they were the three most prominent crimes among athletes facing criminal accusations since 2014 (Brown et al., 2017). Weal's response to the accusations was also presented as one of eight randomly selected series of tweets from Weal, based on IRT typology. The tweets illustrated Weal using mortification, corrective action, provocation, bolstering, or a combination from those four. Twitter was used to present Weal's responses so that they seemed more genuine and personal, as research has found that athletes predominantly use Twitter to interact directly with their fans (Hambrick, Simmons, Greenhaigh & Greenwell, 2010). An example of the blog post is provided in Appendix A.

After reading the blog post, participants were directed to answer a series of scale items. To measure Benoit's (2016) six proposed variables, a three-item, seven-point Likert scale was adapted from Benoit (2016) for each item to measure: (a) the acceptance of Weal's response to the accusations (α = 0.937, M = 3.83, SD = 1.74), (b) Weal's likability (α = 0.9, M = 3.56, SD = 1.41), (c) the amount of blame attributed to Weal (α = 0.827, M = 5.62, SD = 1.17), (d) the perceived offensiveness of Weal's act (α = 0.891, M = 5.08, SD = 1.38), (e) Weal's likelihood to commit the act again (α = 0.937, M = 4.79, SD = 1.29), and (f) the punishment that Weal deserves (α = 0.854, M = 4.81, SD = 1.38).

The perceived image was measured using a five-item, seven-point Likert adaptation of McCroskey's (1966) credibility scale that is used by Coombs and Holladay (1996) to measure organization reputation (α = 0.917, M = 3.95, SD = 1.38). The scale was adapted to specifically measure Weal's overall image. Negative word of mouth was measured using a three-item, seven-point adaptation of Coombs and Holladay's (2007) nWOM scale (α = 0.783, M = 4.06, SD = 1.36). Appendix B provides the scale items used in this study.

Understanding What Predicts Perceived Athlete Image

In order to determine which of Benoit's (2016) variables would predict perceptual and behavioral outcomes, two regression models were performed: one to see which of the variables would predict perceived athlete image ($R^2 = 0.678$, $F (6, 483) = 169.36$, $p < 0.01$), and one to see which of the variables would predict negative word of mouth directed towards Weal ($R^2 = 0.615$, $F (6, 483) = 128.51$, $p < 0.01$). Tables 11.1 and 11.2 provide regression results for each model. This section will discuss each variable's predictability and implications for image management.

First, account acceptance measured a person's willingness to accept Weal's response to the accusations as appropriate. Account acceptance did predict one's perception of Weal's image ($\beta = 0.521$, $t = 11.483$, $p < 0.01$), but not one's willingness to spread negative information and feelings about Weal. Therefore, Weal's image was somewhat dependent on a person's willingness to accept his response. Athletes should keep this in mind while responding to transgression because it provides evidence that their responses do matter in terms of the perception of their images moving forward. The wrong response could be detrimental to one's image, so spending time to make sure that you craft an appropriate response for your fans and stakeholders is important.

TABLE 11.1 Regression Table for Perceived Image

	B	SE	β	t	p
Account Acceptability	0.415	0.036	0.521	11.483	< 0.001
Likability	0.246	0.047	0.251	5.19	< 0.001
Blame/Responsibility	0.039	0.035	0.033	1.107	0.269
Offensiveness of the Act	0.062	0.037	0.063	1.707	0.089
Likelihood to Repeat Act	−0.137	0.037	−0.128	−3.756	< 0.001
Desired Punishment	−0.054	0.045	−0.054	−1.198	0.231

Note: $R^2 = 0.678$

TABLE 11.2 Regression Table for Negative Word of Mouth

	B	SE	β	t	p
Account Acceptability	−0.042	0.039	−0.053	−1.077	0.282
Likability	−0.347	0.051	−0.362	−6.832	< 0.001
Blame/Responsibility	0.018	0.038	0.16	0.484	0.629
Offensiveness of the Act	0.038	0.039	0.039	0.975	0.33
Likelihood to Repeat Act	0.131	0.039	0.125	3.336	0.001
Desired Punishment	0.327	0.049	0.334	6.723	< 0.001

Note: $R^2 = 0.615$

Weal's likability influenced both one's perception of his image ($\beta = 0.251$, $t = 5.19$, $p < 0.01$) and one's willingness to spread negative information and feelings about Weal ($\beta = -0.362$, $t = -6.832$, $p < 0.01$). In other words, Weal's likability does influence how people perceive him and their willingness to talk negatively about him to others. This provides evidence that an athlete's previous image among fans and stakeholders can, in fact, influence his/her image repair process when faced with a transgression. Athletes and their representation should consider previous issues or accolades when planning a statement.

The perception of Weal's likelihood to repeat the act among participants influenced both one's perception of his image ($\beta = -0.128$, $t = -3.756$, $p < 0.01$), as well as one's willingness to spread negative information and feelings about Weal ($\beta = 0.125$, $t = 3.336$, $p < 0.01$). This provides evidence of the claim that one's prior reputation and history of transgressions can play a key role in the repair of one's image during a scandal (Coombs, 2007). Practitioners should consider their client's history of scandals when choosing the most appropriate response to an athlete's transgression. However, the blame and responsibility that participants placed on Weal did not influence the perception of his image nor one's willingness to spread negative information and feelings about Weal. Previous research has found evidence linking responsibility for transgressions and one's perceived image (Coombs, 2007; Kiambi & Shafer, 2016), so this counterintuitive finding could mean that the response Weal provided had more influence in this study than the amount of blame the participants placed on Weal.

The severity of the punishment participants believed Weal deserved influenced their willingness to spread negative information about Weal ($\beta = 0.334$, $t = 6.723$, $p < 0.01$), but did not influence participants' perceived image of Weal. This could be explained by the assumption that the punishment that an athlete deserves is a typical discussion point among journalists, correspondents, and fans when an athlete faces a scandal. Related to this, however, is the usual discussion about how offensive the act in question was according to pundits. The offensiveness of Weal's actions, however, did not influence perceived image or nWOM.

Conclusion

While not a complete list, Benoit's (2016) six common dependent variables is a good starting point to begin exploring what factors determine how a sports fan perceives an athlete after he/she faces a transgression. According to results, the more that respondents accepted Weal's response, the more respondents genuinely liked Weal (based on the information provided), and the fewer respondents believed Weal could repeat the offense, then the more respondents perceived Weal's image positively. In addition, the fewer respondents genuinely liked Weal (based on the information provided), the more respondents believed Weal could repeat the offense, and the stronger the punishment that respondents believed Weal deserved, then the more nWOM that respondents would direct towards Weal.

When exploring the implications for managing athlete image that stemmed from this study, three conclusions stand out based on the evidence. First, the response that the athlete and his/her representation crafts does matter in order to help alleviate some of the damage to one's image caused by the transgression. Practitioners should carefully (while also being timely) consider the response an athlete should take because it can have an impact on his/her image moving forward. Second, practitioners should consider an athlete's prior perceived image and his/her qualities as a public figure when deciding how to respond to a transgression. Finally, practitioners should consider the impact the athlete's actions will have on the amount of nWOM that is generated about the athlete in question, and consider that when crafting the response to the public.

Although the study revealed important findings, it suffered from a few drawbacks that can be addressed through future research. First, some participants might have been familiar with the athlete prior to the study. A real athlete is less likely to skew people's evaluations compared to a fictitious one; however, participants might be a fan of the athlete and closely follow the news. When they read the manipulated news, participants will raise doubt about the situation. The prior perception might influence the relationship between the independent variables and dependent variables, so it is important to control for prior reputation when using real athletes.

Second, all findings are based on a single athlete, so it is difficult to generalize the results. One athlete might possess certain characteristics that potentially influence people's judgment about the dependent variables. Future research should replicate the study using other athletes or situations. The findings can be generalized only if multiple experiments disclose similar findings. Since most of the six proposed variables exert influence on either perceived image or nWOM, future research should look at what crisis response messages or combination of messages will affect these variables. Overall, as an exploratory research, this study produced sufficient evidence to support Benoit's argument and showed it is worthwhile to continue this line of research.

References

Abratt, R. (1989). A new approach to the corporate image management process, *Journal of Marketing Management, 1*, 63–76.

Alexa.com. (2016). *Top sports sites*. Retrieved August 16, 2017 from www.alexa.com/topsites/category/Top/Sports

Amazon.com. (2017). About Amazon Mechanical Turk. Retrieved August 16, 2017 from www.mturk.com/worker/help

Arndt, J. (1967). The role of product-related conversations in the diffusion of a new product. *Journal of Marketing Research, 4*, 291–295.

Bambauer-Sachse, S., & Mangold, S. (2011). Brand equity dilution through negative online word-of-mouth communication. *Journal of Retailing and Consumer Services, 18*(1), 38–45.

Benoit, W. (1995). Accounts, excuses, and apologies: A theory of image restoration strategies. Albany, NY: State University of New York Press.

Benoit, W. (2000). Another visit to the theory of image restoration strategies. *Communication Quarterly, 48*(1), 40–43.

Benoit, W. (2015). *Accounts, excuses, apologies: Image repair theory and research* (2nd ed.). Albany: State University of New York Press.

Benoit, W., & Hanczor, R. (1994). The Tonya Harding controversy: An analysis of image restoration strategies. *Communication Quarterly, 42*, 416–433.

Berger, J. (2014). Word of mouth and interpersonal communication: A review and directions for future research. *Journal of Consumer Psychology, 24*(4), 586–607.

Botan, C. (1993). A human nature approach to image and ethics in international public relations. *Journal of Public Relations Research, 5*, 71–82.

Brown, K. (2016). Is apology the best policy? An experimental examination of the effectiveness of image repair strategies during criminal and noncriminal athlete transgressions. *Communication & Sport, 4*(1), 23–42.

Brown, K. A., Billings, A., & Devlin, M. (2016). Image repair across the racial spectrum: Experimentally exploring athlete transgression responses. *Communication Research Reports, 33*(1), 47–53.

Brown, K. A., Billings, A. C., Mastro, D., & Brown-Devlin, N. (2015). Changing the image repair equation: Impact of race and gender on sport-related transgressions. *Journalism & Mass Communication Quarterly, 92*(2), 487–506.

Brown, K. A., Dickhaus, J., & Long, M. C. (2012). LeBron James and "The Decision": An empirical examination of image repair in sports. *Journal of Sports Media, 7*(1), 149–175.

Brown, K. A., Murphy, B., & Maxwell, L. C. (2017). Tried in the court of public opinion: Effects of involvement in criminal transgressions on athlete image. *Communication & Sport*. doi:10.1177/2167479517697426

Brown, N. A., Brown, K. A., & Billings, A. C. (2015). "May no act of ours bring shame": Fan-enacted crisis communication surrounding the Penn State sex abuse scandal. *Communication & Sport, 3*(3), 288–311.

Bughin, J., Doogan, J., & Vetvik, O. J. (2010). A new way to measure word-of-mouth marketing. *McKinsey Quarterly, 2*, 113–116.

Charlett, D., Garland, R., & Marr, N. (1995). How damaging is negative word of mouth. *Marketing Bulletin, 6*(1), 42–50.

Chatterjee, P. (2001). Online reviews: do consumers use them? *Advances in Consumer Research, 28*(1), 129–133.

Chun, R. (2005). Corporate reputation: Meaning and measurement. *International Journal of Management Review, 7*, 91–109.

Compton, J., & Compton, J. L. (2014). College sports, losing seasons, and image repair through open letters to fans. *Communication & Sport, 2*(4), 345–362.

Coombs, W. (1998). An analytic framework for crisis situations: Better responses from a better understanding of the situation. *Journal of Public Relations Research, 10*(3), 177–191.

Coombs, W. (2005). Image. In R. Heath (Ed.), *Encyclopedia of public relations* (pp. 405–407). Thousand Oaks, CA: Sage Publications.

Coombs, W. (2007). Protecting organization reputations during a crisis: The development and application of situational crisis communication theory. *Corporate Reputation Review, 10*(3), 163–176.

Coombs, W. T., & Holladay, S. J. (1996). Communication and attributions in a crisis: An experimental study of crisis communication. *Journal of Public Relations Research, 8*, 279–295.

Coombs, W., & Holladay, S. (2007). The negative communication dynamic: Exploring the impact of stakeholder effect on behavioral intentions. *Journal of Communication Management, 11*, 300–312.

Coombs, W., & Holladay, S. (2008). Comparing apology to equivalent crisis response strategies: Clarifying apology's role and value in crisis communication. *Public Relations Review, 34*(3), 252–257.

Dichter, E. (1985). What's in an image? *Journal of Consumer Marketing, 2*, 75–81.

Dowling, G. (1993). Developing your corporate image into a corporate asset. *Long Range Planning, 26*, 101–109.

Dunn, D., & Cody, M. J. (2000). Account credibility and public image: Excuses, justifications, denials, and sexual harassment. *Communications Monographs, 67*(4), 372–391.

Dutton, J., Dukerich, J. & Harquail, C. (1994). Organization images and member identification. *Administrative Science Quarterly, 39*, 239–263.

East, R., Hammond, K., & Lomax, W. (2008). Measuring the impact of positive and negative word of mouth on brand purchase probability. *International Journal of Research in Marketing, 25*(3), 215–224.

Forbes' list of the 10 most disliked athletes in sports. (2016, October 20). *FOX Sports*. Retrieved from http://www.foxsports.com/nba/gallery/forbes-most-disliked-athletes-in-sports-020613

Fortunato, J. A. (2008). Restoring a reputation: The Duke University lacrosse scandal. *Public Relations Review, 34*, 116–123.

Gotzi, M. & Wilson, A. (2001). Corporate reputation: Seeking a definition. *Corporate Communication, 6*, 24–30.

Gray, E. & Balmer, J. (1998). Managing image and corporate reputation. *Long Range Planning, 31*, 685–692.

Grunig, J. (1993). Image and substance: from symbolic to behavioral relationships. *Public Relations Review, 19*, 121–139.

Hambrick, M. E., Frederick, E. L., & Sanderson, J. (2015). From yellow to blue: Exploring Lance Armstrong's image repair strategies across traditional and social media. *Communication & Sport, 3*(2), 196–218.

Hambrick, M., Simmons, J., Greenhaigh, G. & Greenwell, T. (2010). Understanding professional athletes' use of Twitter: A content analysis of athlete tweets. *International Journal of Sport Communication, 3*, 454–471.

Harrison-Walker, L. J. (2001). The measurement of word-of-mouth communication and an investigation of service quality and customer commitment as potential antecedents. *Journal of Service Research, 4*(1), 60–75.

Keller, K. (2003). *Strategic brand management*. Prentice Hall, NJ: Upper Saddle River.

Kennedy, S. (1977). Nurturing corporate image. *European Journal of Marketing, 11*, 120–164.

Kiambi, D. & Shafer, A. (2016). Corporate crisis communication: Examining the interplay of reputation and crisis response strategies. *Mass Communication and Society, 19*, 127–148.

Knittel, C. R., & Stango, V. (2013). Celebrity endorsements, firm value, and reputation risk: Evidence from the Tiger Woods scandal. *Management Science, 60*(1), 21–37.

Kruse, N. W. (1981). Apologia in team sport. *Quarterly Journal of Speech, 67*(3), 270–283.

Liu, B. F., Austin, L., & Jin, Y. (2011). How publics respond to crisis communication strategies: The interplay of information form and source. *Public Relations Review, 37*(4), 345–353.

McCroskey, J. C. (1966). Scales for the measurement of ethos. *Speech Monographs, 33,* 65–72.

Manheim, J. B., & Albritton, R. B. (1983). Changing national images: International public relations and media agenda setting. *American Political Science Review, 78*(3), 641–657.

Mayzlin, D. (2006). Promotional chat on the internet. *Marketing Science, 25*(2), 155–163.

Meng, J., & Pan, P.-L. (2013). Revisiting image-restoration strategies: An integrated case study of three athlete sex scandals in sports news. *International Journal of Sport Communication, 6*(1), 87–100.

Meyer, K. (2008). An examination of Michael Vick's speech of apologia: Implications for the study of sports apologia and image repair. Conference Papers—National Communication Association, 1. Retrieved from EBSCOhost.

Nguyen, N., & Leblanc, G. (2001). Corporate image and corporate reputation in customers' retention decisions in services. *Journal of Retailing and Consumer Services, 8*(4), 227–236.

Paolacci, G., Chandler, J., & Ipeirotis, P. (2010). Running experiments on Amazon Mechanical Turk. *Judgment and Decision Making, 5,* 411–419.

Park, S. H. (2015). Factors and characteristics of political likeability as a source of public relations: Focusing on the likeability factors in South Korea. *Indian Journal of Science and Technology, 8*(13), 1–6.

Pillsbury, S. H. (1992). The meaning of deserved punishment: An essay on choice, character, and responsibility. *Indiana Law Journal, 67*(3), 719–752.

Reza Jalilvand, M., & Samiei, N. (2012). The effect of electronic word of mouth on brand image and purchase intention: An empirical study in the automobile industry in Iran. *Marketing Intelligence & Planning, 30*(4), 460–476.

Scott, E., & Jehn, K. (2003). About face: How employee dishonesty influences a stakeholder's image of an organization. *Business and Society, 42,* 234–266.

v. Wangenheim, F., & Bayón, T. (2004). The effect of word of mouth on services switching: Measurement and moderating variables. *European Journal of Marketing, 38*(9–10), 1173–1185.

Westbrook, R. A. (1987). Product/consumption-based affective responses and postpurchase processes. *Journal of Marketing Research, 24,* 258–270.

Appendix A

Sample Manipulation Blog Post

LA Kings' Weal Arrested for Parking Lot Brawl

Tom Jones
October 16, 2015

641

Los Angeles Kings center Jordan Weal was arrested early Friday morning after a fight that seemed to have started over a bar tab bet.

Police and witnesses say that after last call at Casey's Irish Pub, Weal, along with two other people, were seen arguing with another group of bar patrons over a bet the two groups made on the Mets-Dodgers NLDS playoff game. Weal was overheard calling the group out for not "owning up to the bet." The argument spilled into the parking lot, where witnesses say Weal took a foreign object out of his car and pursued the group, injuring one person's leg before police broke the fight up.

Weal was released on bail late Friday morning, and the Kings have confirmed that he will not play in Friday's game against the Minnesota Wild. Weal decided to take to Twitter about the incident shortly after he was bailed out:

After the Kings drafted Weal in the third round in 2010, he played minor league hockey, most recently for the Manchester Monarchs of the American Hockey League. Last season, Weal won the AHL's Calder Cup, awarded to the playoffs' most valuable player, scoring 10 goals and 12 assists. The Kings added Weal to the rotation in hopes of taking major rotation minutes throughout the season; however, his status with the team will be reviewed pending the results of the police investigation.

Appendix B

Scales for Dependent Variables

Account Acceptance

1) Weal's statement was acceptable.
2) Weal's statement was satisfying.
3) Weal's statement was fitting.

Likability of the Accused

1) Weal is likable.
2) Weal would make a good teammate.
3) If I followed Weal's team, I would like him.

Responsibility and Blame

1) Weal is responsible for the incident.
2) The incident is completely Weal's fault.
3) I am willing to blame Weal completely for the incident.

Offensiveness of the Act

1) The incident that Weal was involved in was terrible.
2) The incident that Weal was involved in was offensive.
3) The incident that Weal was involved in was awful.

Likelihood to Repeat the Act

1) I think Weal would be involved in another incident similar to this one again.
2) I think it is probable that Weal would be involved in another incident similar to this one.
3) I think Weal would be involved in another incident similar to this one in the future.

Punishment Deserved

1) I think Weal deserves a tough punishment from his team.
2) I think Weal should be punished greatly for this incident.
3) I think Weal should be criticized by the media for this incident.

Perceived Image (Coombs & Holladay, 1996; McCroskey, 1966)

1) X is being honest about the incident.
2) I trust that X is telling the truth about this incident.
3) In this circumstance, I am likely to believe what X is saying.
4) I would prefer not to trust X about this incident.
5) In light of this incident, X is reputable.

Negative Word of Mouth (Coombs & Holladay, 2007)

1) I would encourage people not to support X.
2) I would say negative things about X to other people.
3) I would recommend someone to cheer for X during his games.

Note: all scales adapted from Benoit (2016) unless noted.

12

IS A REBUILD A REPUTATIONAL THREAT?

The Chicago White Sox in 1997 and 2017

Tom Isaacson

On July 31, 1997, the day of the trade deadline in Major League Baseball (MLB), the Chicago White Sox made a trade. Veteran starting pitchers Wilson Alvarez and Danny Darwin and reliever Roberto Hernandez were sent to the San Francisco Giants for a package of six minor-leaguers. The next day, the *New York Times* reported that the "White Sox Are Flying White Flag" (Vecsey, 1997). The "white flag" label, which was first used by columnist Phil Rogers at the *Chicago Tribune*, has endured for the next 20 years, right up until the printing of this book.

The White Sox, at the time of the trade, were one game under .500 and 3.5 games behind the Cleveland Indians in the American League Central Division. Players were upset. Third baseman Robin Ventura, who had worked hard to recover from a spring training leg injury and had only recently rejoined the team on the active roster, was quoted as saying, "We didn't realize August 1 was the end of the season" (Greenstein, 1998, para. 3). Pitcher Danny Darwin, a veteran of seven different Major League Baseball teams, said, "I've never seen in my 22 years of baseball an owner say that he was giving up on his ballclub" (Schoenfield, 2011, para. 5).

Darwin's quote referred to a frequently repeated phrase from team owner Jerry Reinsdorf, who told *Chicago Sun-Times* reporter Toni Ginnetti, "anyone who thinks we can catch Cleveland is crazy" (Sullivan, 2017b, para. 9). Perhaps an indication of the times—a time when sports talk radio was increasingly popular and cable television had hours of programming to fill—the full quote by Reinsdorf was rarely repeated. In it, he said, "If we keep playing the way we're playing, anyone who thinks this team is going to catch Cleveland is crazy" (Newhan, 1998, para. 4).

In addition to the players, the fans and media were upset as well. Much of the dissatisfaction was directed at Reinsdorf and then general manager Ron Schueler.

Paul Sullivan, a staff writer for the *Chicago Tribune*, three years after the trade, wrote about how "fans and media ripped Reinsdorf and Schueler for surrendering" (2000, para. 12) and how, for Schueler, "the attacks were so overwhelming at first that Schueler was reluctant to even look at his mail or check his voice mail" (Sullivan, 2000, para. 14).

The entire event and subsequent media and fan reactions, produced a reputational threat for the organization. Fan attendance at home games during the following season dropped 25.5 percent, and was the team's lowest total in nine years. The second year after the trade, fan attendance dropped an additional 4 percent (Chicago White Sox, 2017).

Chicago White Sox management and organizational responses to the threat exhibit crisis response strategies outlined by Benoit (1995) and Coombs (1995, 1998). Reinsdorf continued to defend the strategy taken by initiating the trade, when he described how the team was no worse after the trade and how it would be both more interesting and likeable to a Chicago fan base going forward (Newhan, 1998). Schueler defended the trade as his only recourse due to the team's inability to re-sign the veteran players that were traded to the Giants (Sullivan, 2000).

The background and reactions to the 1997 trade, while interesting in their own right—in hindsight the trade was a success when two of the players acquired in the trade, pitchers Keith Foulke and Bob Howry, became key members of Chicago's surprising 2000 division-winning team (Sullivan, 2017b)—are used here to illustrate the narrative and reactions surrounding a team's rebuilding effort. The same organization, 20 years later, is again embarking on a rebuilding process.

Links can and have been made between the two time periods, 1997 and 2017. The *Chicago Tribune* recently published an anniversary article titled, "White Sox engineered infamous 'White Flag' trade 20 years ago" (Sullivan, 2017b). In it, the author reviews the old trade and describes some of the events surrounding the current rebuilding effort, including the statement that "most Sox fans are buying into GM Rick Hahn's current garage sale" (Sullivan, 2017b, para. 6). An article by JJ Stankevitz (2017) for CSN Chicago described how one of the seminal trades launching the current rebuilding effort, that of pitcher Chris Sale to the Boston Red Sox in December 2016 for four minor-league prospects, "was the first rebuilding blockbuster trade the organization had made since the 1997 White Flag deal" (para. 7).

This chapter is developed as a case study that reviews the strategies and tactics developed and implemented by the communications/media relations staff in 2017 to mitigate crisis risk and strengthen the long-term reputation of the Chicago White Sox organization.

2017 Rebuilding Process

Following the completion of the 2016 season—one in which the White Sox finished 78–84, 16.5 games behind the division-winning Cleveland Indians, marking the fourth straight year with a sub-.500 record—the team's now 81-year-old Owner Jerry Reinsdorf, Executive VP Kenny Williams, and General Manager Rick Hahn met with key scouts and decision makers at the annual organizational meetings and agreed on a rebuilding plan (Stark, 2016). Intentionally, this organizational shift was not immediately made public, but some hints of the plan were shared with the media by Hahn at MLB's General Manager meetings in early November, when he stated:

> A lot of what we did in the last few years had been trying to enhance the short-term potential of the club to put ourselves in a position to win immediately. I feel the approach at this point is focusing on longer-term benefits. It doesn't mean we won't necessarily be in a good position in 2017. It means that our targets and whatever we're hoping to accomplish have a little more longer-term fits in nature.
>
> *Hayes, 2016, para. 5*

As the rebuilding plans took shape, the fans were not forgotten. Hahn intended to keep them abreast of the team's efforts as well. Hahn shared, "Once we start making transactions, we'll explain our rationale behind what we're doing and why we did it" (Hayes, 2016, para. 22).

The internal plan became public with two significant trades in December at MLB's Winter Meetings. Starting pitcher Chris Sale, a five-time All-Star, was traded to the Boston Red Sox for four minor-league prospects, including MLB's then top-rated minor-league prospect Yoán Moncada, and outfielder Adam Eaton was traded to the Washington Nationals for three minor-league pitchers, including MLB's then top-rated minor-league pitching prospect Lucas Giolito. The trades were immediately well received by the media, both nationally (Scheinin, 2016; Stark, 2016) and in the Chicago area (Haugh, 2016; Kane, 2016; Van Schouwen, 2016a).

During the same period, beginning in November and continuing on toward Spring Training, the team's top communications and media relations professionals met to discuss upcoming communication challenges associated with a rebuilding team. They were faced with a common problem for sports communicators: a lack of control over the product, at a time when the product was not expected to be good (i.e., the team for the upcoming season was likely to lose, a lot). Strategically, the "sale" of a massive rebuilding effort required close interaction between the five units within White Sox Communications to ensure consistent messaging about the process across earned, owned, and paid media.

The staff decisions would have made Arthur Page smile. Founders of the Arthur W. Page Society, a top professional organization for senior public relations and corporate communication executives, developed seven principles for the effective practice of public relations. The first Page Principle, *tell the truth*, is described as "let the public know what's happening with honest and good intention; provide an ethically accurate picture of the enterprise's character, values, ideals and action" (Arthur W. Page Society, 2017a, para. 2) The second, *prove it with action*, is described as "public perception of an enterprise is determined 90 percent by what it does and 10 percent by what it says" (Arthur W. Page Society, 2017a, para. 3).

The uniqueness of a competitive professional sports environment, where trading assets is a key part of a rebuilding effort, produces a strategic need to flip the order of the two principles. Nonetheless, both of the principles were evident as additional communication strategies were implemented.

The White Sox opened up the books, so to speak. The team was not expected to win in 2017. Once two of the team's top players were traded away during the offseason—with more trades expected during the season—the focal point was on the future, not the present; it was on prospects and development, not wins and standings. The new perspective was described by Senior VP of Communications Scott Reifert:

> We recognized that as we go through this multiyear transition our fans aren't just interested in what is happening at the major league level each night, but they are also invested in following the development of players in our minor league system. Last winter we tried to identify and expand on creative ways to work with our players and each of our affiliates to highlight the achievements of our standout minor leagues, and we think it has been an initiative that benefits the organization and hopefully is a lot of fun for fans.
>
> *Van Schouwen, 2017c, para. 17*

The tactical implementation of the initiative took the form of enabling Comcast SportsNet's broadcast of games by the team's AAA affiliate the Charlotte Knights in the Chicago market; creating a White Sox minor-league player and pitcher of the month award (winners were selected with input from key Chicago area media); generating media attention in the Chicago market by sending team interpreter Billy Russo to nearby Indianapolis when Charlotte played there, enabling top prospects to be interviewed in Spanish; making team General Manager Rick Hahn, Director of Player Development Chris Getz, and Director of Amateur Scouting Nick Hostetler widely available to Chicago-area sports talk radio (allowing for regular updates on the status and direction of the rebuilding process); and arranging for conference calls between local media and minor-league prospects (Van Schouwen, 2017c).

Efforts to support the development of earned media coverage by the media relations staff included the creation of a minor-league FTP site that was uploaded daily with supporting audio and video, increased minor-league inclusions in the team's game notes, conference calls with minor-league and baseball operations staff—an estimated 25 in all throughout the season—and media events in Chicago for two of the team's top minor-league prospects (B. Beghtol, personal communication, September, 19, 2017; R. Garcia, personal communication, September, 13, 2017; S. Reifert, personal communication; September 11, 2017).

Through the White Sox social media channels, the content reflected a shift as well. In addition to expected information about current games and the Major League club, minor-league updates increased. The team's official Twitter page (@whitesox) regularly included minor-league team results, awards won by minor-league players, and media and fan interactions with minor-league players. On Facebook, the trend among sports organizations to produce more of their own video content is evident, and the additional material focused on prospect profiles, fan–prospect interactions and minor-league highlights. "Inside the White Sox," the team's long-running blog, provided content that could frequently be shared through other organizational channels.

The discovery, development and promotion of stories via social media is important, especially when linking time periods 20 years apart. Director of Digital Communication Brad Boron explained the difference:

> More than anything, this allows us a share in our voice, to tell our own story, in a way that 15 or 20 years ago we were relying on traditional media to tell it. We approach our social media in a way that shows we care what our fans think, what they like and what interests them. Then we provide content that matches those needs.
>
> *personal communication, September 18, 2017*

The communications efforts coincided with organizational decisions that demonstrated a commitment to the rebuilding process. In May 2017, the White Sox outbid other teams to sign 19-year-old Cuban prospect, Luis Robert. Throughout the summer General Manager Rick Hahn continued to trade Major League players for minor-league prospects, including starting pitcher José Quintana to the Chicago Cubs for a package of four players that included the Cubs' top two prospects, according to MLB.com.

Impact of Communications/Media Relations Efforts

Unlike 1997, the current rebuilding effort has been well received, perhaps as well as is possible for a rebuilding effort. Public relations metrics such as earned media coverage and key stakeholder reactions can be combined with traditional evaluative measures (e.g., attendance stability, TV ratings) to provide a snapshot.

Earned media coverage, a long-standing indicator of successful public relations, has always been notoriously hard to quantify. However, in this instance, even a simple review of published media coverage reveals large differences between 1997 and 2017. In 1997, the "white flag" reference appeared immediately (Vecsey, 1997), was shared widely, and has endured over multiple decades.

Players' responses demonstrated anger and frustration (Greenstein, 1998; Schoenfield, 2011), and the general manager and team owner were criticized for "surrendering" (Sullivan, 2000).

In late 2016, when the current rebuild was publicly launched, the White Sox and its general manager were hailed as the winners of MLB's Winter Meetings, both by Chicago-area (Haugh, 2016; Van Schouwen, 2016b) and national media outlets (Jaffe, 2016; Scheinin, 2016; Stark, 2016). A review of Chicago-area media coverage from spring training onwards into the 2017 season is highlighted in Table 12.1, showing both initial and growing support for the rebuilding effort.

Both former and current players have weighed in, and have exhibited consistent support for the rebuild. Former first baseman Paul Konerko, a star on the team's 2005 World Series team, called the rebuild "impressive" and one that shows a team commitment to conducting the rebuild in "the right way" (Konerko, 2017). Shortly before he was traded, outfielder Melky Cabrera, one

TABLE 12.1 Sample of Chicago Newspaper Headlines about 2017 Rebuild

Outlet/Headline	Date	Author
Chicago Tribune		
White Sox rebuild goes beyond top prospects showcased in Cactus League	3/30/17	Kane
White Sox's rebuilding status looks good compared to Cubs of 2012	6/5/17	Sullivan
White Sox rebuild taking root in Charlotte and Birmingham	7/17/17	McGrath
Jerry Reinsdorf says he started rebuild to do what was right for White Sox fans	8/15/17	Kane
Chicago Sun-Times		
White Sox rebuild shift to higher gear with trade of Quintana to Cubs	7/13/17	Van Schouwen
Rick Hahn is very, very busy proving his baseball smarts	7/20/17	Morrissey
White Sox look to keep 'winning' the rebuilding process	7/20/17	Van Schouwen
Focus of White Sox' rebuild shifting to player development	8/20/17	Van Schouwen
Daily Herald		
Chicago White Sox rebuild only just beginning	3/8/17	Rozner
Rebuilding Chicago White Sox excited about draft haul	6/14/17	Gregor
Let the Chicago White Sox's rebuild begin	7/31/17	Gregor
Chicago White Sox understand losing is part of rebuilding	8/8/17	Gregor

of the few remaining veterans on the team at the time, told a *Chicago Tribune* reporter, "I like this team and I would like to stay here for a long time, not just until the end of the season" (Kane, 2017b, para. 4).

The positive earned coverage was supported by the team's consistency between organizational actions and communication. After launching the rebuilding effort with the Winter Meeting trades of Sale and Eaton, Hahn traded nine more Major League players for prospects during the 2017 season (Hershkovich, 2017). The impact on the farm system was profound. As recently as two years ago, it was among the worst in baseball; by August 2017 it was ranked as one of the top two in Major League Baseball (Hayes, 2017a).

The organizational turnaround was supported by additional earned media coverage. In early September the White Sox brought top prospects Eloy Jimenez and Michael Kopech to Chicago for media and fan events. Assistant Director of Media Relations Ray Garcia (2017) described the media events: "A normal Tuesday night in September when you're 30 games under .500, there are not going to be a lot of TV cameras out there," said Garcia. "I think we had every single television station from the city represented to cover these two kids who weren't going to be doing any kind of baseball activity" (personal communication, September 13, 2017). Bob Beghtol, Senior Director of Media Relations, added, "It looked like Opening Day or a Cubs series. We were shocked that it was received that well" (personal communication, September 19, 2017).

Fan reactions can be harder to gauge, especially when the rebuild is underway and results of it are not expected on the field until 2019 or later. However, media members have written about encouraging fan reactions to various parts of the rebuild (e.g., Van Schouwen, 2017a). Team spokespeople have discussed it as well. In February 2017 General Manager Rick Hahn commented on the impressive reaction of White Sox fans to the initial steps in the process (Rozner, 2017a), and as late as August 2017 he reiterated his appreciation for the fan support and buy-in (Benetti, 2017). Team owner Jerry Reinsdorf said in August 2017, "We're fortunate our fans have really been forgiving, and have bought into what we're trying to do" (Nightengale, 2017, para. 42). At the end of the 2017 season, Hahn shared with an AP reporter, "I cannot tell you how many various fans have stopped me, or emailed me or mentioned to me that they've never been this excited over a 60-win team" (Associated Press, 2017, para. 3).

Within the team's front office phone calls from frustrated fans, something typically seen with a struggling team, have nearly stopped as fans support the rebuilding launch (S. Quinn, personal communication, September 13, 2017). Director of Advertising and Design Service Gareth Breunlin simply states, "You talk to any White Sox fan, they're on board with this process and the rebuild. They're excited" (personal communication, September 18, 2017).

As Ecker (2017) noted about the White Sox in an article in *Crain's Chicago Business*, "the team is in the early stages of a roster rebuild, historically a drain on TV viewership" (para. 10). The team's internal communications and media relations objectives focused on retaining fans and reducing the financial implications of the rebuild, not on growth during a period when it would be unlikely.

A review of recent TV ratings shows, as of early September 2017, the White Sox have had a Chicago-area rating of 0.80, equal to about 28,000 households per game. This is a 12.5 percent reduction over 2016 ratings (0.92, 32,000 households). For comparison, when the Chicago Cubs embarked on its rebuilding effort in 2011, TV ratings dropped from 2.19 in 2011 to 1.70 in 2012 (Ecker, 2017). A review of attendance figures at home games in 1998, the season following the "white flag" trade, shows that attendance dropped 25.5 percent to the team's lowest total in nine years. In 2017, the drop compared to the previous year was 5.5 percent.

External Factors

Undoubtedly, the success communicating the current rebuilding effort to key stakeholder groups—primarily media members and fans—has been influenced by some external factors. The first, and perhaps most important, is a nearby parallel case example with the Chicago Cubs, something that has not escaped notice of Chicago-area media (e.g., Haugh, 2017; McGrath, 2017; Sullivan, 2017a). In 2011, the organization began a complete rebuild that started on the field with a 101-loss season in 2012, and culminated with a 103-win season in 2016 that ended with the team's first World Series win since 1908. Similarly in the American League, the Kansas City Royals engaged in a long-term rebuild that produced back-to-back World Series appearances and a championship in 2015, and the rebuilt Houston Astros won 101 games and then the World Series in 2017.

For the White Sox, a key structural change took place between 1997 and 2017. In 1997, the communications department was a substantially smaller unit that was located within marketing. Following an external communications audit in the early 2000s, it was recommended that communications—due to its importance as a critical business function—be separated from marketing. At that time, Scott Reifert was promoted from director of public relations to VP of communications. This change to the organizational structure ensured a direct line of communication between the department and the team's top leadership.

In addition, it further enhanced the organization's ability to engage in increasingly proactive communications and media relations strategies. New units were created within the department, including Public Relations and Digital Communications. Most recently, before the 2017 season, an in-house video team was hired. Director of Digital Communications Brad Boron explains:

> I don't think you can understate the role of video in all that we do. We made a huge investment in the video side. It was something new that Scott and I wanted to add, and knowing the strategies and where the story lines were this year, it became even more important.
>
> *personal communication, September 18, 2017*

The benefits of producing its own video, both for organizational storytelling and external distribution to media, was echoed by staff members across all units in the department. Increasingly, the added resources allow the Communications Department to function as its own in-house news agency with opportunities to communicate directly to fans (B. Boron, personal communication, September 18, 2017; R. Garcia, personal communication, September 13, 2017).

The structural change in particular is cited as a contributing factor within organizations that achieve the highest levels of "public relations excellence." In the public relations academic field, the Excellence Study identified major factors that make public relations an effective organizational management function, and provides a guide for the internal structure of a public relations department; this includes the recommendation that the senior PR executive is a member of an organization's dominant coalition (Dozier, Grunig, & Grunig, 1995).

Internally the value is recognized. About the structural changes, Beghtol describes, "It was Scott's vision when he became VP, now senior VP, that we would have the right people speaking on the right issues at the right time, and they're all on the same page" (personal communication, September 19, 2017). When asked about the consistent messaging coming from the White Sox throughout the rebuilding process, Garcia shares, "Honestly, I think the biggest key, is getting everyone on the top on the same page. Rick [Hahn] and Scott [Reifert] are constantly talking and in communication" (personal communication, September 13, 2017).

Conclusion

In a nine-month span, between December 2016 and August 2017, the Chicago White Sox traded 10 veteran players for 19 prospects (Nightengale, 2017). The team's farm system, which had been ranked at 23rd among 30 MLB teams at the start of the process, rose to a number 1 or 2 ranking as of August 2017, depending on the source—MLB Pipeline or Baseball America (Hayes, 2017a). Of Chicago's top 30 prospects, including 2017 draftees, 14 are new to the organization since December 2016 (Hayes, 2017b; H. Sundwall, personal communication, November 1, 2017).

While rebuilding efforts 20 years apart do not provide a perfect comparison—simply too much has changed with the media landscape, expansion of social media, growth in team-produced content, and information accessible to fans—there is enough in common to evaluate how one circumstance differs from the other. In late 2016 and into 2017, the White Sox Communications Department utilized a variety of strategies to make the rebuilding process as transparent as possible for key stakeholders, primarily fans, players, and media members.

David Haugh (2017), in a *Chicago Tribune* article in March 2017, wrote, "the White Sox have shown excellent transparency preparing their fan base for the inevitable struggles ahead" (para. 10). The external view is consistent with perceptions of staff members in the department. Boron said, "I credit everyone from the top on down for creating that direct open dialogue to start it off, and then letting us delve deeper into what this means for our fans and giving them day-to-day updates on watching this investment pay off" (personal communication, September 18, 2017). Beghtol simply states, "We try to be transparent with everything we do" (personal communication, September 19, 2017).

The approach is in line with recommendations made in the Arthur W. Page Society's *Authentic Enterprise Report* (Arthur W. Page Society, 2017b); it has positively influenced the narrative surrounding the rebuild, and minimized the effects of a potential reputational crisis for the organization.

The challenges of implementing and selling a rebuilding process to fans and media will continue to face professional sports teams, and much can be learned from the White Sox's experience. The frequent interactions between team management and senior communications officials helped ensure consistent messaging from the start. The transparency of the process improved media and fan buy-in and made it easier for internal staff to find and develop appropriate storylines to support the rebuilding narrative. The creation of awards, events, and video content, combined with wide availability of key spokespeople, demonstrates a strong understanding of newsworthy elements that were then promoted through traditional and social media. The communications staff is quick to adapt to trends in the field (e.g., expanding in-house video capabilities), increasing the organization's ability to develop its own story for direct distribution to fans.

The final results are yet to be determined. The team is now moving from stage one (trading veterans for minor-league prospects) to stage two (player development—a lengthy process, as baseball fans know) with stage three on the horizon (to compete for championships) (Musick, 2017). During stage one the team has lost, spending most of the 2017 season among the three worst MLB teams. Even this, during a rebuild, can be beneficial since the White Sox's 2018 draft pick will be high. In the midst of the losing, the "wait until next year" narrative—or, in this case, the "wait until the team's prospects develop"—has been widely shared and distributed. Perhaps in the end it will produce a sporting event not seen in Chicago since 1906, a Cubs-White Sox World Series.

References

Arthur W. Page Society (2007a). *The authentic enterprise: An Arthur W. Page Society report.* Retrieved from http://awpagesociety.com/thought-leadership/authentic-enterprise-report

Arthur W.Page Society (2017b). *The page principles.* Retrieved from http://awpagesociety.com/site/the-page-principles

Associated Press (2017, October 2). Rebuilding White Sox see foundation starting to take shape. *USA Today.* Retrieved from www.usatoday.com/story/sports/mlb/2017/10/02/rebuilding-white-sox-see-foundation-starting-to-take-shape/106241032/

Benetti, J. (2017, August 5). White Sox GM Hahn talks about rebuild. *Daily Herald*. Retrieved from www.dailyherald.com/sports/20170805/benetti-white-sox-gm-hahn-talks-about-rebuild

Benoit, W. (1995). Accounts, excuses, and apologies: A theory of image restoration strategies. Albany, NY: State University of New York Press.

Chicago White Sox (2017). *Year-by-year results*. Retrieved from http://chicago.whitesox. mlb.com/cws/history/year_by_year_results.jsp

Coombs, W. T. (1995). Choosing the right words: The development of guidelines for the selection of the "appropriate" crisis-response strategies. *Management Communication Quarterly, 8*(4), 447–476.

Coombs, W. T. (1998). An analytical framework for crisis situations: Better responses from better understanding of the situation. *Journal of Public Relations Research, 10*, 177–191.

Dozier, D., Grunig, L., & Grunig, J. (1995). *Manager's guide to excellence in public relations and communication management*. Mahwah, NJ: Lawrence Erlbaum Associates.

Ecker, D. (2017, July 12). Cubs TV ratings slide during disappointing season. *Crain's Chicago Business*. Retrieved from www.chicagobusiness.com/article/20170712/BLOGS04/170719951/cubs-tv-ratings-slide-during-disappointing-season

Greenstein, T. (1998, July 29). The "white flag" trade hit a nerve with fans and players alike. A year later the question is . . . what did the Sox gain?" *Chicago Tribune*. Retrieved from articles.chicagotribune.com/1998-07-29/sports/9807290111_1_mike-caruso-schueler-american-league-central

Gregor, S. (2017a, June 14). Rebuilding White Sox excited about draft haul. *Daily Herald*. Retrieved from www.dailyherald.com/sports/20170614/rebuilding-chicago-white-sox-excited-about-draft-haul

Gregor, S. (2017b, July 31). Let the Chicago White Sox's rebuild begin. *Daily Herald*. Retrieved from www.dailyherald.com/sports/20170731/let-the-chicago-white-soxs-rebuild-begin

Gregor, S. (2017c, August 8). Chicago White Sox understand losing is part of rebuilding. *Daily Herald*. Retrieved from www.dailyherald.com/sports/20170808/chicago-white-sox-understand-losing-is-part-of-rebuilding

Haugh, D. (2016, December 8). General manager who won winter meetings wants more for the White Sox. *Chicago Tribune*. Retrieved from www.chicagotribune.com/sports/columnists/ct-rick-hahn-rebuilding-haugh-spt-1209-20161208-column.html

Haugh, D. (2017, March 31). As the Cubs drive toward a dynasty, the White Sox quietly rebuild. *Chicago Tribune*. Retrieved from www.chicagotribune.com/sports/columnists/ct-cubs-white-sox-haugh-spt-0402-20170401-column.html

Hayes, D. (2016, November 8). GM Rick Hahn hints that rebuild could be on horizon for White Sox. *CSN Chicago*. Retrieved from www.csnchicago.com/chicago-white-sox/gm-rick-hahn-hints-rebuild-could-be-horizon-white-sox

Hayes, D. (2017a, August 3). Influx of talent from July trades results in No. 1 ranking for White Sox farm system. *CSN Chicago*.Retrieved from www.csnchicago.com/chicago-white-sox/influx-talent-july-trades-result-no-1-ranking-white-sox-farm-system

Hayes, D. (2017b, October 4). The good, the bad and the mixed: What went right and what went wrong for the 2017 White Sox. *CSN Chicago*. Retrieved from www. nbcsports.com/chicago/chicago-white-sox/good-bad-and-mixed-what-went-right-and-what-went-wrong-2017-white-sox

Hershkovich, E. (2017, August 15). White Sox GM Rick Hahn on rebuild: World Series title is the only goal. *Sporting News*. Retrieved from www.sportingnews. com/mlb/news/white-sox-gm-rick-hahn-rebuild-trades-interview-prospects-yoan-moncada/zocdnyxqbrpt1vy2jyjkfwita

Jaffe, J. (2016, December 8). Winter meetings: Winners (closers, Chicago) and losers (Toronto, ex-Blue Jay sluggers). *Sports Illustrated*. Retrieved from www.si.com/mlb/2016/12/08/winter-meetings-winners-losers-aroldis-chapman

Kane, C. (2016, December 7). White Sox send Adam Eaton to Nationals for top-rated MLB pitching prospect. *Chicago Tribune*. Retrieved from www.chicagotribune.com/sports/baseball/whitesox/ct-white-sox-adam-eaton-nationals-20161207-story.html

Kane, C. (2017a, March 30). White Sox rebuild goes beyond top prospects showcased in Cactus League. *Chicago Tribune*. Retrieved from www.chicagotribune.com/sports/baseball/whitesox/ct-white-sox-rebuild-deep-prospects-spt-0331-20170330-story.html

Kane, C. (2017b, July 23). On his way out? Melky Cabrera wants to stay with White Sox. *Chicago Tribune*. Retrieved from www.chicagotribune.com/sports/baseball/whitesox/ct-melky-cabrera-white-sox-trade-potential-20170723-story.html

Kane, C. (2017c, August 15). Jerry Reinsdorf says he started rebuild to do what was right for White Sox fans. *Chicago Tribune*. Retrieved from www.chicagotribune.com/sports/baseball/whitesox/ct-white-sox-notes-jerry-reinsdorf-speaks-spt-0816-20170815-story.html

Konerko, P. (2017, July 31). In my words: Konerko commends Sox rebuild. *MLB.com*. Retrieved from http://m.mlb.com/news/article/245040824/paul-konerko-white-sox-rebuild-will-pay-off/

McGrath, D. (2017, July 17). White Sox rebuild taking root in Charlotte and Birmingham. *Chicago Tribune*. Retrieved from www.chicagotribune.com/sports/columnists/ct-white-sox-plan-future-mcgrath-spt-0718-20170717-column.html

Morrissey, R. (2017, July 20). Rick Hahn is very, very busy proving his baseball smarts. *Chicago Sun-Times*. Retrieved from https://chicago.suntimes.com/sports/morrissey-rick-hahn-is-very-very-busy-proving-his-baseball-smarts/

Musick, T. (2017, September 1). GM Rick Hahn says White Sox beginning next phase of rebuild. *Chicago Sun-Times*. Retrieved from http://chicago.suntimes.com/sports/gm-hahn-says-white-sox-beginning-next-phase-of-rebuild/

Newhan, R. (1998, March 23). Chicago's Reinsdorf has no regrets over trade. *Los Angeles Times*. Retrieved from http://articles.latimes.com/1998/mar/23/sports/sp-31867

Nightengale, B. (2017, August 15). White Sox owner Jerry Reinsdorf wants to repay fans with a winner. *USA Today*. Retrieved from www.usatoday.com/story/sports/mlb/columnist/bob-nightengale/2017/08/15/white-sox-owner-jerry-reinsdorf-rebuild/570393001/

Rozner, B. (2017a, February 14). White Sox GM Hahn has fans on his side. *Daily Herald*. Retrieved from www.dailyherald.com/article/20170214/sports/170219449/

Rozner, B. (2017b, March 8). Chicago White Sox rebuild only just beginning. *Daily Herald*. Retrieved from www.dailyherald.com/article/20170307/sports/170309099/

Scheinin, D. (2016, December 9). The White Sox are the clear winners of baseball's winter meetings. *Washington Post*. Retrieved from www.washingtonpost.com/news/sports/wp/2016/12/09/the-white-sox-are-the-clear-winners-of-baseballs-winter-meetings/?utm_term=.338ea9ccfea8

Schoenfield, D. (2011, July 20). The Rays and the white flag trade of '97. *ESPN*. Retrieved from www.espn.com/blog/sweetspot/post/_/id/13944/the-rays-and-the-white-flag-trade-of-97

Stankevitz, J .J. (2017, January 17). The last White Sox rebuild: Bobby Howry remembers aftermath of '97 "white flag" trade. *CSN Chicago*. Retrieved from www.csnchicago.com/chicago-white-sox/last-white-sox-rebuild-bobby-howry-remembers-aftermath-97-white-flag-trade

Stark, J. (2016, December 8). White Sox nailing the art of the sale. *ESPN*. Retrieved from www.espn.com/mlb/story/_/id/18233692/chicago-white-sox-nailing-art-sale

Sullivan, P. (2000, September 12). On top of standings, world. *Chicago Tribune*. Retrieved from http://articles.chicagotribune.com/2000-09-12/sports/0009120299_1_sox-fans-sox-gm-white-flag-trade

Sullivan, P. (2017a, June 5). White Sox's rebuilding status looks good compared to Cubs of 2012. *Chicago Tribune*. Retrieved from www.chicagotribune.com/sports/columnists/ct-sullivan-cubs-white-sox-rebuild-comparison-spt-0606-20170605-story.html

Sullivan, P. (2017b, July 29). White Sox engineered infamous "white flag" trade 20 years ago. *Chicago Tribune*. Retrieved from www.chicagotribune.com/sports/columnists/ct-white-flag-history-sullivan-around-baseball-spt-0730-20170729-story.html

Van Schouwen, D. (2016a, December 7). White Sox trade Adam Eaton to Nats for top prospects. *Chicago Sun-Times*. Retrieved from http://chicago.suntimes.com/sports/white-sox-nationals-in-trade-talks-for-adam-eaton/

Van Schouwen, D. (2016b, December 8). White Sox win another winter meetings. *Chicago Sun-Times*. Retrieved from http://chicago.suntimes.com/sports/white-sox-win-another-winter-meetings/

Van Schouwen, D. (2017a, July 13). White Sox had no qualms about trading Quintana to Cubs. *Chicago Sun-Times*. Retrieved from http://chicago.suntimes.com/sports/white-sox-had-no-qualms-about-trading-q-to-cubs/

Van Schouwen, D. (2017b, July 13). White Sox rebuild shift to higher gear with trade of Quintana to Cubs. *Chicago Sun-Times*. Retrieved from http://chicago.suntimes.com/sports/cubs-acquire-jose-quintana-from-white-sox-for-four-prospects/

Van Schouwen, D. (2017c, July 20). White Sox look to keep "winning" the rebuilding process. *Chicago Sun-Times*. Retrieved from http://chicago.suntimes.com/sports/white-sox-look-to-keep-winning-the-rebuiding-process/

Van Schouwen, D. (2017d, August 20). Focus of White Sox' rebuilt shifting to player development. *Chicago Sun-Times*. Retrieved from http://chicago.suntimes.com/sports/focus-on-white-sox-rebuild-shifting-to-player-development/

Vecsey, G. (1997, August 1). White Sox are flying white flag. *New York Times*. Retrieved from www.nytimes.com/1997/08/01/sports/white-sox-are-flying-white-flag.html?mcubz=3

13

THE ROLE OF TEAM SUCCESS AND FAILURE IN MITIGATING FAN DISSATISFACTION WITH TICKET PRICE INCREASES

Joseph R. Blaney

As the threatened walkout by the Football Supporters Federation (FSF) (Rumsby, 2016) and the British Parliament's warm reception to the FSF's call for more affordable ticket prices illustrates, sports organizations must be cognizant of fan concerns about ticket prices from one season to the next. To be sure, when the legislative body of a country which considers association football (soccer) a sacrosanct part of its culture even entertains the notion of laws designed to regulate pricing of this entertainment, that country demonstrates just how important economic access to attendance has become. Clearly, ticket prices perceived as gratuitous and/or abusive can threaten a sports organization's reputation and revenue stream alongside other instances of wrong-doing (e.g., player behavior off-field or on-field, doping, dishonesty, etc.). While there is ample evidence (see Bloom, 2014) that many sports teams can raise ticket prices without negative repercussions, scholarship demonstrating the conditions under which sports ticket prices may be safely increased is non-existent.

This chapter aims to illuminate that issue with experimental research designed to examine the ticket price increase privilege afforded to teams that win, lose, and rebuild. The following sections will offer an examination of the intersection of sports and image repair, a discussion of how "organizational reputation" and "intent to purchase" can be impacted by price increases, hypotheses to be tested, and a controlled study of how a team's winning/losing/rebuilding status plays into its reputation and ability to sell tickets after announcing price increases.

Sports and Image Repair

As Benoit's (1995) Theory of Image Restoration Strategies has been described thoroughly elsewhere in this volume, there is no need for a full review of the typology and its many applications here. However, it is worthwhile to review the emerging importance of this approach in sports communication studies.

The rhetorical defense of sports figures can be tracked as early as Nelson's (1984) analysis of Billie Jean King following revelations of an affair with her secretary. She relied on the strategies of bolstering her family life and differentiation of the affair she had from a presumably unacceptable lesbian lifestyle (still broadly frowned upon in the early 1980s). Her responses were generally well received and Nelson's judgment was that surrogates (fellow tennis players, friends, sports media) offered support that helped her cause. This case drew upon earlier incarnations of *apologia*, prior to the image restoration typology offered by Benoit (1995) in *Accounts, Excuses, and Apologies*.

The earliest application of this more developed approach came before release of that book, namely Benoit and Hanczor's (1994) case study of the Tonya Harding controversy. Recall that she was accused of colluding with associates in an assault (striking the knee with a metal baton) on U.S. Olympic figure skating rival Nancy Kerrigan, which left the skater temporarily unable to practice in the run-up to the 1994 Olympic Games. The study found that Harding relied on strategies of bolstering, denial, and attacking her accuser, but that her discourse on *Eye-to-Eye with Connie Chung* was not effective because her credibility leading up to the interview had been damaged by inconsistencies in her explanations and contradictory statements from others familiar with the parties. She also failed to challenge incriminating evidence. Public opinion polling supported their judgment, as Harding's image never recovered and she was banned from the sport for life.

Fortunato (2008) used the approach to study the Duke University lacrosse team scandal, wherein three players were accused of sexually assaulting a dancer who had been hired for an alcohol-fueled party. This study noted that university officials employed mortification, bolstering, and corrective action, while a Len-Ríos (2010) application of the case discovered uses of denial in terms of the players' assault, admissions of wrong-doing (mortification) insofar as the team's penchant for rowdy, disorderly parties, and ultimately the employment of separation (a promise to replace the coach as a form of blame-shifting and corrective action). This study noted that these efforts tended to help repair the team's image with the local audience but did not repair a varnished national image.

Blaney, Lippert, and Smith (2013) offered a comprehensive edited volume with 20 sports image repair studies included. These studies all serve as additional examples of image restoration applied to the sport genre. However, Twork and Blaney (2013) laid the parting shot in that volume when they called for an embrace of empirically testing image repair strategies to discern the veracity of some of the claims made in the image repair case studies. For instance, Blaney and Benoit (2002) claimed that mortification would, as a matter of course, be more effective when combined with corrective action. However, Twork and Blaney's (2013) experiment found that an athlete accused of unacceptable on-field aggression who apologized and promised to take leave for anger management treatment (mortification plus corrective action) experienced no stronger reputation measure than the athlete who merely apologized (mortification only). Pace, Fediuk, and Botero (2010) and Blaney (2016) made similar calls for the testing of these strategies.

Notably, some scholars had been marching to their own beat with quantitative work all along. Jerome (2008) advanced image repair in terms of a "rhetoric of atonement" in the case of NASCAR driver Tony Stewart's physical assault on a newspaper photographer after a poor performance. In particular, she examined the scenario whereby a rhetor could not use denial, justification, or transcendence. This work also pushed the field to begin using quantitative approaches to test the utility of the image restoration typology. Brown, Dickhaus, and Long (2012) found that mortification was a more appropriate strategy for LeBron James than shifting the blame or bolstering, following his image crisis in the wake of his departure from the Cleveland Cavaliers for the Miami Heat. Brown, Billings, and Devlin (2016) found further support for the superiority of mortification over reducing offensiveness and evading responsibility strategies with the additional finding that a white athlete (compared with Asian, Black, Hispanic, and Middle Eastern equivalents) achieved weaker image repair across all three of those image repair responses. Likewise, Brown, Billings, Mastro, and Brown-Devlin (2015) again pointed to both the strength of mortification as an image repair choice and the unexpected higher ratings of black athletes. However, to this day the use of the image restoration typology as a rhetorical lens (rather than strategies to be tested) remains a standard approach. This status as the received approach may be due to the elegance with which the typology may be applied to ubiquitous speech in defense of reputation across many genres (corporate, religious, political, entertainment, etc.). Certainly, as humans remain subject to error and wrong-doing, the need to examine image repair efforts will likely never subside. However, enough IRT casework exists to insist that scholarly efforts move on studies of a generalizable nature for the purpose of strategy prescription for public relations practitioners.

The study described later in this chapter is one more shot at normalizing the study of image restoration choices empirically. While the rhetorical-critical approaches to image repair certainly continue to provide cases for potential transferability (see Benoit's 2015 study of the New Orleans Saints as an example), this program of inquiry will only grow by testing the claims made in the many case study applications.

Aside from the question of reputation, the other relevant factor addressed in this chapter is the question of "intent to purchase" as applied to sports organizations. The next section will review what we know, generically, about the role of price increases in ticket sales and touch on the limited work specifically examining sports ticket sales.

Price Increases and Intent to Purchase: The Basics

This chapter essentially addresses three topics: reputational threat to sports organizations posed by price increases, sports organizational image repair, and intent to purchase sporting event tickets. However, like much communication research, this study must rely on the wisdom gained from other disciplines—specifically, marketing findings about purchase intent come into play.

One helpful place to begin is Spears and Singh's (2004) study merging "attitude toward the brand" and "purchase intentions." They begin by acknowledging the work of Mitchell and Olson (1981) in establishing reliable measures of attitude toward the brand, with tri-partite characteristics: (a) attitude is held toward an object/brand, (b) attitude accompanies evaluation in terms of goodness or badness, and (c) attitude is an internal state of mind, ultimately subject to adjustment/change and reliably reported by human subjects. Spears and Singh (2004) infer that, from these attitudes, particular consumer behaviors will naturally ensue. This is where "intent to purchase" becomes most relevant. That consumers orient their purchasing power at least partially based on orientation to the brand makes tremendous common sense and underscores the reality for most businesses that brand strength impacts revenues.

Drawing on the previous work of Bagozzi, Tybout, Craig, and Stemthal (1979), Spears and Singh (2004) conceptualize purchase intent as "personal action tendencies" involving the brand. This differs from attitude insofar as purchase intent assumes motivation to engage in the act of commerce, whereas attitude toward brand merely takes stock of sentiment toward the brand. It is this connection between brand attitude and purchase intent that made Spears and Singh's (2004) contribution so helpful, as well as their offering of a reliable measure of intent to purchase (more on that later).

Ticket Price Increase Announcements as Threat to Image

This chapter works from the assumption that announcing ticket price increases is inherently a self-inflicted attack on the sports organization. It is true that announcing such increases is not akin to being accused of cheating, doping, or shielding violent and sexually abusive players. These sorts of charges pose threat to image by their dastardly nature and are leveled by second parties. Benoit and Dorries (1996) offered the foundational notion of the rhetorical attack (*kategoria*) as (a) the assignment of responsibility for an act to some person or organization and (b) the assessment that the act was offensive. In this spirit, I argue that the organization which announces price increases functionally performs the following: (a) announces its intent to separate current customers from their finite financial resources (assignment of responsibility to self) and (b) admits to something unsatisfactory in their current business model which needs correction (implying an unacceptable state of affairs). In other words, ticket prices would be going up either because the current business plan was insufficient in generating company profits (failure) or because the amount of profit was insufficient to placate owners (perception of greed). Summarily, the organization has announced *planned* harm to the fan and inadequate business acumen at least for the present.

Conceptualizing the announcement of customer-negative policy changes as an erstwhile attack on self allows our field to address self-announced/self-inflicted attacks to be understood as the first half of Ryan's (1982) notion of the speech-set, with the second being the *apologia*/account/purification/image restoration (all depending on the scholar's approach).

Competitive Sports and Circumstances Beyond Organizational Control

Having established that ticket price announcements are tantamount to attack, the subject of the strategic response can be considered. In the case at hand, a ready response exists: the organization needs revenue. Of course, this need for revenue is never described as a blatant attempt at increased returns on investment for owners. The usual canard speaks to the need to raise revenues in order to field a competitive team in the increasingly competitive world of professional sports. Benoit (1995) would describe this as *defeasibility*, or an attempt to evade responsibility for the wrong-doing by claiming circumstances beyond the party's control compelled the offensive act. Originally conceptualized in Scott and Lyman's (1968) notion of accounts and later included in Benoit's typology, defeasibility is among the attempts to evade responsibility for an action. Logically, if a person/party can be perceived as not responsible for occurrence of a wrong-doing, then it would likely follow that the offended audience might not penalize the person/party. For an innovative treatment of the economics of athlete salaries and necessity of revenue enhancements, see Wolfersberger's (2012) analysis of the relationship between athlete salary increases, consumer purchasing power increases, and revenue sources for major sports organizations. The assessment of ticket price increases as necessary (placing the increase beyond the organization's control) or unnecessary is *not* germane to this study, but the question of defeasibility as a strategic choice when raising ticket prices is most certainly important to scholars and managers.

The logic that defeasibility ought to be effective if, in fact, an audience buys the notion that the "offender" cannot be held responsible due to circumstances beyond their control is solid. However, initial assessment of the strategy does not point to its effectiveness. For instance, Benoit (2006) found that President George W. Bush's use of defeasibility in response to attacks about faulty intelligence leading to the Iraq War, sluggish job growth, and an increasing budget deficit were ineffective because it painted him, chief executive officer of the country, as unable to fix problems if he were to be given another term (the 2006 publication looked at a "Meet the Press" appearance during the 2004 re-election cycle).

In a broad study of the five general image repair strategies on a battery of six different measures (acceptability of strategy, likability of accused, blameworthiness, offensiveness, likelihood of repeated offense, and extent of punishment deserved), Benoit's (2016) study found that defeasibility was relatively less effective than other image repair strategies such as corrective action, accident claim, and expressions of mortification. This work did not claim that defeasibility was necessarily inappropriate; only that other strategies had more inherent potential.

However, Benoit and Brinson (1999) found that Queen Elizabeth's use of defeasibility to counter accusations that the British royal family expressed inadequate public grief over the death of Princess Diana was judged as appropriate and effective. In this judgment, the fact that the defeasibility was plausible (family was shocked and trying to protect the well-being of survivors) was pointed to as the root of its effectiveness.

It is this plausibility scenario, and the inherent logic of not blaming parties who cannot be held responsible, which leads me to believe that defeasibility should remain an important option for those accused of wrong-doing. In the context of the sports organization, the ability to make the financial commitments necessary to field a winning team is fairly well established. Florida (2011) offered a compelling description of the role of market size (read: available revenues) in fielding championship teams. This would appear to offer moral cover for the team needing to raise revenues/prices in order to compete and succeed. Successful athletes are expensive. As such, teams that plan to succeed must plan to spend more. Moreover, given the widespread critique of athletes as overpaid and overvalued socially, the following is predicted: (a) winning sports teams who announce ticket price increases will retain stronger reputations than losing or rebuilding teams who announce ticket price increases; and (b) winning sports teams who announce ticket price increases will enjoy stronger fan intent to purchase than losing or rebuilding teams who announce ticket prices.

How Were Winners, Losers, and Rebuilders Compared?

Testing this hypothesis required four experimental conditions (Winning teams, Losing teams, Rebuilding teams, and Record Not Indicated [control]) following announcement of ticket price increases by the fictional team, the Milwaukee Stormchasers. The news announcement and the manipulation messaging for all subjects is provided in the Appendix. Human subjects would be exposed to one of those conditions via an online survey using Qualtrics.

Social media snowballing produced the following subject responses: 45 in winning team, 46 in losing team, 44 in rebuilding team, and 47 in no record indicated. Demographically, the subjects were 55% men and 45% women; 39% were aged 25–44, 37% were aged 45–64, 17% were aged 18–24, and 7% were aged 65 or older; 8% owned season tickets to a professional or NCAA Division I sports team, 6% attended multiple games per month, 18% attended one game per month, 54% attended one game per month, while 13% attended no such games in the course of a year. In addition, 29% reported that baseball was their primary sports interest, followed by 27% football, 18% basketball, 16% hockey, 6% other, and 4% soccer. It is worth noting that the social media contacts were largely from the United States, which would explain the very low numbers for soccer as primary spectator sport.

Following exposure to the experimental condition, each subject answered a short survey using five-point (Likert-type, 1–5, with 5 as the strongest) adaptations of Coombs and Holliday's (1996) Organizational Reputational scale (five items with Cronbach's $\alpha = .76$ in this study) and Spears and Singh's (2004) Intent to Purchase scale (four items with Cronbach's $\alpha = .83$ in this study). Data collected from the survey was exported into SPSS in order to run analyses of variance (ANOVA) between our four groups on each of the measures. Item scores were reversed-recoded as necessary.

Results? Don't Be a Loser!

Perhaps the heading of this section is a bit trite in its summary. However, the results will underscore the true predicament for the losing team.

Organizational Reputation

Results of the ANOVAs revealed significant ($F(3, 177) = 6.72$, $p < .01$) differences on organizational reputation scores between the Rebuilders manipulation ($M = 3.3$, $SD = .83$) and the Losers manipulation ($M = 2.7$, $SD = .67$). The team which communicated its need to raise prices due to efforts to improve from mid-pack scored higher than the team which merely announced the ticket price increase and were listed as in last place.

Intent to Purchase

Results of the ANOVAs revealed significant ($F(3,177)=5.22$, $P < .01$) differences on intent to purchase scores between: Winners ($M = 2.7$, $SD = .87$) and Losers ($M = 2.1$, $SD = .85$); Rebuilders ($M = 2.7$, $SD=.91$) and Losers ($M = 2.1$, $SD = .85$); and between Record Not Indicated ($M = 2.6$, $SD = .78$) and Losers ($M = 2.1$, $SD = .85$). Notably, mean scores for the Winners and Rebuilders manipulations were identical, and the Losers manipulation actually scored lower than the Record Not Indicated manipulation. These scores point to a "Losers Who Announce Ticket Price Increases" combination that is potentially very hazardous for its business model.

One notable oddity in the data bears mentioning. An ANOVA measuring differences in mean scores for intent to purchase showed that soccer fans (M = 2.6, SD = .87) reacted to price increase announcements more negatively than hockey (M = 3.2, SD = .62), basketball (M = 3.0, SD = .66), baseball (M = 3.0, SD = .68), and football (M = 2.9, SD = .81), albeit the differences were not statistically significant as p = .06, most likely owing to a very small soccer group (n = 7).

Ticket Prices and Refining the Defeasibility Strategy

The results listed in the prior section have important implications both for the effectiveness of the defeasibility strategy and the ticket price increase scenario discussed throughout this chapter. First, consider the implications for sports organizations that, for whatever reasons, must increase ticket prices. The evidence above speaks strongly to the idea that teams perceived as losers ought not raise prices. There may, in fact, be a very legitimate need to increase ticket prices in order to cover costs associated with team payroll and operations. However, raising prices in such a condition could hurt revenues rather than enhance them. Moreover, it may be most intuitive that losers should not raise prices when their product is considered of low quality. This study provides some strong evidence.

Second, it does not appear that winning teams necessarily enjoy a privilege to raise prices any stronger than a team which is positioned as average but rebuilding. Teams who have recently won championships should recognize this potential vulnerability when considering implications for long-term revenue estimates and proceed cautiously. Likewise, a mid-pack team should consider that its ability to raise prices may be as strong as a championship team so long as it can communicate those rebuilding efforts and point to evidence of improvement.

Third, this chapter provides some additional evidence that pointing to circumstances beyond organizational control (defeasibility) may not necessarily help improve reputation or retain sales levels. Consider that Winners (2.7), Losers (2.7), and Record Not Indicated (2.6) all scored roughly the same on intent to purchase. While this study certainly had limitations, evidence here shows that a team with no record mentioned and no explanation for the price increase fared as well as a team with a championship and a team "smack in the middle" of the league standings. As such, pointing to unfortunate circumstances to justify an offensive act may not be helpful.

A fourth contribution of this study came with its re-conceptualization of attack. Organizational image may, in fact, be under attack even when it is not subject to scrutiny of some external party. Specifically, a person/organization announcing a change in practice that will negatively impact an identified stakeholder sets itself up as advancing harm and taking responsibility, meeting Benoit and Dorries' (1996) typology. As such, companies announcing price increases, a government unit announcing reduction in services at same level of taxation, a college announcing a tuition increase, or parents informing a college student of providing less support for the next term all present themselves with threats to image.

Fifth, one might note with curiosity that soccer fans reacted more poorly to ticket price increases than other sports fans, approaching significance (p = .06) but with a group size so small (n = 7) that including more soccer fans in the dataset would likely produce confident claims. Surely, soccer ("football" to most of the world) merits enough international stature that a future study could consider this difference in attitude in the soccer fan population. Because this sample was largely American, researchers should be quick to note potential cultural differences between the United States, Europe, Africa, Asia, Australia, and South America (not to mention the rest of North America). There is no American equivalent of the Football Supporters' Federation of the United Kingdom. It could be that soccer culture (daresay, "industry") varies widely between countries and even regions of countries.

Proceeding Cautiously

While this chapter presents reason for sports executives to take pause when considering increases, there are some limitations that make claims stated here somewhat tentative. First, human subjects for this study were exposed to the ticket price increase announcement and subsequent responses as text, rather than audio and video. Differing distribution channels might exhibit different effects to be considered alongside these results.

Second, as mentioned in the above discussion of soccer peculiarities, the sample was primarily residents of the United States. Generalizability to sports in other regions of the world remains problematic.

Third, the experimental stimuli of a fictitious team in a fictitious league certainly conjured up inconsistent images in the respondent's minds. Were they imagining baseball, football, basketball, hockey, soccer, or something else? Were they imagining a well-funded, major league environment or a modest minor league concern (after all, Milwaukee has both major and minor league sports teams). As this image likely changed from subject to subject, so many variables have to be considered as unidentified (market size, imagined existing ticket price, game-day experience, etc.).

Fourth, given the mental variability of which sport/league was imagined, is the $7.00 ticket price increase mentioned in the manipulation to be considered negligible or substantial? The fan attending a Chicago Cubs game with an infield box seat ticket sold for $99.00 at face value might not fret a $7.00 increase as much as a Peoria Rivermen hockey fan who is used to paying $11.00 or less for tickets.

Fifth, given the growing likelihood that such ticket price increase announcements will be read as part of some social media stream, sports scholars need to consider that the intended audience is likely taking the news alongside immediate feedback (whether positive or negative) from the fan community. As such, the rather clean and controlled presentation of messages and subsequent request for feedback in this study lacks the complication of any social media message cluttering.

Still, the claims presented in this chapter offer wisdom for sports executives. Raising prices while perceived as a loser should be done only with great caution. Likewise, being perceived as a winner does not necessarily present an organization with an advantage over teams still rebuilding. The particulars of fan base and brand strength need to be strongly considered. Finally, pointing to unfortunate situations beyond organizational control (defeasibility) does not result in a more positive audience response.

References

Bagozzi, R. P., Tybout, A. M., Craig, C. S., & Sternthal, B. (1979). The construct validity of tri-partite classification of attitudes. *Journal of Marketing Research, 16,* 88–95.

Benoit, W. L. (1995). *Accounts, excuses, and apologies: A theory of image restoration strategies.* Buffalo: State University of New York Press.

Benoit, W. L. (2006) President Bush's image repair effort on Meet the Press: The complexities of defeasibility. *Journal of Applied Communication Research, 34,* 285–306.

Benoit, W. L. (2015). *Accounts, excuses, and apologies: Image repair theory and research* (2nd ed.). Albany: State University of New York Press.

Benoit, W. L. (2016). Effects of image repair strategies. In J. R. Blaney (Ed.), *Putting image repair to the test: Quantitative applications of Image Restoration Theory.* Lanham, MD: Lexington Books.

Benoit, W. L., & Brinson, S. L. (1999). Queen Elizabeth's image repair discourse: Insensitive royal or compassionate Queen? Public Relations Review, 25, 145–156.

Benoit, W. L., & Dorries, B. (1996). Dateline NBC's persuasive attack of Wal-Mart. *Communication Quarterly, 44,* 463–477.

Benoit, W. L., & Hanczor, R. (1994). The Tonya Harding controversy: An analysis of image repair strategies. *Communication Quarterly, 42,* 416–433.

Blaney, J. R. (Ed.). (2016). *Putting image repair to the test: Quantitative applications of Image Restoration Theory.* Lanham, MD: Lexington Books.

Blaney, J. R., & Benoit, W. L. (2002). *The Clinton scandals and the politics of image restoration.* Westport, CT: Praeger.

Blaney, J. R., Lippert, L. R., & Smith, J. S. (Eds.). (2013). *Repairing the athlete's image: Studies in sports image restoration.* Lanham, MD: Lexington Books.

Bloom, H. (2014, September 8). *NFL increases ticket prices because it can.* Retrieved October 24, 2017, from www.sportingnews.com/nfl/news/nfl-ticket-prices-psls-cost-2014-history-roger-goodell average-spending-games stadiums/5ixmgha1sy2d1 xr597zidhhow

Brown, K. A., Billings, A., & Devlin, M (2016). Image repair across the racial spectrum: Experimentally exploring athlete transgression responses. *Communication Research Reports, 33,* 47–53.

Brown, K., Billings, A. C., Mastro, D., & Brown-Devlin, N. A. (2015). Changing the image repair equation: Impact of race and gender on sport-related transgressions. *Journalism & Mass Communication Quarterly, 92,* 487–506.

Brown, K. A., Dickhaus, J., & Long, M. C. (2012). LeBron James and "The Decision": An empirical examination of image repair in sports. *Journal of Sports Media, 7*, 149–175.

Coombs, W. T., & Holladay, S. J. (1996). Communication and attributions in a crisis: An experimental study in crisis communication. *Journal of Public Relations Research, 8*, 279–295.

Florida, R. (2011, December 30). *Why size matters in pro sports victories.* Retrieved October 24, 2017, from www.citylab.com/design/2011/12/why-size-matters-pro-sports-victories/756/

Fortunato, J. A. (2008). Restoring a reputation: The Duke University lacrosse scandal. *Public Relations Review, 34*, 116–123.

Jerome, A. M. (2008). Toward prescription: Testing the rhetoric of atonement's applicability in the athletic arena. *Public Relations Review, 34*, 124–134.

Len-Ríos, M. E. (2010). Image repair strategies, local news portrayals, and crisis stage: A case study of Duke University's lacrosse team crisis. *International Journal of Strategic Communication, 4*, 267–287.

Mitchell, A. A., & Olson, J. C. (1981). Are product beliefs the only mediator of advertising effect on brand attitude? *Journal of Marketing Research, 18*, 318–332.

Nelson, J. (1984). The defense of Billie Jean King. *Western Journal of Speech Communication, 48*, 92–102.

Pace, K. M., Fediuk, T. A., & Botero, I. C. (2010). The acceptance of responsibility and expressions of regret in organizational apologies after a transgression. *Corporate Communications: An International Journal, 15*, 410–427.

Rumsby, B. (2016, February 9). *Football fans plot mass stadium walkout in protest over rising ticket prices.* Retrieved October 24, 2017, from www.telegraph.co.uk/sport/football/competitions/premier-league/12147445/Football-fans-plot-mass-stadium-walkout-in-protest-over-rising-ticket-prices.html

Ryan, H. R. (1982). *Kategoria* and *apologia*: On their rhetorical criticism as a speech set. *Quarterly Journal of Speech, 68*, 256–261.

Scott, M. H., & Lyman, S. M. (1968). Accounts. *American Sociological Review, 33*, 46–62.

Spears, N. S., & Singh, S. N. (2004). Measuring attitude toward the brand and purchasing intentions. *Journal of Current Issues & Research in Advertising, 26*, 53–66.

Twork, J., & Blaney, J. R. (2013). Reputation differences between mortification-only and mortification/corrective action strategies following a transgression by a professional athlete. In J. R. Blaney, L. R. Lippert, L. R., & J. S. Smith (Eds.), *Repairing the athlete's image: Studies in sports image restoration.* Lanham, MD: Lexington Books.

Wolfersberger, J. (2012). *A long-run analysis of salary inflation.* Retrieved October 24, 2017, from www.fangraphs.com/blogs/a-long-run-analysis-of-salary-inflation/

Appendix

All subjects were exposed to the following announcement:

STORMCHASERS TO RAISE TICKET PRICES

Milwaukee-The Milwaukee Stormchasers of the National Athletic League (NAL) announced today that individual ticket prices would be raised by $7.00 for all seating levels. Additionally, season ticket holders will pay an additional $400 per seat. Concession beverages will also rise by an average of ten percent.

"Winners" group was also exposed to the following:

"The Stormchasers organization places a high value on its fans and wants the game day experience to remain affordable. However, we must increase prices at this time in order to retain a championship roster, meet our expected payroll, and cover other expenses." Stormchasers president Robert Cunningham said in a prepared statement.

The Stormchasers were National Athletic League Champions last season.

"Losers" group was also exposed to the following:

"The Stormchasers organization places a high value on its fans and wants the game day experience to remain affordable. However, we must increase prices at this time in order to meet payroll and other expenses," Stormchasers president Robert Cunningham said in a prepared statement.

The Stormchasers finished in last place of the National Athletic League last season.

"Rebuilders" group was also exposed to the following:

The Stormchasers organization places a high value on its fans and wants the game day experience to remain affordable. However, we must increase prices at this time in order to attract the players necessary to keep rebuilding this team, meet our expected payroll, and cover other expenses," Stormchasers president Robert Cunningham said in a prepared statement."

The Stormchasers finished in fifth place out of nine teams in the National Athletic League last season.

"Record Not Indicated" group was shown no additional message.

In all above groups, emphasis added was the author's to underscore differences in the messages.

14

ABBY WAMBACH

G.O.A.T. (Greatest of All Time) or Just a Goat?

Rachel Allison and Ann Pegoraro

U.S. professional athletes, particularly those in the high-profile, culturally valued sports of American football, basketball, and baseball, are also celebrities. Many embrace this status, leveraging their visibility for sponsorships, television appearances, and other promotional opportunities. As public figures, professional athletes' off-field lives and exploits are often as interesting and as followed as their on-field talents. Consequently, athletes' off-field transgressions and misdeeds are increasingly relevant to their playing careers. While certainly not all professional athletes would identify as role models whose position requires adherence to a code of personal and professional conduct, clear transgression of laws or deeply embedded social norms can be risky. Athletes' careers, their sponsorships, and their fans are at stake (Brown, 2016). When athletes' reputations and, as a result, their livelihoods are at issue following transgression, they commonly engage in communicative actions to repair their public image.

Athletes have increasingly adopted social media for repair efforts because they are direct, immediate, and interactive, and because they give athletes control above team or league gatekeepers (Schmittel & Hull, 2015). Social media also give control to users, allowing for lively, robust, and public discussion on transgressions and image repair efforts that can be captured by researchers. With several exceptions (Brown & Billings, 2013; Brown, Brown, & Billings, 2015; Sanderson & Emmons, 2014), however, studies have neglected social media as sites of image repair communication and reception. The importance of social media in bringing attention to and fostering discussion of women's sports makes this a critical omission, particularly given the lack of attention to women's sport in mainstream mass media coverage (LaVoi & Calhoun, 2014).

With few exceptions (Benoit & Hanczor, 1994; Compton, 2013), studies of athlete transgression have examined image repair processes among men. In contrast, this chapter examines transgression and image repair for a prominent woman in U.S. professional sport, soccer's Abby Wambach. We look at how Wambach was constructed by social media users upon her retirement from professional play in late 2015 and consider how these constructions shifted following a transgression. Did Wambach's arrest for driving under the influence (DUI) several months post-retirement move her from the G.O.A.T. (Greatest of All Time) to just a goat? Or were her efforts to repair her image via social media successful?

Repairing the Athlete's Image

Benoit's image repair theory (IRT) has been the primary theoretical tool to date for scholars who examine how athletes work to redress reputational damage after a transgression. Following Benoit's typology of image repair strategies, research on image repair among athletes has focused heavily on the content of repair efforts, identifying the discursive strategies used to repair image (Blaney, 2013; Meng & Pan, 2013). Less commonly, research has examined the reception of repair work, typically with an eye to the effectiveness of strategies (Brown, Brown, & Billings, 2015; Onwumechili & Bedeau, 2016; Sanderson & Emmons, 2014). As Burns and Bruner (2000) argue, "effectiveness" often implies an "appropriate standard" of how well the means of persuasion were used (p. 35). "Effectiveness" defined as change to public opinion is harder to document, and establishing causality is tricky. Nevertheless, previous studies have used organizational response, career outcomes, opinion polls, newspaper coverage, and experiments testing the attitudes of college student participants to assess responses to image repair (Brown, 2016; Onwumechili & Bedeau, 2016). Which IRT strategy is used, and its effectiveness in repairing reputation, depends on contextual factors such as the nature of the offense committed and the previous reputation of the athlete. However, substantial research has found that mortification is often an effective strategy to repair image, particularly in combination with corrective action (Blaney, 2013; Brown, 2016; Onwumechili & Bedeau, 2016; Sanderson & Emmons, 2014). Athletes may thus be best off taking responsibility for their perceived offensive actions, apologizing, and delineating future action to repair their wrong-doing or prevent future occurrences.

Social Media

Social media have shifted the balance of power among leagues, teams, athletes, and fans. In the decade or so of their existence, social media sites such as Twitter, Facebook, and Instagram have become a "disruptive force in sport communication today" (Pegoraro, 2014, p. 133). Social media disrupt top-down processes of communication by enabling consumers to also become producers. Compared to traditional media forms, social media are used by "ordinary" people (as opposed to "professionals") to create and share content. Social media also enable immediate fan communities by fostering social ties among geographically dispersed individuals. Social media users can quickly find and connect to one another through their shared fandom of sports leagues, teams, and players. Social media are thus important virtual spaces for collective, fan-driven cultural constructions of sporting events and figures (Murthy, 2012; Stavros, Meng, Westberg, & Farrelly, 2014). As a result, social media are advantageous for applications of IRT, particularly those concerned with audience response and the effectiveness of IRT efforts, because they allow researchers to simultaneously examine how social media users assign meaning to athletes, how these meanings change with athlete transgressions, and how social media users respond to athletes' efforts to repair their image. Essentially, social media are apt at capturing the before and after of transgression that allows for nuanced analyses of image repair's effectiveness.

Interestingly, some recent research has documented "fan-enacted" (Brown, Brown, & Billings, 2015; Brown-Devlin, 2017) crisis communication, where fans use social media not only to respond to athletes' or organization's image repair work, but to actively participate in efforts to manage and shape public response to transgression, and often in ways that support the perceived transgressor(s). This may be particularly true among highly identified fans whose self-identity is so tied to their sports fandom that a hit to an athlete's or team's reputation feels like a personal attack to be defended against (Brown-Devlin, 2017; Sanderson & Emmons, 2014). For instance, Brown and Billings' (2013) study of self-identified University of Miami fans' Twitter response to NCAA investigation of the university for impermissible benefits found that, in engaging directly in image repair work, fans became an "extension" of the university. Fans variously used ingratiation (coming together as a collective of fans), reminder (recounting past successes), and attacking the accuser strategies to support the University of Miami and uphold their own fandom. So, too, did Brown, Brown, and Billings (2015) conclude that ingratiation and reminder strategies are likely common "fan-enacted" strategies on social media. Yet few studies have examined fans' contestations over social media in response to athlete, team, or organizational transgression.

Image Repair and Gender

The lack of research on women athletes and image repair is notable for several reasons. For one, public responses to transgression vary by the gender of the athlete (Crosby, 2016; Douglas, 2014; Kramer, 2013). Women are often subject to added scrutiny for transgression compared to men, as many legal

and social transgressions are also at the same time a violation of gender expectations (Brown, Billings, Mastro, & Brown-Devlin, 2015; Compton, 2013).
Women may also use different image repair strategies than men (Compton,
2013; Kramer, 2013). Research on U.S. track star Marion Jones is instructive
on these points. Douglas's (2014) study of Jones's admission of steroid use argues
that the contempt Jones faced reveals the influence of both gendered and racial
stereotypes. Kramer (2013) examined Jones's interview on the *Oprah Winfrey
Show* and concluded that her repair strategies were gender-specific, with Jones
emphasizing her status as a loving mother. Women may also receive different
audience responses to their repair efforts than men. However, few studies have
focused on how social media users construct and communicate the meanings
they attach to women athletes, and none examine responses to women's transgression on social media (Filo, Lock, & Karg, 2015; LaVoi & Calhoun, 2014;
Lebel & Danylchuk, 2012; McDonald, 2002; Pegoraro, 2010).

Our Study

Our analysis is located at the intersection of studies of athlete image repair, social
media, and constructions of women in sport. In line with prior investigations
using image repair theory, we are concerned with audience response to transgression over social media, an understudied component of image repair (Burns
& Bruner 2000; Schmittel & Hull, 2015). How, we ask, is a prominent, elite
woman athlete constructed via Facebook? Do Facebook users' constructions
change between moments of celebration and transgression? To answer these
questions, we analyze the Facebook conversations that surrounded the American
soccer star Abby Wambach on two occasions: Wambach's retirement from professional soccer in December 2015, and her arrest for driving under the influence
(DUI) four months later. The sport (soccer), the player (Wambach), and the
moments (retirement and arrest) were selected intentionally for the study.

It is perhaps only in soccer that a women's team has experienced the attendance
numbers, corporate buy-in, and mainstream media coverage routinely enjoyed in
"Big Three" U.S. men's sports (Allison, 2016). The women's national team victory in the 1999 Women's World Cup is widely considered to be a "watershed"
moment for women's sports in part given these metrics, and this moment of
unprecedented visibility has been repeated in several tournaments since, including
the 2015 Women's World Cup (Christopherson, Janning, & Diaz McConnell,
2002). Women's soccer has enjoyed several moments of national cultural recognition, with the respective members of the national team gaining large fan
followings. However, the media attention commonly given the team in international tournaments dries up afterwards. With the advent of social media, many
women's soccer fans have gone online (Coche, 2016). Social media users have set
the agenda for conversations about sports in mainstream mass media, including
for U.S. women's soccer. During the 2012 Olympics, for instance, controversy

between U.S. goalkeeper Hope Solo and former U.S. defender Brandi Chastain unfolded via social media, subsequently penetrating mainstream media outlets. Social media discussions went mainstream as well during the 2015 Women's World Cup as players and fans chafed at the gender inequality evidence in poor field conditions (Creedon, 2014).

We examine Facebook users' constructions of U.S. forward Abby Wambach. Wambach has been a mainstay of the national team since the 2000s and built a sizable fan base through her talent and leadership. We compare Facebook commentary across two events that took place four months apart in order to examine shifts in fan responses to Wambach based on social context. The moment of retirement was chosen as a celebratory point during which fans, collectively, reflected upon and built Wambach's legacy. In this context, we expect commentary to be positive in tone.

In contrast, we expect a more negative or ambivalent tone to commentary following Wambach's arrest. Moments of transgression, whether criminal or social, may be unique in bringing cultural constructions of gender to the forefront. Athlete transgressions are commonly understood by media and the public through the lenses of gender, race, and sport type (Brown, 2016; Compton, 2013; Douglas, 2014). Deviance violates the cultural positioning of white women as more cooperative and "nicer" than men (Kramer, 2013). This may be particularly true in soccer, where athletes' status as role models encouraging girls to seek playing excellence is believed to be central to the draw of the sport (Allison, 2016). Additionally, women in so-called "sex appropriate" sports (Crosby, 2016) are perceived as less likely to transgress compared to women in male-typed sports. As a white woman competing in the gender-appropriate sport of soccer, then, Abby Wambach's transgression (arrest for DUI) violates a set of sport-specific gendered and racialized social norms. We expect that Facebook users' responses to this transgression may highlight these norms, and in different ways compared to the moment of retirement. In the case of Abby Wambach, post-DUI discussion was also heightened given her public visibility during the 2015 Women's World Cup. Our research questions are as follows:

1. How do users on Facebook construct American soccer player Abby Wambach?
2. Do these constructions vary between moments of celebration and transgression?
3. Do individual fans change their framing of Wambach from moments of celebration to transgression?

Studying the G.O.A.T.

In late October 2015, U.S. forward Abby Wambach announced her intention to retire from professional soccer. Her final game took place on December 16, 2015, as the U.S. Women's National Team faced off against China in the last of their 10-game post-2015 Women's World Cup victory tour. That same day, Wambach posted a photo of herself seated in a locker room with her back to the camera on her public Facebook page (see Figure 14.1). The photo was accompanied by a single sentence of text that read, "Make them forget me." The text referred to a video produced for the retirement (now on YouTube) that exhorted fans to forget Wambach in service of the next generation of players. As Wambach explained in the video, "I want to leave a legacy where the ball keeps rolling forward." Wambach's Facebook post garnered just over 18,000 reactions, with the overwhelming majority of these (17,969) "likes." The post was shared 1,660 times, and drew 1,173 total comments.

Four months later, on April 3, 2016, Wambach again posted to her public Facebook page, this time with a statement regarding her arrest the previous

 Abby Wambach
December 16, 2015 · 🌐

Make them forget me.

FIGURE 14.1   Wambach's Retirement Facebook Post

night for DUI. Wambach wrote, "Last night I was arrested for DUI in Portland after dinner at a friend's house. Those that know me, know that I have always demanded excellence from myself. I have let myself and others down. I take full responsibility for my actions. This is all on me. I promise that I will do whatever it takes to ensure that my horrible mistake is never repeated. I am so sorry to my family, friends, fans and those that look to follow a better example.—Abby." This statement was clearly intended to communicate mortification and promised future corrective action (Benoit, 1995). This statement gained more attention than the post on retirement, with 56,312 reactions. Again, most of these reactions (49,978) were "likes." The post was shared 4,136 times and garnered 8,748 total comments.

We collected comments on both posts using NCapture, an NVivo add-on that scrapes data from public Facebook pages and exports for further analysis. Data were collected from April 3 to April 25 and all collections were merged to create the dataset that included user comments made on both the retirement post and the DUI post. Excluding comments that tagged other Facebook users but did not include text, we collected 1,140 comments from the post on retirement and 8,571 comments from the post on arrest for a total dataset of 9,711 comments. Comments were exported as CSV files and loaded into Leximancer text-mining software for qualitative analysis.

Leximancer is "a computer software tool that conducts thematic and semantic analysis on written words as well as visual text" (Pegoraro, Burch, Frederick, & Vincent, 2014, p. 5). The software first determines the primary concepts present within a set of words, and then determines relationships between themes. Leximancer's algorithm considers both word frequency and co-occurrence to identify families of concepts, or themes. Leximancer generates both a concept list and a conceptual mapping of the relationships between concepts, or the organization of concepts into themes. Leximancer software holds the advantage of coding large datasets that would be impossible for researchers to code manually. It produces highly reliable, replicable results generated from the text. As in previous research using this software (Frederick, Stocz, & Pegoraro, 2016), computer coding with Leximancer was supplemented by human verification. In order to understand themes and their relationships to one another, both authors reviewed Leximancer's concept map and read posts within each theme.

Goodbye, Abby

For retirement, six primary themes emerged from the data: Career & Inspiration, Good Luck, Thank You Abby, Never Forget, We Will Remember, and Not Going to Happen. As the concept map in Figure 14.2 shows, the first three of these themes were most salient in the data, while the final three had a more minor presence. Theme 1 (Career & Inspiration) contained descriptors such as soccer, played, girls, inspiration, amazing, and daughter. Comments within this theme

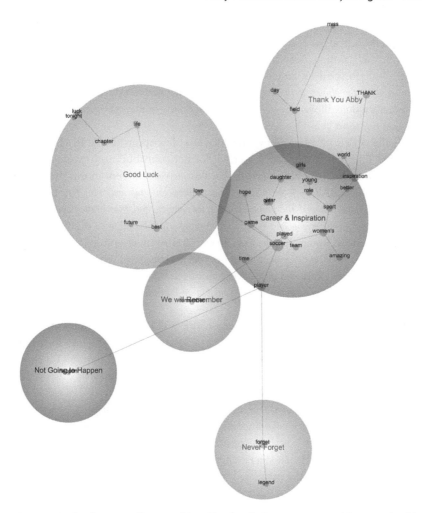

FIGURE 14.2 Leximancer Concept Map, Facebook Comments on Abby Wambach's Retirement

praised Wambach's athletic talents and her status as a role model, particularly for girls and women. Representative comments in this theme include, *You are an amazing athlete and we have loved watching you over the years!* and *Simply the greatest soccer player ever play the game!* Facebook users argued that Wambach's play had inspired both current and future generations of girls who played soccer, saying, for example, *thank you for inspiring my daughter to be an elite soccer player!*

Theme 2 (Good Luck) was largely a forward-looking theme including descriptors like best, life, future, luck, and chapter. Commenters within this theme imagined their own loss of Wambach on the playing field but simultaneously looked to her future, wishing her luck on all endeavors post-professional soccer.

One user focused on the loss of Wambach in professional soccer, writing *Going to miss u on the field so bad :(much love.* Another, in contrast, imagined what was next for Wambach, noting *Abby, I can hardly wait to see what the next phase of your life brings.* Other forward-looking comments, such as *We can never forget your impact, but we must allow the players of the future to write their own stories,* argued that Wambach's retirement would allow a new, younger generation of players to make their own mark on the sport.

Theme 3 (Thank You Abby) included the descriptors THANK, field, day, and miss. This theme thanked Wambach for her contributions to women's soccer both on and off the playing field. An illustrative comment in this theme was *Who you are on AND off the field is what makes you unforgettable!* Another user wrote, *You have changed the game of soccer for women and that makes you a legend and I thoroughly believe you will now "change the world."* Similar to the Good Luck theme, comments under the heading Thank You Abby often took on emotional valence as Facebook users reflected on the past and future of women's soccer. For example, one user expressed bittersweet emotions on the occasion of Wambach's retirement, writing *Sad day for WNT fans but an exciting beginning for the new things u will do!*

The three minor themes (Never Forget, We Will Remember, and Not Going to Happen) are best understood in context of Wambach's stated desire for fans to forget her. In response to Wambach's exhortation that she be forgotten, Facebook users rallied to contradict this message. One argued, *I understand your statement, but sorry, not going to happen, ever!* Wambach would be remembered. *We will always remember you,* one user commented. Another wrote, *Remember kid—heroes get remembered, but legends never die.* In summary, Facebook users' messages on Abby Wambach's retirement post were positive, reflective, and intensely emotional. Users constructed Wambach as a talented and inspirational figure whose play had left a lasting impact on the game and who would be remembered with pride by her fans.

After Arrest

For DUI, eight primary themes emerged: A Mistake, People, DUI, Sh★t Happens, Respect, Still Loved, Thank You, and God. Figure 14.3 presents the concept map of Facebook comments on Wambach's statement post-arrest. The most predominant themes were A Mistake, People, DUI, Sh★t Happens, and Respect. Still Loved, Thank You, and God were more minor themes.

Theme 1 (A Mistake) included descriptors like mistakes, everyone, responsibility, human, learn, actions, role, example, and character. The thrust of this theme was that DUI arrest was a "mistake" of the sort that anyone could make; it was simple human error. Comments to this effect included *You made a mistake like everyone else, Abby everyone makes a mistake every now and then,* and *We all make*

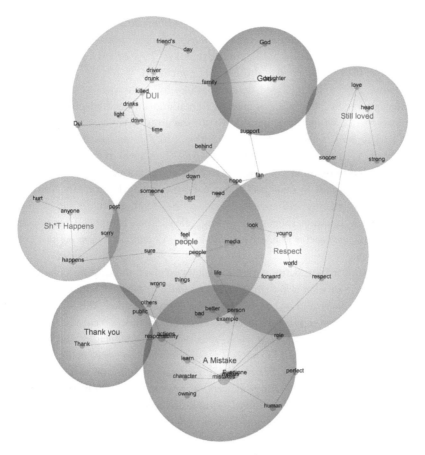

FIGURE 14.3 Leximancer Concept Map, Facebook Comments on Abby Wambach's
Arrest for DUI

mistakes, it's how we own them and grow that makes all the difference. As the last comment hinted at, what mattered to users was not the making of the mistake (here,
arrest for DUI) but the response. Wambach was perceived as having immediately
taken responsibility for her arrest in her Facebook statement. *I call this "woman-
ing up": you made a mistake; you took responsibility for your actions,* one user wrote.
Because of her response, Wambach's reputation was perceived to be untarnished;
one user wrote *People make mistakes but if you use this time to show young kids that
they must deal with the consequences of their actions your legacy will continue.* Similar
comments included *Even in a mistake she is an example* and *The way you are handling your mistake, is an example of leadership.* However, this theme (A Mistake)
was somewhat bidirectional, with a minority of users contradicting the dominant
message of owning up to human error. Here, arrest for DUI was not a mistake,

but a poor decision. *No one mistakenly drinks and then mistakenly drives*, one user commented. *A mistake is washing whites with colors*, another noted, arguing that the arrest far surpassed the threshold defining mistakes. *Your actions were the result of a bad DECISION, not a mistake*, another user concluded.

Theme 2 (People) included descriptors like life, others, best, things, hope, down, and media. "People," as in an external and unspecified group, including mass media, would be judging Abby for the arrest. One user noted that *The press loves to bring famous people down*. Another said, *The media will drag it on like they do, try not to take it to heart, they are brutal*. This level of expected scrutiny was perceived to be unfair, as one user referenced in writing, *I know I would hate to be judged, especially in social media, by the biggest mistake I ever made*. Abby was encouraged to exercise resilience in the face of the judgment and to find meaning in her trials, as one user suggested, writing, *Abby, there's always obstacles in people life but the ultimate goal is to overcome difficulties in life and make them positive in life learning lessons.*

Some expressed sympathy with what they perceived to be Abby's plight. For example, one user wrote, *I'm sorry that you are in the spot light for this, and people feel the need to pass judgement on you because of that.* Others praised Abby for "getting ahead" of the negative press. Illustrative comments included, *You've saved us from the relentless media storm and their always speculation!* and *You did not wait for TMZ or some other nasty media outlet to announce your mistake—you owned it.* Again, a few argued against empathy for Wambach, instead calling attention to the plight of those injured and killed by drunk drivers. In response to a comment describing the death of a family member due to a drunk driver, one user said, *I feel empathy for people like Connie and her son and the many other victims of drunk driving.*

Theme 3 (DUI) included descriptors like drunk, drive, killed, family, behind, light, and friend's. Here, users discussed the nature of DUI as an offense. This was by far the most complex and contentious theme, with roughly equal numbers of comments expressing conflicting opinions. On the one hand, some Facebook users felt that DUI was not a severe offense. Some reported their own DUI arrests. Representative comments included *no big deal I've been arrested twice for DUI but only convicted once* and *I had my one DUI in 2001 so don't worry you will get past this.* Others argued that arrest for DUI was not the same as driving while intoxicated. As one user noted, *The law's definition of DUI does not necessarily mean someone is intoxicated to the point of being unable to drive.* The legal limit for alcohol consumption was the problem, and not Wambach's behavior, one user suggested in writing, *Maybe the amount that we can drink during a meal out at a restaurant should not be enough to be considered "too drunk to drive." I'm saying raise up the allowable amount.* Again, Wambach was praised for the speed and honesty of her response to her arrest and some fans wrote that they continued to support her. Illustrative comments in this vein included *You are not the only one who ever got a DUI but you are one of a few to do it with humility and grace, Kudos to you for speaking for yourself and not hiding behind lawyers like many celebrities do*, and *Be well, Abby, and know that your fans and those who look up to you are still behind you and believe in you.*

On the other hand, some users repeated the assertion that DUI was a poor choice, and not an understandable mistake. Comments to this effect included *getting behind the wheel when you know you're drunk is a choice that could have KILLED someone!* And *Drinking and driving are preventable, there are no excuses that justify this*. The danger of driving after drinking alcohol was stressed, as in *Lucky only to be charged with DUI and not a jail sentence for getting into an accident and murdering someone's children, or parents, or spouse*. Some comments told stories of friends and family members harmed by drunk drivers, such as *However, being that my cousin and her husband were killed by a drunk driver only a few weeks ago, it's very hard for me to have warm fuzzy feelings about anyone who chooses to get behind the wheel of a vehicle after drinking*. Several users avoided the debate over the meaning of DUI entirely, opting instead to provide suggestions for safe transportation after drinking. One user recommended, *Next time you go out with friends or family and you would like to have a couple of drinks, take a taxi home or have someone who is a non drinking designated driver Its the safest way*. Another opined, *We live in an age where a car and a driver is just an app request away.*

Theme 4 (Sh★t Happens) included descriptors like happens, hurt, anyone, and sorry. This theme described the arrest as an event that could happen to "anyone." This argument was best captured in the comment *I'm sorry Abby, don't worry we know shit happens sometimes!* Because DUI arrest was so common, it was wrong to negatively judge someone for it, as one user said in writing: *If anyone judges you by this one lone act, they had be very careful about karma*. This theme was also somewhat bidirectional, with a few users objecting to the argument that DUI could happen to anyone. *Hahahaha this CANNOT happen to anyone*, one person wrote. Another argued, *What a let down. The argument "it can happen to anyone" is a horrible argument.*

Theme 5 (Respect) included descriptors like respect, forward, look, young, and fan. Most users argued that they had gained respect for Wambach because of her Facebook statement and that Wambach's reputation was not harmed by the arrest. One comment read, *Your legacy remains intact, and fans will eventually move past this and be more respectful of you*. Another read, *Abby you owe no one an apology you are human and being a true fan of yours this has no impact on my admiration of you!* However, a few users said that they had lost respect for Wambach. Comments here included, *You made a poor choice, you will certainly pay a price if not in traditional punishment then in the loss of respect and admiration of some of your fans* and *You're fucking pathetic and every fucking fan girl defending you is fucking pathetic.*

The minor themes (Still Loved, Thank You, and God) comprised expressions of support for Wambach, including love for her (*I love Abby she's a good soccer player I hate when people are negative towards her she deserves positive not negative go usa*), gratitude for her candor and speed in addressing her arrest (*Thank you for being transparent and making a public apology*), and professions of God's love and forgiveness *(I'm proud of you and I betcha God is, too!)*.

In contrast to comments on the retirement post, responses to Wambach's Facebook post after her arrest for DUI were far from uniform. The dominant message by far was empathy and support, as users constructed DUI as a commonplace mistake and lauded the speed and tone of Wambach's response. However, a small, but consistent number of Facebook comments post-DUI were negative or unsupportive, with users calling attention to the dangers of driving under the influence and lambasting Wambach for her poor "choice."

Users Who Commented on Both Events

175 Facebook users commented on both retirement and arrest posts, sometimes multiple times. Subsequent analyses examined the 193 comments on Wambach's retirement post and 194 comments on her arrest post, coding them manually as either Supportive of Wambach, Non-Supportive of Wambach, or Other, and then locating them within the themes generated in Leximancer. There was 100 percent intercoder agreement between the authors.

As shown in Table 14.1, the comments on Wambach's retirement post were almost ubiquitously supportive, with most falling into Career & Inspiration, Not Going to Happen, and Never Forget themes. Very few users changed their opinion after Wambach's arrest, with 154 of the 194 comments on her post-DUI Facebook post expressing continued support. The modal theme of these comments was A Mistake.

Remembering the G.O.A.T.

This study examined the responses of Facebook users to U.S. soccer star Abby Wambach's public Facebook statement following her arrest for DUI in April 2016. Given the dearth of research on social media constructions of women athletes, we include an earlier point of comparison (Wambach's retirement from professional soccer) to first understand how social media users constructed Wambach's significance. This counterpoint allows us to capture the "effectiveness" of Wambach's image repair work in terms of audience response. Do Facebook users buy Wambach's arguments? And do their perspectives change between moments of celebration and transgression?

We find that Facebook users unanimously constructed Wambach as a star player on the women's national team who had made a tremendous positive impact on women's soccer. As we examined user comments during a moment designed to reflect upon and celebrate Wambach's career, this is not surprising. There was a notable gendered element to Wambach's significance. As in previous research on women's soccer (Allison, 2016; Christopherson et al., 2002), Wambach was argued to be uniquely inspirational to girls and women. Thus, we established Wambach's reputation in the eyes of social media users as a highly

TABLE 14.1 Coding of Comments From Users Who Commented on Both Facebook Posts

Retirement Coding

Support Codes		Theme Codes	
Supportive	173	Good Luck	8
Non-Supportive	0	Thank You Abby	15
Other	20	Career & Inspiration	42
		We Will Remember	7
		Not Going to Happen	34
		Never Forget	66
		N/A	21

DUI Coding

Support Coding		Theme Coding	
Supportive	154	A Mistake	88
Non-Supportive	13	People	4
Other	27	DUI	6
		Sh*t Happens	4
		Respect	33
		Still Loved	29
		Thank You	2
		God	2
		Other	23

skilled and motivational figure whose fans professed respect and admiration for her accomplishments on and off the field.

After her transgression several months after retiring, Wambach's image repair efforts on Facebook were largely successful by the metric of social media user response. In part, this may have been because she employed the strategies of mortification and corrective action found in previous research to be most effective at swaying public opinion. Certainly, Wambach moved quickly to admit to and apologize for her misdeed. Facebook user comments on Wambach's post lauded her for the speed of her reply and for its content and tone, suggesting that users responded positively to Wambach's message and perceived her apology as sincere.

Similar to previous research on social media users (Brown & Billings, 2013; Brown, Brown, & Billings, 2015), we find that fan response went beyond merely reacting to Wambach's image repair message to actually do some of the image repair work for her. While Wambach herself used mortification and corrective action strategies to uphold her reputation post-DUI arrest, some Facebook users employed denial, accident, bolstering, minimization, and attacking the accuser strategies (Benoit, 1995). Users variously denied that an offense took place, downplayed the seriousness of DUI, framed the arrest as a "mistake" that could happen to anyone, emphasized Wambach's leadership and athletic skills, and positioned Wambach as the one unfairly under attack. In doing so, Facebook users worked to uphold Wambach's reputation. In fact, in many comments the arrest was argued to strengthen Wambach's positive reputation, as she became an example of "taking responsibility" for her actions.

Of course, it is likely the case that those who responded to Wambach's posts are a highly self-selected group; those strongly identified fans of Wambach's or the women's national team are likely overrepresented here (Brown-Devlin, 2017). When fandom becomes tied to self-identity, reputational damage to athletes and teams may "cause fans to act out to salvage their damaged self-esteem" (Brown-Devlin, 2017, p. 173). Thus we should expect to see some segment of Facebook commenters work to repair the reputation of this high-profile player. We also show that Facebook responses were not wholly uniform. A critical minority of comments reflected alternative perspectives and show that Wambach's image repair was not equally successful among all of her Facebook followers.

On the day of her final professional game, Abby Wambach asked her fans to forget her. The fans, of course, will not. But how will they remember her? Does the fact of her arrest a mere four months after retirement have consequences for her reputation in the long term? Our study suggests that the arrest did not, and will not, significantly damage her reputation. While Facebook became a site of fierce debate among users as to the meaning of Wambach's transgression, the predominant user message was one of acceptance and forgiveness. Due in large part to successful image repair, Wambach's legacy will live on.

References

Allison, R. (2016). Business or cause? Gendered institutional logics in women's professional soccer. *Journal of Sport & Social Issues, 40*, 237–262.

Benoit, W. L. (1995). *Accounts, excuses, and apologies: A theory of image restoration strategies.* Albany, NY: State University of New York Press.

Benoit, W. L., & Hanczor, R.S. (1994). The Tanya Harding controversy: An analysis of image restoration strategies. *Communication Quarterly, 42*, 416–433.

Blaney, J. R. (2013). Introduction: Why sports image restoration and how shall we proceed? In J. R. Blaney, L. Lippert, & J. S. Smith (Eds.), *Repairing the athlete's image: Studies in sports image restoration* (pp. 1–8). Lanham, MD: Lexington Books.

Brown, K. A. (2016). Is apology the best policy? An experimental examination of the effectiveness of image repair strategies during criminal and noncriminal athlete transgressions. *Communication & Sport, 4*, 23–42.

Brown, K. A., Billings, A. C., Mastro, D., & Brown-Devlin, N. (2015). Changing the image repair equation: Impact of race and gender on sport-related transgressions. *Journalism & Mass Communication Quarterly, 92*, 487–506.

Brown, N. A., & Billings, A. (2013). Sports fans as crisis communicators on social media websites. *Public Relations Review, 39*, 74–81.

Brown, N. A., Brown, K. A., & Billings, A. C. (2015). "May no act of ours bring shame": Fan-enacted crisis communication surrounding the Penn State sex abuse scandal. *Communication & Sport, 3*, 288–311.

Brown-Devlin, N. (2017). The modern sports fan navigating crises online: An examination of fan-enacted crisis communication. In A. C. Billings & K. A. Brown (Eds.), *Evolution of the modern sports fan: Communicative approaches* (pp. 167–184). Lanham, MD: Lexington Books.

Burns, J. P., & Bruner, M. S. (2000). Revisiting the theory of image restoration strategies. *Communication Quarterly, 48*, 27–39.

Christopherson, N., Janning, M., & Diaz McConnell, E. (2002). Two kicks forward, one kick back: A content analysis of media discourses on the 1999 Women's World Cup soccer championship. *Sociology of Sport Journal, 19*, 170–188.

Coche, R. (2016). Promoting women's soccer through social media: How the U.S. federation used Twitter for the 2011 World Cup. *Soccer & Society, 17*, 90–108.

Compton, J. L. (2013). Unsports(wo)manlike conduct: An image repair analysis of Elizabeth Lambert, the University of New Mexico, and the NCAA. In J. R. Blaney, L. Lippert, & J. S. Smith (Eds.), *Repairing the athlete's image: Studies in sports image restoration* (pp. 253–264). Lanham, MD: Lexington Books.

Creedon, P. (2014). Women, social media, and sport: Global digital communication weaves a web. *Television & New Media, 15*, 711–716.

Crosby, E. D. (2016). Chased by the double bind: Intersectionality and the disciplining of Lolo Jones. *Women's Studies in Communication, 39*, 228–248.

Douglas, D. D. (2014). Forget me . . . not: Marion Jones and the politics of punishment. *Journal of Sport & Social Issues, 38*, 3–22.

Filo, K., Lock, D., & Karg, A. (2015). Sport and social media research: A review. *Sport Management Review, 18*, 166–181.

Frederick, E., Stocz, M., & Pegoraro, A. (2016). Prayers, punishment, and perception: An analysis of the response to the Tony Stewart-Kevin Ward, Jr. incident on Facebook. *Sport in Society, 19*, 1460–1477.

Kramer, M. R. (2013). The image repair media interview as apologia and antapologia: Marion Jones on the Oprah Winfrey Show. In J. R. Blaney, L. Lippert, & J. S. Smith (Eds.), *Repairing the athlete's image: Studies in sports image restoration* (pp. 59–70). Lanham, MD: Lexington Books.

LaVoi, N. M., & Calhoun, A. S. (2014). Digital media and women's sport: An old view on "new" media. In A. C. Billings & M. Hardin (Eds.), *Routledge Handbook of Sport and New Media* (pp. 320–330). New York: Routledge.

Lebel, K., & Danylchuk, K. (2012). How tweet it is: A gendered analysis of professional tennis players' self-presentation on Twitter. *International Journal of Sport Communication, 5*, 461–480.

McDonald, M. G. (2002). Queering whiteness: The peculiar case of the Women's National Basketball Association. *Sociological Perspectives, 45*, 379–396.

Meng, J., & Pan, P. (2013). Revisiting image restoration strategies: An integrated case study of three athlete sex scandals in sports news. *International Journal of Sport Communication, 6*, 87–100.

Murthy, D. (2012). Towards a sociological understanding of social media: Theorizing Twitter. *Sociology, 46*, 1059–1073.

Onwumechili, C., & Bedeau, K. (2016). Analysis of FIFA's attempt at image repair. *Communication & Sport*. doi:10.1177/2167479516633843

Pegoraro, A. (2010). Look who's talking—Athletes on Twitter: A case study. *International Journal of Sport Communication, 3*, 501–514.

Pegoraro, A. (2014). Twitter as disruptive innovation in sport communication. *Communication & Sport, 2*, 132–137.

Pegoraro, A., Burch, L. M., Frederick, E., & Vincent, C. (2014). I am not loving it: Examining the hijacking of #cheerstosochi. *International Journal of Sport Management and Marketing, 15*, 163–183.

Sanderson, J., & Emmons, B. (2014). Extending and withholding forgiveness to Josh Hamilton: Exploring forgiveness within parasocial interaction. *Communication & Sport, 2*, 24–47.

Schmittel, A., & Hull, K. (2015). "Shit got cray cray #mybad": An examination of the image-repair discourse of Richie Incognito during the Miami Dolphins' bullying scandal. *Journal of Sports Media, 10*, 115–137.

Stavros, C., Meng, M. D., Westberg, K., & Farrelly, F. (2014). Understanding fan motivation for interacting on social media. *Sport Management Review, 17*, 455–469.

INDEX